PENTECOSTALISM
AND THE FUTURE OF
THE CHRISTIAN CHURCHES

Pentecostalism and the Future of the Christian Churches

Promises, Limitations, Challenges

Richard Shaull and Waldo Cesar

William B. Eerdmans Publishing Company

Grand Rapids, Michigan / Cambridge, U.K.

© 2000 Wm. B. Eerdmans Publishing Co.

255 Jefferson Ave. S.E., Grand Rapids, Michigan 49503 /

P.O. Box 163, Cambridge CB3 9PU U.K.

Printed in the United States of America

05 04 03 02 01 00   7 6 5 4 3 2 1

Library of Congress Cataloging-in-Publication Data

Shaull, Richard.

    Pentecostalism and the future of the Christian churches:

promises, limitations, challenges / Richard Shaull and Waldo Cesar.

       p.   cm.

    Includes bibliographical references.

    ISBN 0-8028-4666-1 (pbk.)

    1. Pentecostalism.   I. Cesar, Waldo A.   II. Title.

BR1644.S46 2000

270.8′3 — dc21

                                             00-27983

Contents

Acknowledgments

Funding for research leading to this publication was provided by The Research Enablement Program, a grant program for mission scholarship supported by The Pew Charitable Trusts, Philadelphia, Pennsylvania, U.S.A., and administered by the Overseas Ministries Study Center, New Haven, Connecticut, U.S.A.

Translation of Part I from Portuguese by Regina Musselman Shank and the authors.

Preface

This book is the culmination of a process of collaboration in the study of Christian social responsibility that began forty-five years ago. In the mid-fifties, Waldo Cesar and I first came together in Brazil around a common concern: the urgent need we felt for a dynamic response, on the part of the Christian community, to the suffering and struggle of the poor, caused by widespread social injustice and economic exploitation. We discovered that we were struggling with the challenge this presented to us personally. At the same time, as we worked with a new generation in our churches, Waldo as Executive Secretary of the Youth Department of the Evangelical Confederation of Brazil, and I with the Student Christian Movement and students in the Presbyterian Seminary in Campinas, we were aware of the fact that a growing number of these young people were facing the same challenge. They were becoming increasingly aware of the suffering around them and were disturbed in conscience by it. And they found themselves surrounded by dynamic social movements, each offering its own analysis of the situation and its ideological perspectives and response. But how were they to understand and respond to these social realities from the perspective of their faith? When they turned to their churches for help, they found a theology and a form of piety that had little or no connection with what they were confronting daily.

In the face of this situation, Waldo and I realized that a new approach was called for, on the part of men and women whose faith was leading them to become involved in this social struggle: an approach that would combine *in-depth study of social reality from the perspective of our faith with theological and biblical reflection carried on in the midst of this struggle.*

Guided by this conviction, we began our first efforts to bring together small groups for the study of social issues from this perspective. This soon led to the creation of the Sector of Social Responsibility of the Church, in the Evangelical Confederation, under the direction of Waldo Cesar. Within a few years, this approach, quite unique at that time, reached a growing circle of men and women from various Protestant churches, as it began to offer them resources for study and action that they had not found before. Later on, significant sectors of the Roman Catholic Church joined us, unofficially, in this effort. Our experience in Brazil led to our participation in the creation and development of a movement for the study of Church and Society, which spread across Latin America, as well as involvement in a similar program of study by the World Council of Churches.

The military coup in Brazil, in 1964, together with repressive movements in some churches, brought these efforts to a halt, but we continued our work in this area as we went our separate ways. Waldo, after completing his studies in sociology, concentrated his efforts on the study of religion, working first with Christian Lalive D'Épinay on studies of Protestantism in Chile and Brazil, and later at the Institute for the Study of Religion (ISER) in Rio de Janeiro, where he coordinated a project for the study of Protestantism and Ecumenism in Brazil. During this same period, I continued my theological work on social issues at Princeton and in collaboration with theologians of liberation in Latin America.

When I was allowed to return to Brazil in the mid-eighties, after having been excluded for twenty years, Waldo and I renewed our friendship and were surprised to discover how our paths were converging once again. The approach to social issues from the perspective of faith that we had developed early on had set the terms for the work of both of us since that time. More than this, we were coming to the conclusion that this same approach might have a special relevance and make a significant contribution in the new and quite different social and religious situation in Brazil and elsewhere in Latin America.

Vast numbers of people, under the impact of the global economy of the market, are facing ever greater impoverishment and marginalization. At the same time, the most basic structures needed for sustaining human life are eroding more and more, and increasing numbers of women and men are experiencing personal brokenness and social disintegration. In this situation, their central concern is focused on their often desperate struggle for daily survival and the search for the resources necessary for the reconstruction of their lives, individually, in the family, and in the community. Living this reality, they are turning more and more toward religion as their only hope.

In this context, we had each come to the conclusion that Christians concerned about their responsibility in society were facing a new situation that called for new responses. The central question is rapidly becoming, How can the resources of our religious heritage be a source of new life and hope for those now caught up in this daily struggle for survival? For only when these women and men, whose lives are being threatened and often broken by the destructive powers around and within them, find a spiritual power capable of reorganizing their lives will they have the will and the energy to struggle dynamically to change their world. And once again, we cannot ignore the fact that our older, more established churches are largely absent from the life and struggle of these people. More than this, they seem to lack the vitality necessary to respond to this challenge. At the same time, Pentecostal movements have been reaching precisely those in this situation and are growing among them at an extraordinary pace.

Waldo and I not only shared this understanding of what was happening in society and in the religious community. We also realized that this was leading us to engage in more serious study of Pentecostal movements in order to understand what they are doing — or not doing — to respond to this situation of suffering of the poor, to explore the potential they have of contributing significantly to the struggle to transform unjust economic, social, and political structures, and to see what those of us who are not Pentecostals might learn from their experience.

As we reflected together on this, we became convinced that this new situation called for an approach similar to that which we had developed several decades earlier: study that started out from our reading of the present situation in the light of our faith and was motivated by our calling to respond to it; study that gave a primary place to sociological analysis of Pentecostalism while at the same time seeking to understand it as a *religious* reality. This meant a type of social analysis carried on in dialogue with theology, a dialogue in which our theological reflection might well be transformed as a result of this engagement with social reality.

This unexpected convergence encouraged us to dream of collaborating on a new project, an interdisciplinary study *of this type,* in the expectation that it might make possible a number of things we could not accomplish working independently: a more thorough exploration of the complexity of a religious phenomenon full of vitality and ecclesiastic and social challenges; a theological study that would be enriched as it took into account sociological analysis of these movements, a study in which the resources of sociology and theology would be explored while drawing on them to find answers to existential questions regarding the nature of our response to the challenge before us.

While we were trying to find a way to embark on this study, given our very limited resources, Waldo received a grant from The Pew Charitable Trusts, through the Overseas Ministries Study Center, to support our project of interdisciplinary research. This not only made it possible for both of us to dedicate a full year to the first stage of this study; it also allowed us to work together in such a way that the conceptualization and development of all aspects of the project would be the product of our interaction with each other from our respective disciplines. In this way, we were able gradually to define the issues we wanted to study and how we wanted to work on them. We were also able to participate together in attendance at services and in some interviews, to share in our evaluation of the transcripts of interviews, and to discuss what was emerging from them as well as what we were learning from our sociological and theological studies of Pentecostal movements.

Our approach to Pentecostalism through two disciplines gradually became integrated as we worked together in these areas, all of this shaping a methodological procedure as well as leading to a number of changes in the process we had outlined for our research. As a result of this constant interaction between researchers and their two disciplines, each of us, while working within his own discipline, was influenced by the other. Thus, Part I, a sociological analysis by Waldo Cesar, goes beyond the perspectives of studies *exclusively* scientific-sociological. And Part II, my theological reflections on Pentecostalism, has been significantly influenced by this ongoing dialogue with social reality. For those interested in this interdisciplinary dimension, see the short appendix to Part I, *Sociological and Theological Horizon.*

When we initiated this collaboration, we had no idea what would result from it. We are now convinced of the validity of what we have undertaken and realize that each of us has gone beyond what would have been possible without this interaction. At the same time, we realize that, as a result of what we have done, we are facing new issues that call for much more thorough research and reflection. This is evident in at least two respects, in relation to the two areas in which we have been working:

The first has to do with our perception of what is involved in a *sociological* study of a *religious* movement of this nature and understanding what it is *religiously,* as we perceived how important it is, in efforts to understand Pentecostalism, to study it sociologically with a certain *spiritual sensitivity.* Our interdisciplinary study compelled us to take into account the complexity of the issues raised — and of others that emerged in the process of this study. More than a history or a quantitative analysis of the Pentecostal phenomenon, we found ourselves interested in searching for the consequences of this movement in the life of the people who accept its form of worship, the demands of a personal commitment without restrictions, the load of a set financial contribution, intense personal and community emotions, the anticipation of a miracle, the active role of Satan, the obligation to evangelize. This, we believe, calls for sociological analysis that is prepared to take into account the realm of spiritual values and ethics and its meaning for human behavior, its experiences and hopes.

Consequently, while focusing on the crucial issue of the suffering of the poor and the response of Pentecostalism, we could not ignore other issues present in the complexity of a movement that, in the end, directly or indirectly, consciously or not, includes all social issues and the relation of the churches to contemporary history. Thus, our concern about *the future of the Christian churches.*

In the second place, the central question that we posed for our research compelled us, in our theological reflections, not only to look critically at what Pentecostal movements are offering to those who are suffering most in the present situation but also at the challenge this might present to those of us who are not Pentecostal. But we were hardly prepared for an unexpected discovery. As we tried to understand the Pentecostal movement from an interdisciplinary point of view, we came to the conclusion that we were dealing with a new expression and form of Christian faith and life, quite different from anything we have known until now in Brazil, in traditional Protestantism, as well as in Catholicism.

If this is the case, then our theological objective had to change: it was no longer simply a matter of evaluating this movement from our given paradigmatic perspective; quite the contrary, it was a matter of discovering a new interpretive paradigm of Christianity and its emergence among the poor of the Third World. And if we are capable of grasping the full meaning of this change for Christian faith and life, then we are compelled to identify theologically what this new religious impulse brings to the mainline churches — to capture what the Holy Spirit may be trying to say through all of this. At the same time, while seriously considering this new paradigm, we cannot avoid asking if the Pentecostals themselves are aware of the new spiritual reality they experience — and if they are examining this fact in the light of our common biblical heritage. Such is the purpose and the content of Part II, *The Reconstruction of Life in the Power of the Spirit*. Once again, in this area, we find ourselves forced to deal with new issues in new ways and to seek new ecumenical relationships for such theological reflection.

It is also necessary to mention here another unexpected result of the process of study we have followed: our decision to write in the first person — which is closer to the experience each one of us has had with the present reality of the Pentecostal movement. When entering the almost always crowded churches, we did so as *researchers* of a religious and social phenomenon. However, the emotion that involved the multitude of the faithful would always touch us. In a different way, certainly. But it was not possible to ignore the contagious power of this collective movement — gestures, cries, prayers, songs, offerings, hugs, confessions; or the manifestations which exploded around us — the bodies involved in the common search for a new way of being a Christian and of living in the world.

This work represents an endeavor to which innumerable persons contributed, among whom we point out the people interviewed from several branches of Pentecostal churches as well as scholars of this movement. Besides the long interviews with women and men (thirty, with an average length of one hour and a half) and attendance at approximately forty services in churches of poor as well as middle-class and rich neighborhoods, we examined an extensive scientific and religious bibliography. We also attended numerous lectures and debates and collected ample documentation from evangelical and secular newspapers and magazines. And we are grateful to the Institute for the Study of Religion — ISER — for the opportunity to take part in their analysis of the responses they received to 1,332 questionnaires on "Evangelicals at Home, in the Church and in Politics," which was given the suggestive title "New Birth."

While we cannot mention here the names of all those who contributed, in one way or another, to this effort, we have a special word of gratitude for the contribution of the anthropologist Clara Mafra, as well as the help we received from our wives — Nancy Johns and Maria Luiza Cesar — who accompanied us in our many visits to churches, conducted a number of interviews, and participated in our study of them, enriching the research with observations pertinent to gender and other matters that derived from the visits and personal contacts.[1]

From the moment of initiation of our project, we had the privilege of being financed for one year of work (July 1995 to June 1996) by a grant from The Pew Charitable Trusts, administered by the Overseas Ministries Study Center. Our warmest gratitude for this cooperation, without which the research and this book would not have become a reality.

Richard Shaull

1. Maria Luiza, who died in July 1997, was unable to see the final result of the research and the publication of this book.

PART I DAILY LIFE AND TRANSCENDENCE IN PENTECOSTALISM

Waldo Cesar

Introduction

A t the beginning of the twentieth century, precisely in 1904, the jour-nalist João do Rio[1] published a book entitled *The Religions in Rio*. In it, he writes, in a somewhat disorderly way and without scientific preten-sions, about the various religions established in Rio de Janeiro. "The city abounds with religions," he affirms in the introduction. "It suffices to stop at any corner and ask. The diversity of services will surprise you." He writes further: "Rio, as all cities in this time of irreverence, has a temple on each street and a different belief in each person."

1. Pen name for João Paulo Alberto Coelho Barreto (1881-1921), famous chroni-cler of the customs of Rio de Janeiro and of Brazilian society of his time.

Some chapters of Part I are partially based on a presentation of mine at a seminar on "Popular Religions: Insights and Learnings for Latin American Ecumenism, A Look at the Decade of the '90s," held in Santiago, Chile, in January 1991, and sponsored by the Unit of Work, Justice and Service, of the World Council of Churches. That paper, entitled "Survival and Transcendence: Daily Life and Religi-osity in Pentecostalism," was published in *Religião e Sociedade* (ISER) 16.1-2 (1992).

The exaggeration of the journalist contained a symbolic projection. What wouldn't he say today? In the Evangelical universe alone, including what today is called Neopentecostalism, five new churches appear each week in Greater Rio.[2] In three years around three hundred thousand people have joined these churches. What is the origin of so many converts? Sixty-one percent were Roman Catholic, 16 percent had left either Candomblé or Umbanda (Afro-Brazilian religions), and the rest belonged to Spiritism or the historic Protestant churches. In 1996, the number of Evangelicals had reached 1,500,000 — corresponding to approximately 15 percent of the population of the state.[3]

After a century of demographic growth and of urban transformation of Rio, a few religions and churches have disappeared, while several others, not even imagined during the times of the dazzled chronicler of the beliefs of the Brazilians, found fertile ground for expansion here: oriental, esoteric and syncretistic religions, ecumenical churches, ethnic religions, native creations. In the dispute for the conquest of the souls of the inhabitants of Rio de Janeiro, after nearly four centuries of colonial Catholic preeminence (and as the established church between 1824 and 1857), religions sprout with vigor and challenge researchers, historians, and theologians.[4] At this

2. These data proceed from two sources, originating in research conducted by the Institute for the Study of Religion (ISER), under the coordination of Rubem César Fernandes: Evangelical Institutional Census of the Metropolitan Region of Rio de Janeiro (CIN; 1991-92) and New Birth Research (NN; 1992-94). The latter, by residence sampling, was based on visits to 40,172 homes in 4,787 neighborhoods. The fifty-three denominations found by the sampling were grouped into six sets: Assembly of God, Universal Church of the Reign of God, other Pentecostal Churches, Historic Churches, Baptists, and "Renewal" Churches. A summary of the results of this research was published in *Religião e Sociedade* (ISER) 17.1-2 (1993).

3. Other data reveal that Evangelicals occupy all the possible spaces in the area being studied, which can be projected to other states. In some municipalities Evangelicals now outnumber Catholics. The CIN census took data from the Notary of Legal Persons, where 118 Evangelical temples were registered in a short period of six months. In thirteen municipalities of Greater Rio, the census found 3,300 Evangelical temples, more than twice the 1,251 Catholic parishes and communities in the same region. The *Favela do Lixão* (a very poor slum), in the municipality of Duque de Caxias, with 4,000 inhabitants, has fourteen Evangelical churches and one Catholic, with four Pentecostal temples on one street.

4. A recent book, *Struggle for the Spirit* (Oxford: Polity Press), by David Lehmann, director of the Latin American Center at Cambridge University, analyzes

point the chronicler seems to have some advantage in his attempt, marked by disinterestedness and a bit of humor, barely to "uncover a little of the mystery behind the beliefs in this city."

Origin and Nature of Pentecostalism

The mystery continues — and becomes even more complex with the implanting of Pentecostalism, with its insurmountable popular appeal and challenge to the historic certainty of traditional branches of Protestantism and even to the Catholic Church. A new form of church never stopped growing. And now, in these last decades, almost a century after the arrival of Pentecostalism in Brazil (a few years after the publication of João do Rio's book), it seems to be renewing its power, multiplying itself in innumerable groups and factions throughout the whole country.

Within a period of one year and independent of each other, the first Pentecostal churches in Brazil appeared, both having their origin in the Sanctification Movements, which arose in the United States at the beginning of this century. The names of the churches and leaders that marked this upheaval on the Protestant scene, in the beginnings of Pentecostalism in the United States and Brazil, have been well studied and published. However, it is important to remember the meaning of those events, for the historical as well as the theological itinerary of these new forms of church in the last decades. In the United States, the most known dates are the years 1901 (Topeka, Kansas), 1906 (Los Angeles), and 1907 (Chicago). Soon afterward, the movement arrived in Brazil. The Congregação Cristã do Brasil [Christian Congregation of Brazil], founded in 1910 in the Brás neighborhood, in São Paulo, and the Assembleia de Deus [Assembly of God] in 1911, in Belém, in the state of Pará, established the national framework for a new type of church and religious experience. In very little time, Pentecostalism spread throughout the country, in the same way it spread all over the world, from the unusual happenings in North American Protestantism.

---

contrasts between Catholics and Protestants in Brazil (Christian base communities and Pentecostals, with emphasis on the Universal Church of the Reign of God) and stresses the relations between religion and popular culture.

Those were years of great scandals in the religious scene, in the United States (with intense repercussion in the secular press) as well as in Brazil (and certainly in other countries). What was happening? How did this new movement — considered heretical, sectarian, limited to a few persons unsatisfied with their religious experience, members of a black church of humble origin — develop and arrive in Brazil? Even though the new expressions of spirituality were somewhat similar to other moments of renewal in the history of the church, the emphasis on the action of the Spirit empowered Pentecostalism in a way that allowed it to shake up old church structures, placing their own theological formulations in check.

"They were all filled with the Holy Spirit and began to talk in other languages, as the Spirit enabled them to speak." This was the text (Acts 2:4) of the sermon of the young black pastor William J. Seymour in a Church of the Nazarene, in Los Angeles. The preacher said that God had a third blessing, besides conversion and sanctification, and this blessing was the baptism of the Holy Spirit. Seymour's sermon resulted in his being excommunicated by the female pastor of the church, Neely Terry, also black, leading him to hold meetings in private homes in the city. It was 1906 — and on the 6th of April an eight-year-old boy, along with other people, began to speak in tongues. Some days later, Seymour and his followers rented an old church, formerly of the African Methodist Episcopal Church, and there began a movement that took the name of "The Apostolic Faith." The address — 312 Azusa Street — became famous and is recognized as the base for the creation and worldwide spread of the modern Pentecostal movement. Protestants of several countries came to see what was happening and left from there to go to other countries as missionaries.[5]

---

5. According to Walter Hollenweger (*The Pentecostals* [Peabody, Mass.: Hendrickson, 1988], p. 23), "They shouted three days and three nights. It was the Easter season. The people came from everywhere. By the next morning, there was no way of getting near the house. As the people came in, they would fall under God's power; and the whole city was stirred. They shouted there until the foundation of the house gave way, but no one was hurt." Carmelo E. Álvarez (*In the Power of the Spirit. Pentecostals in Latin America: A Challenge to the Historic Churches,* ed. Benjamín F. Gutiérrez and Dennis A. Smith [Mexico City: AIPRAL, 1996], p. 30) says: "The movement was so large and influential that within a decade Pentecostal phenomena were reported in Asia, Africa, Europe, and Latin America."

New Pentecostal tendencies arose from the doctrinal differences between the Baptist pastor W. H. Durham and Seymour. Two converts, the Swedish Daniel Berg and Gunner Vingren, through a revelation in a dream received by the former, were called to preach the baptism of the Holy Spirit in Pará. After locating the city of Belém on a map in a library in Chicago, they left for Brazil in 1911. There they connected with a Baptist church, pastored by Euric Nelson, also of Swedish origin, owner of immense herds in the Amazon, an activity that was associated with the expansion of the Baptists in the region.

In no time the news spread: a woman had spoken in tongues, followed by other persons. Strong argument followed Sunday service. In the absence of the pastor, the deacon in charge of the work declared that such manifestations were things of *those* times. Vingren calmly argued that "*who* brings souls to God is a matter of secondary importance. What is important is the fact that more and more souls are saved. I would not want to say that the brother does not stand in the truth but that he has not found the whole truth. [He does not have] the truth of the baptism of the Spirit and of the healing of the sick by Jesus, as we can experience them today."[6] Berg and Vingren, however, were excommunicated. Outside a group of Baptists was waiting for them — and thus the Assembly of God[7] began in Brazil. Today it is two times larger than its equivalent in the United States.

Similar to what happened to the American and Brazilian pioneers, preaching about the baptism of the Holy Spirit in a Presbyterian church in Brás, in the city of São Paulo in 1910, caused the excommunication of the Italian laborer Luigi Francescon, also a disciple of Durham, and marked the founding of the Congregação Cristã do Brasil. The noticeable growth of this church, from a popular neighborhood of Italian origin, opened the way for the expansion of this Pentecostalism to the southern part of the country and later to other countries of South America.

6. Hollenweger, *The Pentecostals,* p. 76.
7. The name has its origin in the Greek biblical expression *ekklesia tou theou* (church of God).

Unceasing Growth

Although still close to their North American origin, two separate forms of Pentecostalism developed in Brazil because they originated in extremely distant geographical regions, one in the north and another in the south. Shortly the situation came to be what Agnelo Rossi would speak of, almost three decades later, in his vibrant warning about the "Protestant danger": "This baptism was followed by such an intense zeal, that in a few years, the movement spread worldwide."[8] In their first years in Brazil the new believers, full of a contagious enthusiasm, did not cause any worry to the historic churches, whether they were fruits of European immigration (Anglicans, Lutherans) or of North American missions (Congregationalists, Presbyterians, Methodists, Baptists, Episcopalians). Some of these confessions had been in existence for more than half a century and had relatively stable national structures, despite their great dependency on their countries of origin. The arrival of the Pentecostals was considered an "invasion of sects."[9]

Twenty years later (1930), the phenomenon began to cause fear and controversy. While Protestantism had a total of approximately 1,100 temples, the Pentecostal newcomers already had 267 places of worship and totaled 27 percent of Brazilian Evangelicals. These numbers increased to 58 percent in 1970, with 11,000 temples, a difference of only 3,000 temples in relation to the non-Pentecostal churches, which had 14,000 temples. A graph published in 1932[10] already registered the existence of 9.5

8. Agnelo Rossi, *Diretório Protestante no Brasil* (Campinas: Tipografia Paulista, 1928). The then Father Rossi adds: "At the end of the nineteenth century and beginning of the twentieth some persons in the U.S.A. and Canada realized that it was necessary to awaken the church from its lethargy. Groups were formed dedicated to prayer *(Prayer Bands)* and to propagate, by lectures and through the press, the need for a revival. A small group, persuaded about the urgency of this return to the primitive doctrine, asked God for a manifestation of the Holy Spirit. And, to give them credit, the Holy Spirit came to baptize them and, before that, made itself known with the gift of tongues and the glorification of God" (p. 107).

9. In ch. 3, "Survival and Transcendence," as well as ch. 5, "Only One Space of Life," I return to the analysis of other relations between the church and the street as integral parts of a renewing Evangelical practice.

10. Erasmo Braga and Kenneth Grubb, *The Republic of Brazil: A Survey of the Religious Situation* (London: World Dominion Press, 1932), p. 71.

percent Pentecostals on the Protestant scene, while the Methodists reached no more than 11.5 percent, surpassed only by the Presbyterians (24 percent) and Baptists (30 percent). The Independent Presbyterians, fruit of a division within the Presbyterian Church, in 1903, represented 10 percent of the Evangelicals, and the rest (Adventists, Congregationalists, Episcopalians, and others) added up to 15 percent of the total.[11] Currently, at the end of the nineties and the beginning of a new millennium, the Assembly of God is still the most important Pentecostal group in the country, perhaps in the world, with its five to seven million practicing members. With the development of hundreds of new churches, the current number of Pentecostals has been estimated at between fifteen and twenty million, that is, 10 to 20 percent of the Brazilian population. The historic churches have a total of around 2 percent of the population.[12] And even if the Catholic Church maintains the majority of the Brazilian population, in absolute terms, it is at an evident disadvantage with respect to its growth and the number of priests. Since Pentecostal pastors need little or no theological education, it is not surprising that there are more of them than there are Roman Catholic priests in the country; and that, contrary to what is happening in the Catholic Church, almost all of them are native Brazilians. This does not mean that Roman Catholicism or historic Protestantism are stagnant. Many churches maintain great vitality, but those that cultivate a charismatic renewal or those that are able to combine tradition with renewal are especially so.[13]

---

11. CIN-ISER presents a similar graph, based on their research in Greater Rio, in which it registers percentages of the Evangelical churches by the main denominations: Baptist, 23.3 percent; Assembly of God, 18.6 percent; other Pentecostals, 13.7 percent; other Baptists, 6.4 percent; IURD, 5.8 percent; Congregationalists, 5.3 percent; Presbyterians, 5 percent; House of Blessing, 4 percent; Methodists, 3.9 percent; Adventists, 3.6 percent; other Methodists, 3.4 percent; Christian Congregation, 3.1 percent; Foursquare Gospel, 2.6 percent; other historic ones, 1.3 percent.

12. As some historians of Pentecostalism note, the statistics are neither sufficient nor precise enough for a definition closer to reality, which is one reason why, many times, the numerical references are so dissimilar. The above data is based on the studies by Francisco Cartaxo Rolim (*O que é Pentecostalismo* (São Paulo: Editora Brasiliense, 1987) and André Corten (*Le Pentecôtisme au Brésil: Émotion du pauvre et romantisme théologique* (Paris: Editions Karthala, 1955), both based on several other authors.

13. *Isto É* (24 December 1997) has as its cover article, under the title "A Igreja Católica que faz milagres," a long report focusing on charismatics who "cure illnesses

This growth in the Pentecostal Church has a growing impact on Brazilian society and culture, and particularly on politics. Today's Brazil, considered the largest Protestant community in the world after the United States, has a contingent of around fifteen million Evangelical voters.[14] In the case of the Pentecostals, especially the Universal Church of the Reign of God (IURD), it is not only a matter of voting for the candidates indicated by the leaders, but of favoring on the ballot their own members in electoral campaigns. Thirty-two persons of Evangelical origin were elected to the National Constituent Congress, eighteen of whom were Pentecostals.[15]

Studies, Criticisms, Defenses

This whole complex religious-political-cultural picture has moved some scholars to consider the Pentecostal movement — dispersed but in a way united in its emphasis on the power of the Spirit — as a fourth major phase in the history of the church, after the Reformation, the missionary movement, and the ecumenical movement. Now would be the time for a new manifestation of the Spirit, through the various forms that Pentecostalism has taken in its almost one hundred years of existence. No matter what classification these forms receive — sects, autonomous churches, classical Pentecostalism, Neopentecostalism, the third wave, and so forth — their characteristics as the "religion of the masses," together with an individual and community enthusiasm, suggest a time of the primitive church and constitute, as mentioned, a challenge for the

---

and fill masses using the same techniques as the Evangelicals," estimated at eight million persons divided into sixty thousand prayer groups.

14. Datum from Paul Freston, in *Ultimato,* February 1990, p. 19. The "charismatic movement" (from the Greek *charismata,* gifts of the Spirit) began in February 1967 with Catholic lay professors at Duquesne University, who declared that they had received "the baptism of the Holy Spirit." The movement arrived in Brazil more or less at the same time, having reached the historic Protestant churches as well, and has produced divisions and new denominations among some confessions.

15. Antônio Flávio Pierucci and Reginaldo Prandi (*A realidade social das religiões no Brasil* [São Paulo: Editora Hucitec, 1996]) dedicate the third part of their book — "Religion, Partisan Politics, Vote" — to the question of the participation of Evangelicals in national politics.

historic churches, for theology, and for the ecumenical movement in particular.

However, the critics are not few — and not limited to historic Protestantism and the Catholic Church. The secular press has given a great deal of space to the negative and problematic aspects of Pentecostalism, with emphasis on the IURD. These churches are accused of exploiting financially and spiritually the oppressed, men and women who in their daily anguish search for immediate solutions to their unending problems — and for their own survival.

In the Protestant realm, the rapid expansion of certain Pentecostal groups has renewed the Protestant spirit of controversy, historically more oriented toward combating Catholicism and Spiritism (although sometimes also against Evangelical rivals). This reaction, meanwhile, faces today a much more complex situation, which goes beyond ecclesiological limits and penetrates into the real world in a way totally different from that defined by the heritage of the Reformation.[16] These churches do not seem to realize that the "emotional insurrection" of Pentecostalism, "to which 150 million people from the Third World have been converted," "is not a haystack fire, it is a permanent insurrection."[17] The dynamism of this new religious phenomenon has reached even the world of fiction through soap operas for a mass audience — which means another type of insertion into the media and into the cultural scene of the country.[18] In

16. The Presbyterian pastor Caio Fábio d'Araújo Filho, from Visão Nacional de Evangelização (VINDE) and founder and president of the Associação Evangélica do Brasil (AEVB), has pronounced himself vehemently against the IURD. Having tried for ten years to solve the controversy internally, including speaking with Bishop Edir Macedo, Filho declared publicly his break with the Universal Church: "But it came to the point that the problem reached the international media. It was no longer possible to continue behind the scenes and I had to go public" (*O Globo,* Rio de Janeiro, 23 September 1995).

17. These expressions are from Corten, *Le Pentecôtisme au Brésil,* p. 12.

18. In September 1995, Rede Globo, the most powerful TV station in the country, put on the air a miniseries entitled "Decadence," by Dias Gomes, in which a poor young fellow becomes a charismatic pastor and gets rich from the money of the faithful in a church he started — "The Divine Spark." The broadcasting of the soap opera caused a strong reaction from IURD and Evangelical churches, and it got headlines in the secular press. The next month, it was the Universal Church that provoked a wave of protests by the Catholic Church, when one of its bishops kicked an image of Nossa

general, these criticisms do not recognize or mention the personal transformations taking place within this complex phenomenon, nor do they
perceive the spiritual and social space that opens up to those who surrender themselves — body and soul — to the challenge of a faith that sym-
bolically — in many cases in an effective way — removes the mountains
of day-to-day problems of the marginalized in society.

This heterogeneous set of manifestations, which goes beyond the
ecclesiastical sphere and the social reality of the parish, could not go
unnoticed by the social scientists of Brazil and abroad.[19] There are numerous doctoral dissertations, articles, and books about Pentecostalism,
lately with a greater emphasis on the Universal Church of the Reign of
God. The themes of analysis range from worship services and the behavior of the multitude of followers, to the testimonies of healing and a
"new life," to matters of gender or of emotion as a fundamental element
in Pentecostal culture and spirituality.[20] Other studies analyze how
Pentecostalism has penetrated the mass media, be it by their own radio
and television networks or religious programs on secular TV and radio
stations, which cover daily the immense Brazilian territory.[21] It is a

---

Senhora Aparecida (the patron virgin of Brazil) on a program of Rede Record TV,
owned by IURD. (The *secular* media, furthermore, have adopted religious language
and images in their publicity, announcing several types of products through a religious
appeal, leading to controversy and protest on several occasions.)

19. An analysis of these studies is beyond the scope of this work. Besides the references to several works and articles throughout the text, the bibliography lists some
books and theses of Brazilian as well as foreign authors.

20. On this point, the dissertation of Maria das Dores Campos Machado,
Carismáticos e pentecostais: Adesão religiosa na esfera familiar (Campinas: Editora
Autores Associados/ANPOCS, 1996), stands out. See also Corten, *Le Pentecôtisme au
Brésil.* Guillermo Cook ("Interchurch Relations, Exclusion, Ecumenism, and the
Poor," in *Power, Politics, and Pentecostals in Latin America,* ed. Edward L. Cleary and
Hannah W. Stewart-Gambino [Boulder, Colo.: Westview Press, 1997], p. 78) quotes
Everett Wilson: "Social scientists . . . are apparently more willing than religious observ-
ers to recognize the indigenous and reconstructive character of Pentecostalism," as well
as to emphasize Pentecostals' "subjective experience, freedom of action and view of reality," which non-Pentecostal Evangelicals are likely to reject.

21. André Mello (*Mídia evangélica e interdenominacionalismo,* mimeo., 1995) has
worked on this theme, showing the evolution of the participation of Evangelical organizations and churches in the use of the media. In this area, the work of VINDE stands
out, under the leadership of pastor Caio Fábio, who launched Vinde TV in Rio de Ja-

matter of a revolution of methods, of a deep insertion into modernity.[22] The "open-air service," to mention a traditional experience, is being displaced by more modern, technically effective ways of spreading the message. Other new methods of evangelizing include large public demonstrations: filling enormous football stadiums, parading through urban centers, proselytizing in the multitude that pays homage to Iemanjá at the beaches on New Year's eve, and forming Evangelical blocks that parade in the midst of carnival with Christian messages, which has caused much controversy.

There are, however, areas less studied, such as the production of these churches — newspapers, magazines, books, T-shirts, records, CDs, objects representing Bible stories, special versions of the Bible *(Biblia de Estudo Pentecostal)*[23] — sold in churches and bookstores. And even though there is research about the results of conversion in personal and family life,[24] there is a lack of more thorough studies of the *process* and the instruments of conversion. What motivated the change of religion or church? What was the critical moment in which the drama of personal transformation and affiliation with a new experience of faith, the Pentecostal faith, took place? The answers, touched on in all the personal interviews we made, bring an important contribution to some of the conclusions we reached. But perhaps this "transformation I felt inside of me, of a life filled with more peace, happiness, contact with God . . . , some-

---

neiro in December 1996, the first Evangelical channel by subscription in Brazil, "with 100 percent Christian programming."

22. It is interesting to note this statement of pastor J. Cabral, of the IURD, in an article in the *Folha Universal,* 21 January 1996, under the title, "Uma Igreja pós-moderna": "No subordination to large institutions; practical religiosity with emphasis on individuality; a break with certain values and principles patterned on a legalistic, bourgeois, and conservative ethic; openness to the new, the different and the unusual; abandonment of rigid and bureaucratic methods, and adherence to the simple, the clear, the objective and the direct, are some of the characteristics of the spirit of post-modernity." "In a sense the Universal Church of the Reign of God is moving in this direction, more than any other Evangelical denomination. This move makes it different from the others and, as always happens, what is different causes fear."

23. Edited by the Casa Publicadora das Assemblias de Deus, translated by missionary Donald Stamp.

24. See, for example, Cecília L. Mariz, "Alcoolismo, género e pentecostalismo," *Religião e Sociedade* (ISER) 16.3 (1992): 80-93.

thing in my heart"[25] could be explored not only in a superficial way but also for its deeper meaning.

This conviction, expressed by a woman, introduces another important field in the study of Pentecostalism — that of gender, emphasizing the role of women. Our research does not dedicate a special chapter on the role of women, as we had intended; however, it emphasizes the participation of Pentecostal women through the interviews and refers to their participation in practically all chapters. And we hardly need to mention that besides the research of ISER (NN), there are recent theses and books that contain relevant information concerning the increasing importance of women in the expansion of Pentecostalism.

Whether it be a woman or a man, everything indicates the existence of a *before* and an *after,* be it a conversion or re-conversion: from religious routine to the leap of emotion of a radical faith.

Much of what we have presented here may be well known by many in Catholic and Protestant communities. For the objectives of this book, however, we have considered it important to present this brief sketch of the origin and growth of Pentecostalism and, more specifically, its origin and expansion in Brazil, as well as some current reactions to it, in order to approach the issue that is central to this study: What is the response, or responses, of Pentecostalism to the suffering of the poor?

25. Interview with a teacher and member of the Assembly of God of Duque de Caxias.

1 *The Church and the Street*

A large vestibule precedes a long stairway that gives access to the huge meeting hall of the Universal Church of the Reign of God, situated in a middle-class neighborhood in the southern zone of Rio de Janeiro. Two uniformed young people, wearing gray pants, a blue casual shirt, and tie, receive the believers and the visitors. It is a day dedicated to healing, one of the emphases of the weekly calendar. Other days, four or five daily services are dedicated to personal prosperity, the family, liberation from demons, the search for the Holy Spirit, emotional problems, and praise to God. Today it is healing, the miracle that takes place without doctors or medicine. The receptionists have small plastic cups in their hands, simple objects and not at all sacred — even so, they make it difficult for me to resist the invitation to approach them. I am blessed with some drops of the scarce water, with words of salutation, and with pronouncements of the healing of my ailments. Never before, in all my years of going to many churches, had I been touched by such a gesture, unassuming and confident, anticipating what might occur inside the church. I climb the steps alongside plain, poor people, who are filled with a contagious happiness. Inside, a multitude awaits the spectacle of the entrance of the pastors, of the mediation between heaven and earth — and of the participation of all in the delirium of a contagious emotion.

The First Time . . . I Was Scared

The gesture comes first. Later, the words. And one legitimizes the other in a constant reciprocity. Something new always happens. The expectation is fulfilled. Apparently nobody leaves a Pentecostal service frustrated, no matter how well they know the ritual, the songs, the altar calls, the messages, the offerings. What happens in the pulpit (on stage) is only the first act. Next, the whole auditorium becomes a stage of action. The roles are switched momentarily: the pastor becomes an attendant, a spectator of the ecstasy that fills the souls and bodies of the crowded hall with personal and collective manifestations. Each one for him/herself, God in all. From the moment of entering the church, everything is submission; but on the way out, it is mission. After the surrender — surrender of oneself, of material goods, and of money — it is necessary to communicate the many blessings to the world outside, to divide the overflow, to announce the cure, and to free others from alcoholism, from Umbanda (an African-Brazilian religion), from hate, and from disbelief. The daily routine becomes a place of real experiences, of another dimension of life, of the breaking of the routine, and of the capacity to transcend the same situation that leads most people to despair or misery.

This unexpected but impacting experience was repeated on other occasions, in different contexts, even though, as a researcher, I tried to limit myself to observe the people and their intense mobilization — it was the only way to endure the waves of emotion that filled all the corners of the comfortable meeting rooms. After a series of visits it was sometimes tiring — and uncomfortable — to follow two or three hours of an apparently improvised and repetitious ceremony, especially the requests for contributions: "Who can give one hundred *reais* [Brazilian currency], fifty, twenty, ten, five, or at least one or two? Those who give more receive more."

The comparison with other "sacred spaces" was unavoidable: other services, briefer, solemn, formal; and with those attending other churches. In the Pentecostal churches, perhaps especially in the Universal

Church, the poor always make up the vast majority and black women and men are not few in number. Here we have one of the most intriguing issues that the Pentecostal advance has raised: How can we understand this extraordinary capacity to generate enchantment and happiness in lives deprived of the minimum resources for personal and family fulfillment? How do these people survive? How can participation in a religion with such radical demands — including financial ones — offer conditions of resistance to the many forms of adversity imposed by the dominating system? To what can we attribute this hope against all present and future evidence?

> The first time I went to the Universal I was scared, because, when I arrived there, the pastor, at the beginning of the service, was excellent; but in the middle he began to ask for a very large contribution that I was not in any condition to give. What am I going to do in this church? And then they started to ask for more money: to buy the newspaper, to help in the remodeling of the church — and I couldn't respond. I thought that only those who were able to help could stay in that church. I thought: I'm not going anymore. Later, with time, I decided to return to see what was going on and to talk with the pastor. Then he told me that you only give if you are able and desire to do so. Because they do not force anyone to give. Only those who have the means, if they have faith and want to give to help. At the beginning I also didn't like it because there was a lot of screaming, people falling on the floor and I was scared. . . . At the Universal, prayer is strong and I was scared. But later I got used to it and I liked it. I plan to continue in this religion until the end. . . . Before going to church I had many problems. I was very nervous, so I would get upset about anything. At church they do a cleansing. It seems like we change. . . . I got many things in life that I didn't have.[1]

This first impact of what happens in a Pentecostal[2] church and in the life of its followers, led me to suggest some real — and symbolic —

1. Interview with Leila, IURD.
2. The initial research project did not necessarily include the Universal Church of the Reign of God (IURD), which became fundamental due to the importance of this branch of Pentecostalism in the whole of the conversion experience and the transformations occurring in the life of its followers, as well as its marked worldwide growth.

correlations, which I call *antagonisms and similarities.*[3] Beginning with the rupture with the traditional Protestant churches, there are several areas in which differences, especially differences, manifest themselves. A substantial part of the progress of Pentecostalism lies in the differences or antagonisms with the historic churches and also with the society in which it is inserted. The theme is an old one, but it has taken on new and shocking dimensions. Max Weber used the word *rupture* to refer to the tension between the radical striving for salvation and the institutionalized secular order.[4]

We Take the Word to Another

I will begin with the most evident correlation, which applies to the majority of the Pentecostal churches: the visibility of their temples — huge, noisy, crowded — face to face with the street. The confrontation might suggest the old dichotomy sacred versus worldly. However, the antagonism between Christian faith and secular life, so marked in the history of the church — and in Pentecostal fundamentalism — is overcome or at least relativized by a mission that reaches out to the street, to the transformation of those passing by, whoever they may be, into new creatures. What I am saying can be illustrated by another correlation, elaborated by the anthropologist Roberto daMatta, when he mentions a type of opposition between the house and the street. He says that "one cannot mix the space of the street with that of the house without creating some kind of serious confusion or even conflict."[5] In the case of the temple and the street, if we have traditionally a much greater distance between one and the

---

3. The term *antagonism,* according to the *Novo Dicionario Aurelio da Lingua Portuguesa,* means "opposition of ideas or of systems, rivalry, incompatibility." Apparently strong, the word expresses many of the facets of some Pentecostal tendencies, especially the IURD.

4. Compare Max Weber, *Sociología de la comunidad religiosa,* 2 vols. (Mexico City: F.C.E., 1964), vol. 2, pp. 328-492. These conflicts do not exclude, in certain circumstances, approaches of convenience, in the religious as well as in the political or economic field, as can be deduced from other chapters.

5. Roberto daMatta, *A casa e a rua: espaço, cidadania, mulher e morte no Brasil* (São Paulo: Editora Brasiliense, 1985), p. 43.

other, paradoxically the space is reduced when there is commitment to the *other,* who needs to be *saved.* The believer, many times, was also one of *them* and knows the street codes. The "metaphors and symbols in which the house is contrasted with the street,"[6] in the relation church-street, obey other categories, equally filled with meanings, as we shall see in the chapter "Only One Space of Life."

Here I want to point out that it is only the physical *extension* that establishes a spacial, metaphorical link. There is nothing special from an architectural point of view, and in many cases large movie theaters, rented or bought, which do not even have the appearance of a church, are meeting places. However, in the IURD the name of the church and a Bible verse stand out — Jesus Christ is the Lord — curiously always in gothic letters. The *link* with the street is achieved by means of a large facade, usually a long stairway establishing a certain territorial *continuity,* an invitation for free entry. The flow of the multitude entering and leaving repeated in the succession of several worship services on the same day, reminds us of the incessant walking of people on the sidewalks. The sidewalk seems to extend up to the church, a place of refuge and for the renewal of strength so that the worshipper can go back to the daily routine. Men, women, and children walk naturally between the public and the religious space — and the distance between one and the other is transformed into a bridge, into a relation not always experienced in other churches or religions. Caio Fábio, referring to the IURD, asserted that it is "only a door. The IURD does not have a door, it is a door. Its architecture is a door . . . wide open, greedy mouth, open and on the sidewalk."[7]

At certain moments in the history of the church, beginning perhaps with the theology of the "social gospel," the conflict between church and society was accentuated. One church turned inward, limiting itself to the spiritual needs of its members, and another sought to act in the world, running the risk of losing its identity in doing so. Will the tension be re-

6. DaMatta, *A casa e a rua,* p. 43. DaMatta contrasts the house and the street: the former is "a space that can shelter equals," and the latter is the place where "the vagabonds, the scoundrels, and the marginalized in general" live, even though he emphasizes the fact that the opposition between one and the other is very complex and "is not at all static or absolute" (p. 47).

7. Interview with Caio Fábio, in the Spanish summary of the book by Anders Rooth about the IURD, mimeo., n.d.

solved through the Pentecostal experience (although with an apparently limited vision of the relations between church and society)?

We do not know how much weight converts give to this missionary practice in their daily routine. The task seems to be accomplished easily, as a command from heaven. The internal spaces of solidarity (of social class, of common needs) are extended out to the world, to the street — and in this way, consequently, they are open to other instances, such as direct participation in electoral politics with their own candidates.

> We take the Word to others, we walked to many places, where no buses went. I had a place that was far away. Once we made a campaign for everybody to give anything, beans, rice, cookies, meat. And they made those bags, those boxes that we would distribute in those places, . . . we took food, clothing — and there was a lot of happiness. . . . It was like this, a comparison: I am here with you, right? Then they divide like this: I, you, and another person go on one street; another goes on another street, and another on another. And we hand out the things, we pray for the people, anointing those people.[8]

But who are these pedestrians of faith? Their appearance is of poverty. Many times they are visibly sick. Or they could be drunk. Or their tired faces show distress. There are also healthy, well-dressed people. The search for a new life — material and spiritual — produces a human chain, the people who before only walked the sidewalks now have penetrated a new space of life.

8. Interview with Sra. Juliana, IURD.

2 Poor and Rich

I n this chapter, and in the following one, I intend to explore the possibility that converts to Pentecostalism may have found a way of overcoming the day-to-day hazards of the poor.[1] How can we explain the intense search on the part of alienated people in society (or those coming
from other churches or religions) for a new type of religious experience?
We are possibly observing the manifestation of an ecclesial practice of the
"option for the poor," many times a discourse without larger consequences in the historic churches. Here the antagonisms stand out more
than the similarities.

The human mass present in the churches, be they members or just
sympathizers, is made up of men and women who are part of the great
multitude that circulates on the city streets, the poor that form the bulk of
the Brazilian population. Only some type of extraordinary transformation of life can lead them to this radiant acceptance of a providence capable of cohabiting with the most humble members of the human species

---

1. The theme is a recurring one, which will be obvious in other chapters, especially ch. 6, "One Day, a Thousand Years," as well as in Part II.

— and to offer them a hope that transforms into victory situations normally associated with frustration and despair. Alienation? Fanaticism? Naivete? It would be more accurate to ask, What do the Pentecostal poor think about the poor?

Brazil: A Poor Country

I believe that Brazil is a poor country. This country is not developing because people do not help each other. . . . I don't know where the money from the campaigns done in the church goes, but we also do campaigns for the people who need help for food, people who do not have any possibility of eating right. So we help with two kilos of beans and rice. We take it to church and the church distributes it. Last week a truck went out from here. And it's not for people from the church, it's for the poor community. . . . We do campaigns to collect clothes, clothes we don't wear anymore, and the pastor asks that they be distributed to the children that need them, street children. And we also help people from the street that ask for food.[2]

There is a group of businessmen who attend the church, and the pastors already know them, they know that they work, they are already well known. So, if there are unemployed people, the pastor himself asks: Can you help this young fellow, who is a father with a family and is unemployed? What church does this? I don't see any other church doing it. So this is what it means to help people.[3]

Those interviewed, without exception, poor as they were, not only spoke of the help they received, but also demonstrated solidarity with other poor, sick, and unhappy people, inside as well as outside the church. Some, in this context, mentioned the national reality, such as this member of the Assembly of God:

In terms of politics, the economy, I feel that our country cannot have too much hope. Brazil is a poor, badly administered country. There are

2. Interview with Leila, IURD.
3. Interview with Carlos, IURD.

no great hopes, especially when we consider the Word of God that each year we are approaching the end time. . . . The way things are going, the poor will continue to be poor, unless some choose, as many have, the road of violence, of robbery. Because sadly, all those who have been placed in power look out for their own and their family's benefit. . . . God helps the poor. The Word of God says that he is our shepherd, and we shall not want. It is he who supplies all our needs. He helps by giving us enough to survive. When we are going through difficulties, I believe God always sends someone to help us. God helps the poor and he can even come and give them a better life. If they believe this and strive. Ask God. God also helps the rich. God helps everybody.[4]

This help, for all of those interviewed, is also the result of conversion — an experience that is mentioned a lot by the Pentecostals but is *silenced* or not lived by those *born* in the church, be they Evangelicals or Catholics by tradition. It is good to remember that this type of individual change has radical connotations. In its Hebrew and Greek origin conversion translates the radical idea of a change of direction, of turning around, of staying away from evil and turning to God, and of having a new behavior. The Greek Bible registers a distinction between the interior sign of conversion and the actions that arise from it. It is *metanoia,* true repentance, to which God responds with the forgiveness of sins, sealed, according to the Pentecostal ritual, by the baptism of the Holy Spirit and the manifestation of its gifts: "Each one receives the gift of manifesting the Spirit for the benefit of all."[5]

Researchers have done little to explore the integrative significance of this personal revolution — not excluding variants of it in other manifestations of popular religiosity — as a part of a process that points to other values and another vision of the world. In general, the phenomenon of conversion is understood in a dualistic way, two worlds in juxtaposition, the sacred and the profane, religion and faith, the spiritual and the material. This is a trap in which some theologians have fallen when they refer derogatorily or indifferently to these strange products of a faith that, in the end, removes mountains of obstacles in daily life and leads even members of the historic churches to this "wild happiness" of the Pentecostal churches.[6]

4. Interview with Janete, Assembly of God.
5. 1 Cor. 12:1-11, 28-31 (Jerusalem Bible).
6. I partially use the expression of Roger Bastide, "wild happiness of the gods,"

However, one must not take the signs of radical conversion in Pentecostalism as generators, on their own, of a personal experience that would lead to an ascetic life, favoring economic savings and creating more chances of survival in the midst of the chronic poverty to which the immense majority of these believers belong. Even while taking into account the mechanisms of solidarity and of mutual help, which are characteristic of the majority of the Pentecostal communities, this *victory* over the daily routine cannot be reduced to an economic expression. The difficulties of life, which in the case of the poor classes are manifested on a daily basis, are growing and are cumulative. There is the increase of the cost of the basics of life (food, transportation, shelter, and health), there is unemployment, and wages are less and less adequate. In Brazil, the eighth largest economy of the world (in terms of gross national product) and the fifth largest world producer of food, more than forty million people are undernourished. More than 50 percent of the economically active population of the country belong in some way to the informal economy. According to the 1999 Human Development Report published by the United Nations Development Program, the distribution of income in Brazil is among the worst in Latin America, on a par with Paraguay. The poorest 20 percent of the population receives a mere 2.5 percent of the national income, while the wealthiest 20 percent enjoy 63 percent of the national income. In additon, 15 percent of the Brazilian population (26 million people) have no access to the bare minimum of benefits such as health care, education, and other basic public services. According to the Comision Economica para America Latina (CEPAL), the number of poor and destitute in Brazil, in relative and absolute terms, is greater than the average of nineteen Latin American countries.

The Doors Will Open

These few facts are sufficient evidence of the extremely low quality of life of a very poor population. However, beyond the statistics now published regu-

---

when he refers to the manifestations and catharsis in the sessions of Afro-Brazilian religions (*As religiões africanas no Brasil* [São Paulo: Universidade de São Paulo, 1971], p. 259).

larly is the reality of what is seen daily in the cities and in the countryside. I am not saying that all the poor indicated by these statistics belong to some sort of popular religion or to Pentecostalism. Adults and children without faith also survive by the work and grace of their daily strategies; or they become thieves; or they die of hunger. But it is also a fact that the number of conversions grows day by day — and the strategies of survival of these "new creatures" rely on more than just simple budgeting or an inclination to cut expenses on vices, women, and other "worldly" things.

It is not a matter, of course, of a totally new focus. As Cecília Mariz[7] reminds us, Max Weber pointed to certain affinities between religious belief and material improvement that may come as a result of a new style of life. Moreover, Weber admitted, as did Karl Marx, that a substitution of reason for myth can help the poor to find solutions to their problems. And he conceived of the possibility of religion contributing to the development of a critical attitude in relation to the economic and political system as a whole, especially among the sects.[8]

Mariz considers religion more as a cultural concept, affirming that it tends to be useful in providing *daily solutions* to the problem of poverty. And she establishes a significant distinction between Pentecostals and Catholics in this regard, affirming that Pentecostals solve their relation with poverty better than the Catholics in the Christian base communities (CBC). The Pentecostals are less secularized, she says. For the CBCs, culture and religiosity are submitted to rational analysis and critique — which, according to the pastoral agents, can separate the truth from the dominant ideology. Thus the importance of popular education in the CBCs.

Consequently, these popular religious movements are not autonomous but are linked to the political, economic, and cultural processes of global society. However, I believe that it is possible to add to these components of social reality — Brazilian or Latin American — the spiritual and transcendental dimension that permeates the daily routine of significant segments of the population — which, in a certain way, paradoxically cre-

---

7. *Coping with Poverty* (Philadelphia: Temple University Press, 1994), pp. 7-8.

8. This last dimension, as we shall see in ch. 5, "Only One Space of Life," offers contradictory aspects and is limited, in general, to the election of persons to state and national legislative bodies, whose actions, with rare exceptions, have been the most conservative.

ates conditions for a personal (and community) autonomy as an alternative to the limits imposed by the concrete situations of real life.

> I believe that the doors will open for a converted person, God will bless his or her bread, his or her money. God will multiply it, will give health. I believe that, in relating to social issues, the greatest charity to be done for a person is to convert him or her to Christ, for him or her to be born again. Then comes the human part — the sharing. . . . This house [the church] is a family. Each one gives advice, helps. . . . In the preaching that I sometimes do, I say that when a person accepts God, he or she is no longer a beggar, no longer begs. He or she is blessed by God.[9]

To be blessed by God, as in the Old Testament, means also to have many material goods, to become rich. "Human life according to the will of God, an authentic life, is that in which humans own and enjoy the good things of the world. Prosperity, health, and love are inherent to human nature and are signs of the fulfillment of the destiny that God gave to humanity; just by enjoying these goods, humanity is living according to the will of the Creator."[10] Bishop Macedo and preachers in the services of the IURD insist on this point: God has the "obligation" to give an immediate answer to those who contribute. "Jesus did not want anyone to be sick or poor." The IURD assumes that money is of fundamental importance. I heard a pastor also say that "everybody needs money and runs after it, but does not do this openly." An editorial of the *Folha Universal* (21 January 1996) could not be any clearer when it affirms that for the IURD, as an institution, "money is the blood of the Church."[11] The "theology of prosperity," which emphasizes the importance of money, in several Protestant denominations (not only in the Pentecostal churches) is already well known, and much has been written about it. In the IURD there is even one day each week dedicated to material well-being and riches — the "Day of Prosperity."

This is the *other side* of the relation of the poor with Pentecostalism,

---

9. Interview with pastor Claudinor, Assembly of God.

10. Wilson Gomes, "Demônios do fim do século: curas, ofertas e exorcismos na Igreja Universal do Reino de Deus," *Cadernos de CEAS* 146 (July-August 1993): 47-63, on p. 50. Gomes calls the demand made with the offering a "cosmic deal."

11. Caio Fábio declared (in an interview) that as a matter of fact, "in its practice the IURD is stronger than the Catholic Church."

especially with the Universal Church. The financial power of this church is known as a source of institutional and personal enrichment (for the leaders) and a cause of scandals that have been widely publicized by the press in newspapers as well as on radio and television. As we saw in one of the interviews,[12] the appeals for money can scare and even distance people who, in their situation of poverty, cannot agree with the insistence on a contribution — the largest possible — repeatedly justified by the pastors: "Whoever does not give the tithe is robbing God. The tithe and offering are not for the pastor, they are for the church, for Jesus." "The root of all evil is not money, but the attachment to money." "There is no other way for us to receive blessings in our economic life if we do not first give to God. But when the offering time comes people get stuck!" Another pastor hit his extended hand on a Bible and cried: "The world is criticizing us because of the tithe, but this is not a thing of the church, it is God's. It is here!" It is curious — and frightening — that sometimes they talked about *tithing* 20 percent, 30 percent, and even 50 percent.[13] This happened in a church of the IURD (Copacabana), when they announced a trip of the bishops to the Holy Land, where they would take envelopes with the requests of the believers, in order for them to be anointed and to receive an answer. But it was necessary to contribute.[14] One of the strongest critics of the IURD, the ex-pastor Mário Justino, declares that he is convinced that "two things are essential in order to be a successful pastor in the Universal Church. The first is to have the capacity of channeling impressive offerings."[15] One reporter for the *Folha de São Paulo,* writing

12. Interview with Leila, IURD.

13. The same has been observed in other cities, where some pastors insist on a tithe of 50 percent. The tithe of 30 percent is justified as being 10 percent for each person of the Trinity (*O Globo,* 16 August 1992). Compare Ricardo Mariano, "Os Neopentecostais e a teologia da prosperidade," *Novos Estudos* (CEBRAP) 44 (March 1966): 37.

14. Requests in the IURD of Catete, Botafogo, Copacabana, and Abolição.

15. Mário Justino, *Nos Bastidores do Reino: A vida secreta na Igreja Universal do Reino de Deus* (São Paulo: Geração Editorial, 1995), p. 41. The second quality mentioned by Justino "is to know how to entertain people and hold on to them by their 'leashes.'" Further on, he affirms: "During the meetings in the church, we would distribute envelopes and we would make the faithful deposit in them what we called a 'sacrifice offering' (something like the wages for a month) and a prayer request, which the bishop would take to Israel, the Holy Land."

about the IURD in the United States, used the expression "temple is money," a new version of a saying of Douglas Monteiro: instead of "sellers in the temple," we would have a "temple of sellers."[16]

Poor Believers, Rich Church

How can we understand this correlation between poor believers and a rich church, between a visible congregation of humble workers and a leadership that parades in imported cars and lives in palaces, in this country or abroad?[17] As observers of the services of the IURD, the moment of these appeals for money was the one that disturbed us the most. But what can be said about those who would get up, apparently without hesitation and full of confidence, to take their maximum offering to the altar? The usual answer of the critics is that they are being exploited, taken advantage of in their good faith.

First of all, it is important to clarify that the pathetic financial appeal of the Universal Church is not common in all Pentecostal currents, although the doctrine of the tithe is part of the moral commitment of the majority of its faithful. The research of New Birth (Novo Nacimento; ISER) verified that the biblical principle of the tithe is more generalized than is supposed and even predominant in the Protestant churches. It showed that, during the month prior to the interviews, 71 percent of those interviewed had contributed to their church (29 percent were "owing" the church), while 45 percent gave the tithe (26 percent) or more than the tithe (19 percent), "an elevated percentage in the world of voluntary contributors." The classification of those interviewed according to income revealed another sig-

16. "Igrejas, seitas e agências: aspectos de um ecumenismo popular," in *A cultura do povo,* ed. E. Valle and J. J. Queiroz (São Paulo: Cortez/Instituto de Estudos Especiais, 1988).

17. Walter J. Hollenweger has an interesting chapter about "The Pentecostal Elites and the Pentecostal Poor: A Missed Dialogue?" in *Charismatic Christianity as a Global Culture,* ed. Karla Poewe (Columbia, S.C.: University of South Carolina Press, 1994). In it, he analyzes the affluent character of Pentecostalism in the West and asks what happens when the Pentecostalism of the poor majority, predominant in the Third World, does not agree with the Pentecostal theology of a minority in North America or in Europe. And he adds that "from a Pentecostal perspective, it is surely time to organize a transnational inter-Pentecostal ecumenical debate" (p. 206).

nificant fact: among the poorest (up to twice the minimum wage, R$100.00, corresponding to the same value in US$), 77 percent contributed during that month, and 53 percent gave an amount equal to or more than the tithe. Among those with higher incomes (more than five times the minimum wage) 91 percent declared they had contributed, with 70 percent giving an amount equal to or larger than the tithe. Although the research was done at the homes of those interviewed, without the dramatic atmosphere of a worship service, the data are revealing and indicate that the contribution for the church is part of the personal or family budget and does not depend on the pleas for money that are so much in evidence in the services of the IURD — which naturally places it in a privileged financial situation, opening *spaces* not accessible to other churches. However, its *theology* of giving so that God will respond is not always present or explicit in other confessions.

> We have to give a percentage per month. We have to give 10 percent of our income to the church. I spoke to the pastor: "Pastor, I think that I'm not in a position to be able to stay in this church because it asks for a quantity that I can't give. I don't earn enough." He turned to me and said, "My daughter, you are in the church because you like it and here we ask for money because all religions ask. So we ask. Now, a person gives if they can. If you cannot give, don't give, but do not leave the church, continue your journey here. When you feel that you are in a position to give, then you go ahead and give. But all churches ask for the tithe."[18]

> During a time when I was doing well financially, I was able to give the tithe. I went to a conference in São Paulo and I heard the testimony of a missionary who mentioned that he only gave 10 percent, but later he started to give 20, 30, and in the end he gave almost all his salary to the church, which is for the work of God. I was very impressed, that touched me, and I was able to give 10 for the church and 10 for the Children's Department. But now I am only investing in the children.[19]

There are, however, other elements involved in the act of contributing, of giving, which are very distant from this logic of the market, although it may include some of this *exchange* with God. By *giving* many

18. Interview with Leila, IURD.
19. Interview with Esmeralda, Assembly of God.

times the impossible, the believer *gives* of him or herself. Contrary to the "promises" made by Catholics, when the believer *pays* for what he or she received, the Pentecostal offering is an anticipation of God's response.[20]

> And it was not really with sacrifice. We have to believe in God. If we be-
> lieve in him, for example, the pastor gives the envelope, says that if we
> take that envelope we are going to succeed in getting what we want; but if
> the person doesn't have faith, that is as if you weren't getting anything.
> Because for Jesus, reaching for the envelope, good, putting money inside,
> handing it in, placing a request, and handing it in. Without faith it's not
> going to happen. Having faith that it is going to happen, it happens.[21]

A more comprehensive analysis of this courage to give what normally is lacking, will be further developed, in the chapter "Survival and Transcendence." However, it is worthwhile here to recall the reflection of the psychoanalyst Jurandir Freire Costa concerning the radicalism of the Universal Church precisely in reference to the financial contribution of its poor parishioners. For the big bosses of the church, he says, "the tithe of the believers is a business, [but] I am not so sure that for the practitioners the same act means the same thing." The believers are not necessarily "buying" something (logic of the marketplace), but "giving," participating in a cause. According to their reasoning, this changes everything, even if the faithful are thinking about their material well-being. The sacred values have priority. The main thing "is that giving, instead of buying, is a gesture of 'waste', a 'luxury', . . . imagining that one is consuming." And this act of generosity creates in the one that gives a style of life superior to the unfaithful; it gives them an image of moral greatness. Freire Costa asks: what does "our public and private culture offer, above all the culture of the elite?" Beer, football, carnival, and a trip to Miami. And what about the IURD? It offers a global perspective on life — a sign "that our culture does not have only one rule of the game; it has several" — and things that give meaning to life and death.[22]

20. Observations by Pierre Sanchis and Rubem César Fernandes in a debate about Pentecostalism, at ISER, on 26-27 September 1996.

21. Interview with Leila, IURD.

22. Article in *Folha de São Paulo,* 21 January 1996, under the title "The hidden logic of unreasonableness."

During the service they ask for a certain quantity of money, and then if you can, you give it; now if you can't, they're not going to check anybody's pockets. What the people attack the Universal most about is money. Money and growth. But they don't know that that's where the growth comes from. It is through the money, the donations. How did the church buy Record TV? With money. How did it buy this lot in Botafogo? With money. . . . It was a sacrifice; it was not easy. The majority of the people left the church. . . . The Record was bought with a lot of sweat from maids and day laborers; it was a lot of sweat from the common people. . . . But during the same time we made a campaign to take food to the northeast. We were there until more or less midnight filling the truck with food to take to the northeast. . . . It is so good to share your bread with another person. To satisfy someone's hunger. This feels very good. I give an "A" to this work at the Universal.[23]

Oscar Lewis points out: "Any movement, be it religious, pacifist or revolutionary, that organizes and gives hope to the poor and effectively promotes solidarity and a sense of identification in big groups destroys the social and psychological heart of the culture of poverty." With a new awareness of their class and their worth, "or when they adopt an international viewpoint about the world, they no longer belong to the culture of poverty even though they are still desperately poor."[24]

23. Interview with Rosa (IURD) by Clara Mafra. The purchase of Record refers to a national television channel, at the cost of $48 million. The woman interviewed added: "Many people that were not from the Universal also helped."

24. Oscar Lewis, *La cultura de la pobreza* (Barcelona: Cuadernos Anagrama, 1972), p. 19.

3 *Survival and Transcendence*

The issue of poverty and the conversion of the poor to Pentecostalism lead me to speculate about another type of antagonism, not between churches, but in the even more complex field of the relations of the disinherited with the merciless structure of Brazilian neoliberal society. How do the poor survive the day-to-day assaults on them? If in the comparison between the church and the street the former prevailed, in this case the street is the main scene. But here we will go beyond the physical limits between the sidewalk and the church stairway.

Everything Changed

Speaking more specifically, I would ask, How can we explain the way those converted to the Pentecostal faith overcome these daily contingencies? The human conglomerate that fills the churches, members of the church or just sympathizers, in their great majority are men and women who are part of the multitude of the poor who make up the majority of the Brazilian population. Only some type of extraordinary transformation of life can lead them to this radiant acceptance of a providence capable of co-habiting with the humblest members of the human species — and offering them a hope that transfigures situations normally associated with frustration and despair into victory. Alienation? Fanaticism? Naivete?

> Because the time comes in our lives when we need to find a religion to stick with. Because the world is closed, is becoming closed. So, whoever doesn't have a religion to hold on to ends up falling. I looked for Jesus because I thought it was about time.[1]

> After I entered the Universal everything changed. Even with my very rigid boss it was also possible to change. I used to work very depressed and then I started to take everything in a natural way. I went on to have Jesus alive as I do, so why worry about it. If the boss only knew the God I know today he wouldn't be like he is. . . . And also the doctor said that I would never be a mother. So I took part in a prayer chain at the church and by the seventh session I got pregnant.[2]

The interviews express what many other converts revealed — radiant and confident faces — in the informal conversations. God, Jesus, and the Holy Spirit solved or will solve their problems: sickness will be cured, food will arrive, money will multiply, a child will be born.

But, be careful, this is not a matter of a univocal phenomenon. There are many Pentecostalisms, and not all the answers are coherent or reveal an awareness of the oppressions of the secular world. There is a "plurality of meanings"[3] in the Pentecostal phenomenon, which can oscillate between alienation, growing awareness, and liberation. The point in common in this universe of "deviant ideas," the central mark of Pentecostal religiosity, seems to be an orientation toward another reality — the transcendent world of faith and spirituality. Paradoxically, it is in this dimension, so many times labeled alienating, that resistance and protest are manifested: the cry of the oppressed creature that frees itself from the world, from other religions, or from the very church left behind. The great paradoxes of the religious life become *bearable* and the antagonisms

---

1. Interview with Leila, IURD.
2. Interview with Rosa, IURD.
3. Christian Lalive D'Épinay, "Religião, espiritualidade e sociedade," *Cadernos do ISER* 6 (March 1977).

can be overcome as the immanent and transcendent *familiarize themselves* with each other in the daily reality of the believer. The theoretical and ethical enigmas of religions, the disputes, and the errors and heresies bring us — in the words of Kierkegaard when speaking about the great paradox of the religious life — "a promise and a perspective of a transcendent world, situated beyond the limits of our human experience," but which "remains human, excessively human."[4]

How is this possible? How can the afflictions of the daily routine, in the inexorable striving for personal and family survival, be manifested in happiness and peace, in celebration and witness to the sacred? It is through this *process,* strange or less eloquent in other religious forms, that subjectivity is introduced into "the objective realm of things."[5] Through this path, religion *(re-ligare)* can become basically the *instrument* of the survival-transcendence relation. The hard reality of existence, as we commonly say, and what transcends it, merge into a unique experience. "Religious life and daily life intersect each other."[6]

Max Weber established a clarifying difference by mentioning the religions that adapt people to the world, "making the disorder of the experience tolerable through law and ritual; and the religions of salvation, which accept the disorders and the dangers of existence with resignation, repudiate the pleasures of the world and seek a transcendent and supernatural objective."[7] As in the current Islamic resurgence, religion means a form of life: "You are a Muslim every day and at all times." In the same way, the Pentecostal universe offers a new dimension of religiosity, which may make it possible for us to go beyond a superficial understanding of a phenomenon that cannot be explained in itself nor defined in exclusively sociological terms.[8]

---

4. Quoted by Ernst Cassirer, *Antropologia filosófica* (Mexico City: Fondo de Cultura Económica, 1992), p. 114.

5. Expression of Paul Tillich, *The Courage to Be* (New Haven: Yale University Press, 1952).

6. Compare Peter Berger and Thomas Luckmann, *The Social Construction of Reality* (New York: Doubleday, 1966).

7. Quoted by Donald G. MacRae, *Las idéias de Weber* (São Paulo: Cultrix/USP, 1975).

8. Marx insisted on the risk of remaining at the superficial level, enchanted by the immediate and concrete form — which meant, for him, entering into total illusion. And

The Daily Routine and Transcendence

The concept of daily life, however, has its ambiguities as an integral part of the social structure. As Norbert Elias shows us, it is difficult to give a sociological concept the stature of a universal notion.[9] It's not a matter of characterizing daily life as having "a special structure more or less autonomous" or of saying that the daily routine is "totally different from other domains of life in society"[10] but of penetrating into its meaning as a pronounced dimension of human experience. This is especially true of the poorer classes, for whom the daily struggle for survival transcends the norms that regulate the socially established relations, opening a new symbolic horizon (a future), which before conversion was reduced to a struggle without any meaning other than daily survival. It is, thus, a matter of pointing out a vital relation in a space of time usually stripped of greater meaning.

Here the symbolic, as a revelation of the sacred, occupies a central place in the Pentecostal experience, manifesting itself in a concrete way in the daily struggle. The great cosmic symbols that are referred to by scholars of religion — creation, the heavens, the waters, the earth, hell — are present not only in word but in objects that are representative of the mystery of transcendental things. "The 'symbolic' designates the common denominator of all the ways of objectifying, of giving meaning to reality," says Paul Ricoeur.[11] The material representativity of doctrinal elements in

---

he spoke of the superficiality of an analysis of the circulation of money that does not take into account the process developing behind it, that is, the transformation of money into capital.

9. Norbert Elias, "Elias et la vie quotidienne," *Cahier Internationale de Sociologie* 99 (1995): 237ff.

10. Elias, "Elias et la vie quotidienne," p. 240.

11. Paul Ricoeur, *Freud and Philosophy: An Essay on Interpretation* (New Haven: Yale University Press, 1970), p. 9. The materialization of biblical themes is very much present in the IURD: miniatures of Noah's ark, of Peter's net, and so forth, that the faithful take home with the promise of great blessings and solutions to domestic problems. In Ricoeur's words, "a symbol is a double-meaning linguistic expression that requires an interpretation, and interpretation a work of understanding that aims at deciphering symbols" (p. 9). In spite of their simplicity — or for this very reason — the miniatures representing the great biblical events carry an enormous meaning (a "hermeneutical field") of mediation between the transcendental and the more immediate apprehension of reality.

many ways reveals the concreteness of the daily struggle. "In the short run the individual strives for subsistence, in which task he/she can count on the aid of the meta-social and the transcendental. Directly or indirectly the religious contributes to a symbolic solution of the contradictions of real life," notes sociologist Christian Parker.[12]

Actually, the solutions go beyond the symbolic. The survival of the poor, a material happening, measured empirically, is subjected to another value, of a supernatural order — and this fact alone seems to offer effective solutions in the sphere of daily life. The objects of personal use themselves can become symbols. The purses or wallets that during the service are raised toward heaven, for a special blessing, are taken home with more than a few thin *reais* (Brazilian currency): now they also hold a hope, which allows the believer to even empty them in response to the appeals of the leader. The word is not his, it comes from heaven, and it is better to obey it with happiness. Although, in this case, Roger Bastide was not referring to the Pentecostal service, his words can be applied here when he speaks of the "wild liberation of daily life, from the miseries of existence, of the wild happiness of being possessed by the gods, of leaving the profane realm in order to participate in supernatural exaltation."[13]

In this tangled web of emotions, in the experience of merging in one gesture the transcendent with the immanent, perhaps the greatest *miracle* of the Pentecostal proposal of faith is engraved: survival in the midst of the marginality of life. Even if not everyone goes through the questionable experience of a miracle, everyone testifies to it or considers it a real and immanent fact, be it through an extraordinary cure, through a job that appears suddenly, or through the victory over another day of struggle. All parts of the service emphasize the miraculous and feed the souls along their path in the world. The symbolism of baptism (which many converts experience, and in many cases they are rebaptized) as a resurrection from the dead, represented by the immersion and recuperation of the body in the water; or the gift of speaking strange tongues, symbol of powerful communication with the supernatural — both manifest, as in the past,

---

12. Mimeo., Santiago, Chile, 1986, p. 33.

13. Roger Bastide, *As religiões africanas no Brasil* (São Paulo: Universidade de São Paulo, 1971), p. 259.

the real presence of the Holy Spirit. In other words, the fantastic is integrated into and re-creates daily experience.

Faced with so many extraordinary manifestations, the community response is always festive and without liturgical formality. The faithful appropriate the transcendent — or the transcendent appropriates them — and the result is ecstasy, rapture. Peter Berger says: "It is in worship that the prototypical gesture of religion is fulfilled again. This is the gesture in which humankind, in hope, lifts up its arms to reach transcendence."[14] A powerful link is established among people and between them and the outside world (relatives, friends, real situations), giving to these symbolic forces the concrete potentiality of life or of survival. "The religious conscience," says Paul Tillich, "the state of being concerned unconditionally, must affirm both the unconditional transcendence of its god and the concreteness which makes possible an encounter with him."[15]

We can thus speak about another interdisciplinary implication, now between theology and philosophy, which I find again in Paul Ricoeur. When theology, he says, offers symbols of transcendence capable of producing *reflection* on human existence, it gives food for thought to philosophy. "Theology places before the philosopher the tremendous fact of the mystery which surrounds all the ideas and situations within the reach of philosophy."[16] In a certain way it is what Peter Beyer has told us recently, remembering the empirical nature of the immanent faced with the mystery of the transcendent, while at the same time it can only be spoken of (understood) in terms of the immanent. Transcendent-immanent, in short, he says further, constitute the main polarity (or dichotomy) of communication in religion.[17]

14. Peter Berger, *A Rumor of Angels* (New York: Anchor Books, 1990), p. 116.

15. *Systematic Theology,* vol. 2 (Chicago: University of Chicago Press, 1951), p. 169. Tillich adds that "the mediator-gods have grown out of this tension. They make the transcendent divine approachable for men, and they elevate man toward the transcendent divine. They unite in themselves the infinity of the transcendent divinity and the finitude of men."

16. Compare Jaci C. Maraschin, "A questão do Mito em Paul Ricoeur em relação com a Sociologia do Conhecimento," in *Simpósio* (São Paulo: ASTE, 1972), pp. 23-36.

17. Peter Beyer, *Religion and Globalization* (London: Sage, 1994). "Many sociological definitions of religion operate with a basic dichotomy such as profane/sacred (Durkheim), natural/supernatural (Parsons), nomos/cosmos (Berger), and empirical/

In historic Protestantism symbols are used with such ceremony that their meaning or the meaning of the words that antecede their presentation ends up being reduced. In this way, the dimension of transcendence that makes of them a gift from heaven is lost. A mythical-symbolic narrative is primarily hermeneutical and therefore contains a "reserve of meaning," which cannot be grasped in a *rational* narrative or in "profane historiography."[18] Transcendence, as a quality of what exists or acts on its own, above knowledge or the world of experience, needs symbols in order to express the ineffable, the indefinable. A gift of oneself is only explained through the mystery of a personal surrender that goes beyond the logic of the marketplace and can rejoice in the giving even of everything one owns (Mark 12:42). Another existential dimension is revealed, which surpasses the dialectic between individual and structural poverty (poverty is always personalized). The religious commitment involves the *whole* person, just as the *whole* (or the transcendent) can be manifested in a person. "Proper conceptualization of the immanent whole requires the transcendent."[19] Acting on the daily routine is important in facing vital issues, above all if

---

super-empirical (Robertson). . . . I prefer to use *immanence/transcendence* to label the central religious dichotomy" (p. 5). Although this perspective of Beyer applies to all religions, it can illumine the Pentecostal phenomenon in an exemplary manner. Even though the author does not refer to this particular confession, we can see in this Protestant current its capacity of insertion into the *globalization* that characterizes today's society. It is worthwhile to remember here the international conference about religion, in Toulouse (1997), with the theme Pentecostalism and Transnationalization (the term preferred by the organizers instead of *globalization*), sponsored by the Societé Internationale de Sociologie des Religions. In this sense it is also appropriate to refer to the chapter "New Perspectives: Globalization," by Otavio Velho, where he refers to fundamentalisms as one of the symptoms of globalized modernity, substituting "exclusivist logic and stratifications" for "multiple functional differentiations," leaving "open gaps and 'residues' not covered by the institutional spheres and which create a demand through means of communication (such as religion) which, at a disadvantage from the point of view of modern institutional dynamics, can, nevertheless, gain a new 'performative' role, as 'cultural resources' for social movements" (in *Besta-Fera: Recriação do Mundo* [Rio de Janeiro: Relume Dumar, 1995], p. 225).

18. Compare J. Severino Croatto, *Êxodo: uma hermenêutica da liberdade* (São Paulo: Edições Paulinas, 1981), p. 64.

19. Beyer, *Religion and Globalization,* p. 31. The author adds: "But, as every major religious tradition shows only too clearly, the transcendent is not anything that can be talked about except in immanent terms" (p. 82).

this action refers to the world of the poor and to the struggle for survival. When one advocates a new style of life, starting from day-to-day experience, a future is idealized, different from the contingencies of a restricted time, offering the glories, and responsibilities, of a future full of promises of a transformed life.

Here I am parodying the psychoanalyst Jurandir Freire Costa when, turning to Agnes Heller, he speaks about the action over a (past) contingency as an implication for an idealized future, which automatically makes the subject responsible for what he or she will become. That is, "transforming a contingency into *destiny* implies, simultaneously, defining the human actor as a moral subject who deliberates about alternatives and creates an ideal image of the world capable of ethically orienting his/her decisions."[20] And although the author is not referring explicitly to religious behavior, as in other writings, his reflection furnishes elements for understanding the phenomenon I am analyzing. Moreover, he reminds us that it is not *guilt* (as in the majority of the Protestant confessions) but *responsibility* (here in a positive sense) that establishes a new line of conduct. Even, or perhaps mainly, in relation to others, if the convert feels responsible for those who have not accepted the new faith.

All of this, however, does not mean that the people touched by this supernatural power do not make use of the survival strategies common to the poor population; rather that they submit the multiple forms of management of the informal economy to a new relation — precisely in the context of their faith and absolute trust in divine providence. In the introduction to *Receitas caseiras,* Leonardo Boff says: "No matter how high the flights of the spirit may be, no matter how intimate the emotions of the heart are, they depend a little on material things: a piece of bread, a handful of rice and a glass of water. The spirit need not be ashamed of its cosmic roots. At the human level, material things are never strictly material. In fact, they are sacramental: they are the bearers of meanings which nourish the spirit besides nourishing the body."[21] Rubem Alves says more or less the same thing: "transcendence is revealed in a concrete way not only in the cries for freedom but also in the struggle against all that op-

20. *Tempo e presença,* March/April 1996.
21. Leonardo Boff, ed., *Jornal do Brasil* (Rio de Janeiro) 1982.

presses humanity."[22] And in the words of our Christian poet Murilo Mendes, "one can also reach God through the five senses."[23]

Peter Berger has perhaps captured in a more powerful way the deeper meaning of transcendence in the mystery of certain religious practices. In his book, *A Rumor of Angels* (an almost transcendental title), he has two paragraphs of well-humored reflections about sociology and theology that can offer other dimensions to the effort to relate the survival of the poor — their day-to-day struggle — with the infinite richness of the transcendental. I conclude these considerations with his words:

> I would suggest that theological thought seek out what might be called *signals of transcendence* within the empirically given human situation. And I would further suggest that there are *prototypical human gestures* that may constitute such signals. What does this mean?
>
> By signals of transcendence I mean phenomena that are to be found within the domain of our "natural" reality but that appear to point beyond that reality. In other words, I am not using transcendence here in the technical philosophical sense but literally, as the transcending of the normal, everyday world that I earlier identified with the notion of the "supernatural." By prototypical human gestures I mean certain reiterated acts and experiences that appear to express essential aspects of man's being, of the human animal as such. I do *not* mean what Jung called "archetypes" — potent symbols buried deep in the unconscious mind and common to all men. The phenomena I am discussing are not "unconscious" and they do not have to be excavated from the "depths" of the mind; they belong to ordinary everyday awareness.[24]

22. Rubem Alves, *O enigma da religião* (Petrópolis: Vozes, 1975).

23. Quoted by Santiago Silviano, *Nas malhas da letra* (São Paulo: Companhia das Letras, 1989), p. 65.

24. Berger, *A Rumor of Angels,* pp. 74-75.

4 *Word and Reality*

We arrived a little before the beginning of the service. The hall of the Universal Church was not full as on other occasions, but many lively people were already gathered in the lobby (a room as large as many church sanctuaries). In this intermediate space, between the church and the street, I observe the people. They talk in small groups. I try to hear them, but the noise of the cars is stronger. A bulletin board announces routine things alongside the wonders: worship services, young people's meetings, a meeting of evangelists, a "strong prayer service" on Sunday at 3 P.M.; and a service for curing all evils, for liberation, and for salvation. In the heat of the large lobby, between the noise of the street and the murmur of those who have still not gone through the large glass doors, I catch a glimpse of the movement inside. The first seats are already taken, while many people walk through the immense hall. A lay worker invites us to enter. I am with a group, and I suddenly find myself enjoying the comfort of air conditioning, an easy chair, and fantastic lighting. And then I am aware of the noise inside, which was inviting me on in this researcher pilgrimage through the Pentecostal realm: the exuberance of the *word*. The spoken, sung, cried, and murmured word. The pastor is not the only one who speaks. All can express themselves in some way: in hymns, hallelu-jahs, greeting of the brothers and sisters, testimony, strange tongues, and in choral response to the question shouted out on the speakers, after an affirmation of faith: "Is it or isn't it so!?" and the prolonged echo of the congregation: "It is!"

The word dominates the Pentecostal service. The pastor already has a microphone in his hand. Nobody escapes from the sound that the speakers distribute throughout the enormous space of the service. Orality, the maximum expression of worship, predominantly improvised, mobi-lizes those present. But it is as if everything were programmed ahead of time: prayers, songs, appeals, testimonies, offerings, confessions, expul-sion of demons, Bible readings, hallelujahs, the sale of books and newspa-pers, distribution of symbolic objects, and strange tongues.

This verbal and musical, individual and collective diversity, men-tioned at random, does not obey an ordered sequence. Sometimes the various moments intersect each other, at first soft, now in contrast, much louder. The tone of voice of the leader, between deep and sharp, hurts my ears; and it can reach dramatic moments, as in the sermon, in the appeals, in the "strong prayer," or when expelling demons. Many times neighbors complain and bring suit against the church if the decibels go above the normal level.[1] This powerful network of internal communication, under the mediation of the pastors, links together the gestures of the people, their own voices, their most intimate problems, their deepest hopes, their poverty, and their unusually generous contributions. In general, there is not a single moment of silence or personal reflection. For a stranger, or a passerby, the confusion is notable.

In this chapter I want to explore the issue of orality, one of the most debated themes concerning the Pentecostal experience. Be it in the ser-vices or in the radio and television programs, the power of the untiring

---

1. "Decibels can bring legal problems for churches" is the main article of the *Jornal do Brasil* (4 November 1997), which notes that the Secretariat for the Environ-ment of Rio de Janeiro is investigating the excess of noise of religious services: "The Universal Church of the Reign of God, in Realengo, has already been fined twice, first for R$500, then for R$1,000. The last measurement, on January 17, registered a level of 94 decibels when the maximum permitted at that time and place was 70 decibels." Other churches of the city (Baptist, Assembly of God, and Congregação Cristã) were also fined for the same reason.

word has *internal* and *external* effects. Starting from their manifestations within the spacial limits of the church, these "multiple speech acts" (Corten) project themselves outward, be it through political action or personal commitment to evangelism.[2]

> With unbelievers our work is to evangelize. To preach the gospel of salvation. To preach Jesus Christ as Savior. Only this. We do not offer anything to these people to get them to come to church. We preach, we go to where they are. We do this in open-air services, conferences, crusades, not only in our church, but we are in union with other churches and we hold big events in order to reach the people that need the gospel. We also have personal work, we have sisters who visit hospitals, who visit slums.[3]

> I speak to many people, including my ex-boyfriend. When I entered the church I wanted him to enter with me. He even went about ten times. He didn't like it. He said that the Universal Church was of no use to him. He even preferred the Assembly of God. So, it's a matter of each person. I got tired of calling people, of those I have called no one has come. But I don't get discouraged. I try my best, I evangelize, I give out newspapers . . . at the jail, in the police offices, in the hospital.[4]

> Whenever I have the opportunity to enter homes and speak about the gospel, I do speak. More for friends. I begin with informal conversation, speaking about work issues, general issues. Generally people always complain about something in their life, personal or professional — and that's what I take advantage of to tell them. Yes, I believe I already have won several people for Jesus, not many, but I already spoke of Jesus to many people. I know that the seed was planted. But I already have won three people for the Lord. All my family are in the church, some in the Baptist, but all of them are Evangelical.[5]

It is not a matter of a merely verbal engagement with others, but of the use of language adequate to the situations of life. Personal evangelism

---

2. The political projection of Pentecostalism is the object of analysis in ch. 5, "Only One Space of Life."

3. Interview with Josiel, evangelist of the Assembly of God.

4. Interview with Leila.

5. Interview with Janete.

repeats the *technique* of the sermons — a popular speech, turned toward the day-to-day routine of the people. I believe that this is what Walter Hollenweger refers to when he describes the extent and the strength of the Pentecostal word, "not only due to loyalty to its own tradition but also because it deals with the language of the poor." And he adds: "Here the Pentecostal option automatically becomes political. Using an oral language, they express their solidarity with their own roots, with the poor and the persecuted in their country."[6]

It is opportune to remember that the extension of the word beyond the ecclesiastical sphere, currently not very evident in the historic churches, has reached and continues to gain enormous space in the media. And although news reports (and even editorials) are predominantly quite negative, especially when referring to the Universal Church, nothing seems to diminish the fame or slow the advance of this Pentecostal movement; and the frequency of attendance at its services has not declined. In the midst of the 1992 crisis that sent Bishop Edir Macedo to prison, accused of having used the IURD to carry out illegal financial operations, the faithful simply considered him a victim of persecution, "as happened with Jesus and the prophets." Something similar happened after the kicking of the image of Nossa Senhora Aparecida[7] in 1995, which provoked public and official repulsion from the Catholic Church, the secular press, and the Protestant sector, and even something of an internal crisis. But the IURD was able to keep the faithfulness of its members, including those who criticized the tactless gesture of the bishop.

> He [the bishop] shouldn't have done this. But since nobody is like anybody else. . . . Isn't that so? He did something which has no explanation, because it was he who did it. But nobody liked it. He made a mistake, he made a mistake. He is wrong, as Bishop Macedo said. There is no explanation, neither for me nor for the founder himself.[8]

6. Walter J. Hollenweger, "The Pentecostal Elites and the Pentecostal Poor: A Missed Dialogue?" in *Charismatic Christianity as a Global Culture,* ed. Karla Poewe (Columbia, S.C.: University of South Carolina Press, 1994), p. 205.

7. The violent gesture of the bishop, on a program of Record TV, property of the IURD, was aired on the religious holiday on which the patron saint of Brazil is worshipped (12 October).

8. Interview with Rosa, IURD.

He [the bishop] did something right at the wrong time, and failed ethically. . . . If you are Catholic and you convert to Christ, and you have an altar in your home, and if you allow it, I can go to your home and break that altar. Because you already abandoned that and embraced the faith. . . . For that really isn't worth anything, it's made of plaster, it's made of wood, it's made of metal. . . . Now, if the image has not left the heart of the person, it's no good to break the image. That is why he did the right thing at the wrong time.[9]

What happens *inside* has repercussions outside; and this projection echoes back, institutionally and personally in many cases. This double movement of the effect of words (and actions) reflects another facet of the Pentecostal movement, above all in the most aggressive version of the IURD. If internally the vocabulary of the church service has been re-created, giving emphasis and new power to doctrines and words somewhat neglected by the Protestant tradition, externally the Pentecostals have been labeled "sectarians," "intolerant," "conservatives," "arrogant," and "fanatics" — another display of the use of worn-out terms in the religious realm.[10] But it is in the heat and the vibration of the experience of worship where everything seems to start — and at this point I want to explore the meaning of this noisy orality in reference to the sermon, to glossolalia, and to music.[11] And, naturally, its external effects, especially in the political area.

9. Interview with Josiel, IURD.

10. I take into account this reference of Clara Mafra, in an article, "Apprentices of the Spirit."

11. Prayer occupies many moments in the worship service, and it would be important to have a specific analysis of its role in Pentecostal religiosity. According to Marcel Mauss, prayer is an oral religious ritual, whose origin, little studied, might be seen as a late product of the evolution of religions. He notes: "the prayer-word, as it is closer to thought and more mobile than gestures, makes the relevance of conscience possible and the relation of the individual to God is brought into the realm of free conversation" (commentaries on the works of Mauss, among them, *Institución y culto* [Barcelona: Barral Editores, 1971], in *Sociologia de la religión y teología — Estudio bibliográfico* [Madrid: Instituto Fé y Secularidad, 1975], p. 37).

The Worship Service and the Sermon

The Pentecostal service includes a whole set of verbal manifestations in which the sermon is not always the culminating point, as is the case in the traditional Protestant liturgy. I am not sure if one can really speak of a *sermon* in a Pentecostal service since all the liturgy seems to have the same emphasis, the same doctrinal and catechetical strength. In reality, the *word* goes beyond the sermon, is complemented by the other acts of the service and means more than the exegesis of a biblical text — many times only a pretext to reinforce commitment to the tithe, to evangelization, or to the norms of conduct of the believers. By all means, preaching is a high point, the central theme of which is the fight against evil through personal sanctification. "It is by speaking about evil, giving messages about it, that it is possible to overcome it. The speaking, the giving of messages or only transmitting them, is a central ritual act in the process of liberation at Universal."[12] Or remembering the devil:

> There are people that are not converted. They leave here and go and drink wine. They don't have Jesus. They don't worship the God I worship, but a god invented by them. They have the devil. Here we don't say anything to please people, but what we need to say. That's why many people don't like the Universal Church. Right or wrong?[13]

At the IURD of Botafogo a pastor asked everyone to open the Bible to Philippians 4:1-8; lay workers helped some people find the text. Since in the Universal preaching from the Old Testament seems to predominate, I was curious to hear a message about the last recommendations of Paul and Timothy "to those who are in Philippi." After a long introduction, the leader read the text and pointed out the verse "do not be anxious about anything": "Anxiety is a lack of faith. Whoever has faith does not have anxiety." After speaking about the daily distress of those who awake thinking about the money they have to earn, he went on to speak about women and their feelings: "Women suffer more in their feelings because

---

12. Patricia Guimarães, "Ritos do reino de Deus: Pentecostalismo e invenção ritual" (master's thesis, University of Rio de Janeiro, 1997), p. 59.

13. A section of the sermon preached at the IURD of Barra da Tijuca, with the majority of people in attendance from the middle class, on 15 November 1995.

they take their relation with others more seriously. They are more responsible, men aren't."

However, the sermon, sometimes more than one, is part of the orality that fills the two hours or more of each ceremony. It moves people. It stirs their reality. And although in Pentecostal churches the pulpit occupies the center of the religious space, just as in the majority of the historic churches, its impact on the gathering is incomparably greater. While the traditional preacher is solemnly immobilized behind a small pulpit, the Pentecostal leader has at his disposal a whole platform facing the audience, and therefore he can walk from one side to the other, microphone in hand, his theatrical gestures more easily performed due to the absence of a suit coat. (It is not like this in the Assembly of God, for example, where the pulpit is normally occupied by several pastors and lay persons, wearing coat and tie, who arrive and kneel in prayer until the service starts.) The space of the altar in the IURD, where the same phrase, "Jesus Christ is Lord," is reproduced on the façade of each temple, is filled with a table of objects (difficult to identify at a distance): a candleholder with seven candles and a large cross illuminated from behind with a neon light. In the background, covered by a curtain, is the baptistery for baptism by immersion. When the voice tires, the microphone is passed to the hand of another pastor.

Contrary to what happens in a Protestant service, where according to Rubem Alves discourse takes the place of religious life and experience,[14] here the word is linked to the day-to-day routines, gains new dimensions, and produces, as in the drama of conversion, immediate results. In an interview with our team, Caio Fábio referred to the sermon of the IURD as a "war cry": "the biblical teaching has diminished and has been replaced by the war cry, 'The Lord is the Savior! He is the liberator!' Therefore the war cries function as elements of inspiration for the people. They take the place of teaching. Teaching is more work; it demands study, articulation, and research. The war cry doesn't." It is inspiration and "nourishment":

> What I look for the most in each service is the true worship of God. . . .
> What grounds me the most in faith is the word. Well, the hymn is good,

14. *Protestantism and Repression* (Maryknoll, N.Y.: Orbis Books, 1985).

we get happy, we worship God, but what grounds us is the word. We are nourished each day; it makes us walk, step firmly in faith, walk in this way in deep faith in the word that nourished us.[15]

But the individual is submerged in the collectivity of an auditorium where a certain social and cultural sameness predominates. Dispersed in the world and in the city (on the street), here men and women are united in the emotion of a shared striving. They do not need to make a great intellectual effort, only to repeat the words and gestures. The repetition gives assurance. "Everybody say: 'Glory to God, thank you Lord, in the name of Jesus!'" The murmuring rises; the loudspeakers reach the last seats as the echo of thunder. Perhaps the visitor or the convert had no voice at all, but now he or she has many: singing, wailing, crying, gesturing, and speaking in tongues, in an ecstasy that is just beginning. In this hallucinating rhythm, the word is multiplied by hundreds, by thousands of mouths. The vocabulary is poor, frequently the grammar is incorrect, but the strength of the word is in the immediate answer to the daily distress: health, prosperity, work, the solution to family problems — in short, liberation from vices, from sin. At last there exists an exemplary life, control over the devil, and the certainty of total salvation, for each one and for all, as one single body. "Put your hand on your heart — and let us pray." These first words of some Pentecostal services (I heard it several times at the Universal), with the soft sound of a keyboard, stir each one deeply and unite the whole congregation in a beautiful gesture of emotion and trust in what is going to happen. In the words of Michel de Certeau, popular religious discourse uses "the vocabulary of a hope, a desire to live."[16] Several elements are established: a "system of values" (Barthes), a semantic field, a circuit that begins with the word, provokes the gesture, reaches the body (sick or healthy), and opens in the spontaneity of emotion. Or, evoking Saussure, we can refer to the participation "of the physical, of the physiological and of the psychic, of the individual and of the social," at the same time, in this "unclassifiable reality" that is language.[17]

15. Interview with Esmeralda, Assembly of God.
16. "Cultura popular e religiosidad popular," interview with Michel de Certeau, *Cadernos do CEAS* 40 (November-December 1975): 54.
17. Cited in Roland Barthes, *Elementos de semiologia* (São Paulo: Editora Cultrix, 1971), pp. 17-18.

It is difficult for me to enter completely (in body and soul) into this circuit of emotions. I can put my hand on my heart, lift up my arms, sing, or embrace the brother or sister beside me; but the *reading,* the code of this personal and community happening, is certainly different for *them* than for the researcher. (Among the many lay workers who circulated through the church, one stopped beside me during the prayer for healing — "Now put your hand where you have an illness and Jesus is going to cure you" — put his hand on my head, recited a blessing, and told me to close my eyes.) But will that communion, that happiness of solidarity, only belong to the dispossessed of the world or to the disillusioned in life or to the incurably ill? I believe that it is more than this. Incorporating the reality of life "as it is," the Pentecostal service becomes a new liturgical and hermeneutical key.[18] The popular culture, dominated by orality, "creates a sense that the spoken word has power" and mobilizes the people . . . for Pentecostalism.[19] But this power, although relativized, could reach other cultural and social levels, such as is happening within Catholic and the Protestant churches enthusiastic about the charismatic movement.

> Sometimes you arrive there, you are so sad, you leave happy, you leave light. You arrive there heavy. You leave there light, with a light body. There seems to be something leading you, do you understand?[20]

To what can we attribute such exceptional results, coming from repetitive services and preaching, the themes of which the majority of listeners have already heard hundreds of times?

The Pentecostal discourse is *factual* — and the more it is linked to facts, the more it penetrates the daily routine. In the IURD of Abolição, one pastor was praying with fervor in the following way: ". . . may all that they see be guaranteed to them. Give prosperity to this people of faith. A new salary. A new job. Their own home." And everyone raised high and

18. Carmelo E. Álvarez, in *In the Power of the Spirit. Pentecostals in Latin America: A Challenge to the Historic Churches,* ed. Benjamín F. Gutiérrez and Dennis A. Smith (Mexico: AIPRAL, 1996), pp. 42-43.

19. Quentin J. Schultze, "Orality and Power in Latin American Pentecostalism," in *Coming of Age: Protestantism in Latin America,* ed. Donald Miller (Lanham, Md.: University Press of America, 1994), pp. 67, 76.

20. Interview with Rosa.

shook stems of wheat, symbol of prosperity. "Tomorrow," the pastor continued, "bring wine, and the day after tomorrow, oil." He wasn't speaking of next Sunday, it was the *next day*. This discourse creates a "relation of equivalence"[21] between faith and life and offers a contextual dimension that goes beyond the circuit or the mere relation between the speaker (the preacher) and the listener (the believer). And so we can speak about another type of *antagonism*[22] between what was and what is going to be. This means, once more, that the traditional line separating the sacred space and the profane world is broken by the word. Wittgenstein has said, concerning precisely the limits of language, that religious discourse in general loses its meaning because it is not factual. And even if it does not reach the totality of day-to-day problems, only one element — a simple "elementary proposition" — is sufficient to lead to other propositions and in this way reach the daily universe,[23] and to surpass the anguish and limitations of daily life.

The word, then, acquires a high symbolic value, even more if it is accompanied by objects and ornaments (a miniature of Noah's ark means hope and trust; Peter's fish net, abundance; the floor covered with salt, purification), making the biblical texts *tangible*. Symbolic value also exists in appeals to representations of national folklore (ribbons to tie on your wrist), anointings "with oil from Israel," T-shirts with affirmations of faith, and billfolds or purses raised toward heaven in order for the pastor to bless them and for them to be filled with valuable bills. This unity of the word with the thing expresses the "objective connection of the linguistic structure with the conception of the world" (Habermas). Referring to the Catholic Charismatic Renewal Movement, until now a phenomenon that has been studied very little (in spite of its five to six million believers in the contemporaneity of the Holy Spirit), André Corten points out its central role "in the formation, drawing from popular religiosity, of

---

21. Charles W. Lachenmeyer, *El lenguaje de la sociología* (Barcelona: Editora Labor, 1976).

22. The word *relation* or *network* could be used, as André Corten (*Le Pentecôtisme au Brésil: Émotion du pauvre et romantisme théologique* [Paris: Editions Karthala, 1995]) seems to prefer; however, I believe that the term *antagonism* reflects better the radical separation between a *before* and an *after*.

23. Compare David Pears, *As idéias de Wittgenstein* (São Paulo: Cultrix, 1973), ch. 2, "Limites da Linguagem."

a new religious language." For the same author, however, the Universal Church "functions more and more as an organization with its own discourse machine"; and the effects of this *discourse machine* (Corten's italics), as in certain types of novels or soap operas, portray a definitely new characteristic: a "discourse constructed not to transmit a truth, the effect produced by prophetic discourse, but to assure success."[24]

This success lies in the multiple ways in which the Pentecostal discourse is manifested in the structure of its services; but above all, I insist, by its insertion into the day-to-day reality. Again, the fusion of *internal-external,* by the word, takes place, and what was divided in the consciousness and in the actual life of the believers acquires meaning. The message of the traditional churches does not have, for the popular strata, either the flavor or the content of daily bread. In this sense, Pentecostal services have for the individual and the community a strength that has apparently long since been lost by the main currents of Protestantism. For Pentecostals, things heard are, after all, things seen. I open a parenthesis here to remember Father Antonio Vieira, the great Jesuit preacher of the seventeenth century, for whom this double function of preaching was very much present (a fact that does justice to other forms of worship that value engagement with reality, with the "outward-oriented" movement). For Vieira, the sermon had a *secular destination.* An "internal" elevation was not sufficient. In an analysis of Vieira's "sermon about sermons," Luiz Felipe Baêta says: "Here, the preached sermon has a vocation for the *external,* for *public exposition,* for *political efficacy,* for the modification of a previous situation." And he quotes Vieira himself, in his classical style: "*Ecce exiit seminat, seminare:* Christ says that the Evangelical preacher went out to sow the divine word. . . . He doesn't just mention the act of sowing, but also of going out: *Exiit,* because when the time comes for harvest, we will be measured by our sowing and our steps will also be counted."[25]

24. André Corten, *Le Pentecôtisme au Brésil.*

25. See a remarkable study about "Word, myth and history in the sermon about sermons of Padre Antônio Vieira" (Sermon of the Sixtieth, preached at the Royal Chapel in 1655) by Luiz Felipe Baêta Neves Flores, *Narrativa, ficção e história,* coord. Dirce Côrtes Riedel, Coloquium UERJ (Rio de Janeiro: Imago Editora, 1988), pp. 170-240.

A Pentecostal Language?

In the set of symbolizations that are part of the Pentecostal discourse, perhaps we can go beyond what characterizes language and speak about *a* language. By encompassing all forms of communication — words, gestures, symbols — Pentecostal speech develops new cultural expressions, which suggest a certain style of life. Any speech, Saussure has said, "from the moment it becomes a process of communication is already a language."[26] Experience that is lived is codified, that is, it is symbolized, and it has the power of transforming those who receive it into communicators, as pointed out by Alice Brill: "The symbolic function gives humanity the possibility of capturing its personal experience, expressing it, in order to memorize it for oneself or to transmit it to others."[27] And although not all symbols are inscribed "alongside language as factors of immediate expression," as Paul Ricoeur affirms, "it is in the universe of discourse where these realities acquire a symbolic dimension."[28] A language, being "at the same time a social institution and a system of values,"[29] becomes "something superior to individuals . . . in a relation of reciprocal understanding" between "individuals belonging to the same community."[30] "Religion is a language," affirmed Cassirer and other specialists.[31]

These various references speak, in different ways, about the relations and the power of words in the religious universe, for the individual as well as for the community — a type of *polyphony,* innumerable voices overlapping, although not always in harmony. The person is reached in the mind (the conscience, the spirit) and in the body (gestures, dance,

26. Cited in Barthes, *Elementos de semiologia,* p. 20.

27. Alice Brill, *Da arte e da linguagem* (São Paulo: Editora Perspectiva, 1988), p. 35.

28. Paul Ricoeur, *Freud and Philosophy: An Essay on Interpretation* (New Haven: Yale University Press, 1970), p. 17.

29. Barthes, *Elementos de semiologia,* p. 17.

30. V. Brondal, *Essais de linguistique générale,* cited in Barthes, *Elementos de semiologia,* p. 19.

31. See Antônio G. Mendonça, in *Religiosidade popular e misticismo no Brasil,* ed. Jaci C. Maraschin (São Paulo: Edições Paulinas, 1984), p. 9. Barthes (*Elementos de semiologia,* pp. 23-24) speaks of the concept of *idiolect* "as the language of a linguistic community, that is, of a group of persons who interpret all linguistic utterances in the same way."

trances), with immediate effects on the community (collective catharsis). Each participant seems to be immersed in him or herself, but the total communication established by a common *language* creates communion and trust, which is reflected in all of those present. All the senses participate in the "beat" of the discourse and its repetitive effects.

> I trust because I see. Every day I see preaching, Bishop Macedo preaches every day. I see, I have trust, I trust.[32]

I really believe the expectation becomes so real that the faithful remain in the church even though the promised answers are not immediate, or never come. The miracles or the experiences of radical changes in life (all the promises are radical) do not come to all, but the waiting continues. They don't have yet, but they will have some day: ". . . having nothing, but owning everything" (2 Cor. 6:10). And it is not a matter of a message for the future, for heaven, but for today, here on earth.[33] Bishop Robert McAlister recalls the questions of John Wesley to the evangelists who were presenting a report about their evangelistic journeys: "Was anyone saved?" And then: "Did anyone get angry?" Whoever wasn't saved would get angry. And McAlister concludes: "It is difficult to be neutral when faced with a Pentecostal message. The preacher always has as his objective a decision by all his listeners. He does not make a speech, but presents a challenge."[34]

The symbolic strength of words is extended also to the institutional. The names by which the new Pentecostal churches are called exert a direct, pedagogical function, which has nothing to do with the designations lost in the past of the historic churches, difficult to explain even for the majority of the faithful themselves. The official terminology in the Pentecostal language has a certain special, appealing enchantment. There are more than a thousand names, but a few examples suffice: Church of the New Life, Brazil for Christ, Crusade of Faith, Marvels of Jesus, Signs and

32. Interview with a member of the IURD.

33. We can establish a parallel with what I believe Foucault said, while analyzing totalitarian discourse: under the control of the system this discourse has a real effect, and in its repetition it acquires power.

34. Roberto McAlister, *A esperiência Pentecostal — A base bíblica e teológica do Pentecostalismo* (Rio de Janeiro: Igreja da Nova Vida, 1977), p. 139.

Wonders, God is Love, Alliance with God, Rebirth in Christ. Some names are almost amusing, but they contain a direct message concerning the purpose of the church: First Aid of Jesus, Two-edged Sword, Prepare Yourself, The Last Ship for Christ.

In this explicit terminology the indicative as well as the imperative moods are present,[35] making the Pentecostal discourse radical through a grammatical symbiosis that blends or even confuses word with reality. The ease with which lexical forms are used and the frequency with which the signs of their meaning are changed surpass common language and give voice to those whose speech was submissive and in conformity with the glossary of their marginality and despair. Here lies one more of the secrets of Pentecostal growth. In popular religions (Michel de Certeau's observation, I believe) one speaks *to* God and not, as in the traditional preaching, *of* God. Perhaps one can say, after hearing so many sermons, hymns, prayers, and strange tongues, that in the Pentecostal language one speaks *of* God and *to* God in the simultaneity of its multiple expressions. It is a language that transcends the usual parameters of religious language and is manifested, among other gifts that the Spirit graciously distributes, in *other tongues.* Does faith remove mountains? "No," a Pentecostal preacher said, "it is the *word with faith* that removes mountains."[36]

The Worship Service and Strange Tongues

It is moreover in the inside of the church, in the middle of the service, where "the supernatural gift of speaking in strange tongues" is manifested.[37] A determined moment is not preestablished. Any person, suddenly, can produce sounds the meaning of which she does not know, nei-

35. Rubem Alves (*Protestantismo e repressão* [São Paulo: Ática, 1979], pp. 117-18), in his analysis of Protestant discourse, makes pertinent observations about the indicative and imperative use of certain texts, proceeding from biblical literalism. The indicative form must be interpreted literally (the creation of the universe in six days, the words of the serpent, and so forth), while verses making imperative affirmation (do not accumulate treasures on earth, cut off and throw away the hand that committed sin, and so forth) need not be interpreted literally.

36. Quoted by Ricardo Mariano, in an interview, November 1995.

37. Definition from the *Novo Dicionário Aurélio da Língua Portuguesa.*

ther she nor those around her. It is glossolalia (*glossa,* tongue; *lalia,* speak). What up until that time was understandable in the simplicity of a message geared toward daily problems, becomes, paradoxically, unintelligible. What was at the reach of all is inserted again into the world of transcendence and is no longer an object of rational analysis. We leave the rationality of the message (always very simple, direct) and go toward the mystery of its internalization, at the same time as it is externalized "in the double emotion: religious emotion and esthetic emotion" — as if it were a matter of a "divine rhapsody," which "produces an effect of an emotional peak among those assembled."[38]

The word *glossolalia,* as with many other characterizations or emphases about Pentecostals, comes from outside the Pentecostal Church; that is, it is not a part of their relatively simple linguistic repertoire. For those who receive the gift of speaking in unknown tongues, the phenomenon means surpassing language itself, creating, improvising, and living the ecstasy of an unspeakable grace. After a service in an Assembly of God church, in a suburb in Rio, a presbyter asked me if I had already received the baptism of the Holy Spirit and spoken in tongues. He had an air of challenge, of certainty — which surpassed our curiosity as researchers — affirming that only then would I really be "converted." The production of meaning that comes from the free and unlimited use of sounds — where the voice of each one is lost and added to the group of other voices in the multitude — offers a sign, a signal that is translated and materialized in personal as well as collective liberation. This form of communication, which apparently is unintelligible, becomes deeply communicative and establishes a strong connection with the social as a multiplying instrument of the self.[39]

Glossolalia, as we saw in the introduction, may come from the beginnings of the history of Pentecostalism, or, according to some

38. Corten, *Le Pentecôtisme au Brésil,* p. 126.
39. See Roberto Cipriani, "Masse, peuple et religion," in *Ciência e cultura* (SBPC), São Paulo, November 1989. Cecília Mariz and Maria das Dores Campos Machado observe that "Pentecostal emphasis on individual will reflects a new conception of the individual. Thus conversion changes not only believers' attitudes toward themselves but also their attitudes toward others" (in *Power, Politics, and Pentecostals in Latin America,* ed. Edward L. Cleary and Hannah W. Stewart-Gambino [Boulder, Colo.: Westview Press, 1997], p. 47).

scholars, it may have already been manifested previously in other places and religions, which could undercut the widely propagated belief in its New Testament origin.[40] What matters, however, is the permanence and expansion of an experience that shook the church at the beginning of the century; and its continuity within and beyond the Pentecostal circle. All history of Pentecostalism makes reference to this strange power, which descends on the people at some moment in the service and changes what before was normal and understandable into something unspeakable and mysterious. The glossolalia phenomenon through time shows no signs of lessening (except, perhaps, in some middle-class Pentecostal currents). On the contrary, as we have seen, it penetrates and spreads in the historic Protestant churches and in the Catholic Church (many of them predominantly middle- and upper-class). This growth has led students of glossolalia into long discussions not only of the peculiarity of its unusual speech but also of the mystery of the believer's surrender to it, which includes a mixture of praise, emotion, and liberation. André Corten characterizes glossolalia as "a song of praise" or "a divine tongue."[41]

I believe that we have here the most expressive symbolic dimension of the Pentecostal worship service. It's not a matter of "one more way of speaking, but of being," in the words of an American linguist (Herder), quoted by Octavio Paz. But the writer and critic goes beyond this and says that "speaking in tongues among early Christians and the Gnostics combines various linguistic elements that reflect more than their meanings, which produce a meaning beyond meaning. This meaning we can see and hear, but not translate, except through poetry and art — they also untranslatable." He recalls further that there was an old dream, based on the Kabala, of discovering a first and universal language, endowed with ex-

40. Compare Robert G. Gromacki, *The Modern Tongues Movement* (Grand Rapids, Mich.: Baker Book House, 1972). The author tries to limit the Pentecostal meaning of glossolalia, reducing its importance in the New Testament through examples of its manifestation in other religions and in antiquity.

41. See Corten, *Le Pentecôtisme au Brésil,* pp. 57, 159, as well as other references. Corten quotes several authors, confirming the long line of studies and debates about this gift without "any mediation," "an exclusively personal relation between God and the individual," a sign "of community as well as a point of rupture with the worldly environment" (p. 57).

traordinary properties such as the correspondence between sound and meaning.[42]

Paul the Apostle dedicates 1 Corinthians 12–14 to the charisms (*charisma,* free gift, which Thomas Aquinas defined as something "supernatural granted by God to humanity"), apparently not defining a rigid hierarchy among them. He points out, however, the value of prophecy (". . . aspire to the gifts of the Spirit, especially of prophecy." "For he who prophesies speaks to men and women."). But Paul goes further into this theme, emphasizing the matter of "speaking in tongues" and expressing the desire that all speak in tongues, preferably with interpretation, "for the edification of the community." However, one must not forbid "that someone speak in tongues." He who "speaks in tongues edifies himself," "does not speak to human beings, but to God." And Paul himself gives thanks to God for speaking "all the tongues that you speak" — a text that has been used to affirm that the apostle had spoken in tongues but was trying to correct the excesses; and so he insists that one should pray and sing with the "spirit" and with "reason." Taking these recommendations into account — his dialectic, the "very extensive use . . . of indirect modes of speech"[43] — perhaps we can say that the Pentecostal service of today fulfills another double function: speaking *to* God and *to* human beings. The moment of ecstasy provoked by the gift of tongues (that not all have, but aspire to have — since they are edified when they speak with God) is combined with an *interpretation* (messages, songs, in which all participate — for one speaks to men and women). There is a certain subtlety in the distinction between the two things, since the whole service is dedicated to God; but in some way the *abuses* are probably relativized — and the Pentecostal community lives and grows.

42. Octavio Paz, "Hablar y decir, leer y contemplar," *Vuelta* (Mexico, March 1982). Ricoeur (*Freud and Philosophy,* p. 15), in the same direction, although in another context, recalls that dreams "attest that we constantly mean something other than what we say" — which transforms every dreamer into a poet. And he quotes Gaston Bachelard: the poetic image "becomes a new being in our language, it expresses us by making us what it expresses" (Gaston Bachelard, *La poética del espacio* [Mexico City: F.C.E., 1965], p. 15).

43. Wayne A. Meeks, *The First Urban Christians* (New Haven: Yale University Press, 1983), p. 122.

Nevertheless, it is important to recognize, as seems evident in these chapters of 1 Corinthians, the difficulty created by a break of this nature in the ritual of a Christian service. Even in Paul's time it seemed to be a matter of a radical separation from traditional culture or from the very forms of worship that were being implemented in the new communities. For regulars in a Pentecostal church, as well as for those who enter its doors for the first time or those outside who hear these strange sounds — "a noise as the movement of an impetuous strong wind" (Acts 2:2) — the phenomenon is always uncommon. Even among the faithful. One woman referred to the possibility of the devil using persons that speak in tongues:

> I'm afraid of that person; that person is not with the Holy Spirit. Sometimes what's there is a big devil that is with that person. Because the devil is evil in the business of tongues. Strange tongues is what it is called. He is the first in this business. Only a very anointed pastor can distinguish if it is the devil or if it is really the tongue of the angels. . . . The search for the Holy Spirit is called tongue of the angels. You are glorifying God at that moment. But you have to be very careful. Because the devil also loves strange tongues. I'm tired of seeing it there at the church. They are speaking in strange tongues and when the pastor raises his hand, it's a big monster there that is manifested.[44]

The most common experience, however, is related to the manifestation of the Holy Spirit, which produces intense emotion and a deep feeling of peace and happiness.

> Then I started to go to church, I started participating in the meeting, participating in the services of the Holy Spirit, and soon I surrendered myself to Jesus and was baptized. . . . Then you see something like a wind, you know? You feel that little noise like the wind. Then he [enters] in you and you don't know what you are saying. You speak but you don't understand. Even the person in front of you doesn't understand. This happened to me . . . two times. . . . Another day I felt like this: When I started to search, to search, I felt my tongue curl up and I didn't

44. Interview with Rosa, who, in a long interview, made several references to the devil as a constant presence in her life and in the church.

see anything of what I was saying. . . . There are times when you speak in tongues and you don't see what you are saying.

Here we don't have the custom of clapping hands, but of speaking in strange tongues, yes. I feel very excited, I feel shuddering, I cry. I also glorify. This is very good. But I still haven't spoken in strange tongues. I get excited and speak out loud: Glory to God! Hallelujah!

Because you have the freedom to speak with God, to speak out loud, to scream, so I cry. Everything that I have that's bad during the day, I let it out at night. Then I leave church another person. Everybody is speaking, but nobody listens. You can be screaming . . . only God. A person can be beside me screaming, really screaming, and I am not listening. I am concentrated on the talk I'm having with Jesus. Then I feel good, I leave a different person.[45]

All Pentecostal services speak of liberation, but it seems as if "speaking in tongues" is the supreme moment of ecstasy for the majority of the participants. Patricia Guimarães, in a recent thesis, actually speaks about a "ritual of *liberation* as a ritual system of construction of the person." For the sociologist, liberation "is structured inside the worship service, in the space of the church, as if intended for beyond it, in the spaces outside the church."[46]

The Worship Service and Music

What can we say about the songs, the Pentecostal music, another expression of emotion and, many times, ecstasy? Pentecostal believers sing profusely. Curiously, those interviewed did not refer to the hymns in a specific way, even when faced with the question about which moment touched them the most during the service. A member of the Assembly of God, an evangelist, mentioned the musical group as "one of the best in the city," which attracted musicians and people from outside the church. One woman interviewed included the hymns when speaking of her experience in the worship service, to which, on the invitation of a neighbor, she took her daughter to be healed:

45. Interview with Janete.
46. Guimarães, *Ritos do reino de Deus,* p. 59.

There he prayed for her; then he anointed her with that anointing oil. So I liked it, I liked the service, those songs, I found something different. . . . they have song, they have those groups that praise the Lord, they have a choir, and people think it's very pretty.[47]

The fact is that song, always doctrinal, with very simple words and melodies, is woven into the whole service. In the Assembly of God, it is common to use an orchestra, large or small, which transforms the hymns into an intense collective vibration. At the Universal Church the musical instrument is basically a keyboard, the sound of which is amplified through powerful loudspeakers. The people are led to sing constantly. Sometimes the sermon is interrupted, the preacher initiates a song, the keyboard follows the tune and the people accompany with enthusiasm, in general without any hymnbook in their hands, even though a songbook is available. To help memorization, the director announces the phrase and immediately it is sung repeatedly. In many instances, Pentecostal songs have provoked the anger of those outside, above all those living close to the churches or meeting halls. On not rare occasions the issue ends up at the police station.

What catches my attention, faced with what might sound like poor melody and content, is the power of communication of these songs, in addition to their doctrinal and edifying function. Although the words are efficient bearers of meaning, evoking even "diffuse sensations and feelings (difficult to explain)," they do not completely satisfy a human being's yearning for "total communication." Only music offers this dimension.[48] Ernst Bloch goes beyond this and sees in music "the possibility of a definitive victory over death. Of all the arts, it is the most Utopian . . . it removes humanity from time and the perishable."[49]

Harvey Cox is one of the few scholars of Pentecostalism who dedi-

47. Interview with Terezinha, Assembly of God. Her conversion took place in the Salvation by Christ Church. Terezinha attended several Pentecostal churches before choosing the one with which she is currently affiliated.

48. Expressions of the anthropologist Gustavo Lins Ribeiro, in an article, "O poder difuso da música," *Humanidades* (Editora Universidade de Brasilia) 5.16 (1988): 65.

49. Quote by L. Hurbon in "Ernst Bloch: Los fundamentos de la accion revolucionaria," mimeo., p. A13.

cates a whole chapter to Pentecostal music, recalling its origin in and intimate relation with jazz.[50] Improvisation, as a key quality of jazz, is in many ways present not only in Pentecostal songs but also in glossolalia. Cox quotes the parallel that Walter Hollenweger makes between a type of "scat singing,"[51] which Louis Armstrong made famous, and glossolalia: vocal improvisation in jazz and disconnected syllables. Although they are used in different contexts, and for different ends, "both are forms of verbal expression that transcend the normal limitation of language." From there comes the clapping, which in general accompanies the songs, and the swaying of the body in the need to express the power of music in the totality of the religious emotion.

This new form of singing can also be found in traditional worship services, whose "choruses" express a new rhythm, with a repetitive characteristic that leads to clapping and to the participation of the body. As in the beginning of jazz, perhaps it is a matter of a breaking with a certain melodic order and of a greater proximity to new rhythms, influenced by the dynamics of contemporary music — a "dissonant symphony . . . capable of creating a 'moral community' marked by diverse perceptions of the dissonance, where harmonies are created and re-created."[52]

Words "From Outside"

All of this — the sermon, glossolalia, singing, alongside other moments of the Pentecostal service (offering, expelling of demons, healing) — sounds like a distortion of the traditional experience of the Christian churches and has repercussions in the *external* vocabulary. Just as the emphases of Pentecostal religiosity created an internal language — a *tongue* — peculiar to its form of worship and communication, in the same way certain terms have marked the reaction of the external world, ecclesiastical or not,

50. Chapter 8 of *Fire from Heaven* (New York: Addison-Wesley, 1995), from which I have made several quotes. Hollenweger ("The Pentecostal Elites and the Pentecostal Poor") also analyzes Pentecostal music, comparing it, as Cox does, to jazz and the blues.

51. Cox, *Fire from Heaven,* p. 139. "Scat singing" is a type of song without lyrics, which uses the voice as an instrument.

52. Guimarães, *Ritos do reino de Deus,* p. 39.

to the charismatic experience. They are words "from the outside," in general derogatory, that seek to disqualify this bewildering spiritual universe.

Such a reaction comes from long ago. When "the disciples were called Christians for the first time in Antioch" (Acts 11:26), the label probably had a negative or even a subversive connotation. The interesting thing is that this happens, according to the biblical narrative, after the unusually rapid growth of the church, that is, after Pentecost, a series of miracles, and the conversion of Paul and of the multitude that joined the new communities. Likewise the term *Protestant,* applied initially to the followers of Luther, was coined during the period of the expansion of the Reformation movement, when the clash with traditional Catholicism and with public authorities became irreversible. In the short history of Protestantism in Brazil, the labeling of people as "Bibles," "believers," coming from the popular belief that converts would acquire "billy goat feet," also arose as a consequence of the aggressive evangelization by missionaries; the cost was persecution and suffering. However, I do not intend to enter into the meaning of this type of reaction, very common among political and cultural factions, but rather to call attention to a possible fallacy not only in the vision of Protestant and Catholic groups (and of other religious currents), but also in the media concerning popular adherence to the new churches. (It is evident that the Pentecostals in general are not charitable in their criticism of the historic churches and other religions.)

Some of the words from the outside, mentioned at the beginning of this chapter (sectarians, intolerant, fanatics), are evidence of a more radical judgment of certain Pentecostal manifestations, especially the IURD. In reference to it, in particular, the most constant topic in the secular or religious press, national or international, is the scandals. Faced with the sanctification and spirituality announced by the Universal Church of the Reign of God (I am referring once more to this Pentecostal current precisely because of its constant presence in the media), how can one deal with the breaking of ethical and moral norms that should guide the conduct of its leaders and followers? Corruption, sexual deviations, swindling, false miracles, and exploitation of the poor are some of the accusations that are leveled against the leaders of the church, in general the most prominent ones. These are in addition to the controversial political positions defended by the "Evangelical Caucus," in which parliamentarians from other denominations participate. The sins that the Universal

Church combats take on alarming proportions. Even the editorials of the secular press have covered this issue.[53]

It is not easy to go more deeply into this matter, even in relation to other churches or religious entities, where the scandals may exist in a more discreet way or not have the repercussions associated with institutions or leaders at the center of public attention. Without wanting to minimize the significance of these clear deviations in conduct, I believe that it is possible to establish a distinction between leaders (not all of them!) and those who are led. The leaders who consider themselves above suspicion end up victims of the freedom and power granted by their proclaimed mediation between heaven and earth, of the demand of sanctification, and of the temptations of the spiritual and emotional dominion over a flock many times submissive to their voice and their weaknesses. There are cases in which these sins are condemned by the church itself. However, once the leaders have been removed from their positions, they generally return to them after they have confessed their guilt and repented. Concerning charismatic leaders, Max Weber said that "failure is their ruin." Re-conversion, however, seems to restore credibility and their place in the body of the church. In general the faithful forgive their leaders, or simply do not believe the news reports or the truth of the suits that are brought against them. As we have said, the followers of the IURD remember that the prophets, Jesus, and his disciples were accused of many things, imprisoned, and killed, even though they were innocent. Others, although they recognize the validity of the criticisms, prefer to point out positive aspects about the Universal Church.[54]

This is an ongoing problem. Periodically, as conversions grow, new scandals are announced. Or else, surprisingly, issues arise that indicate the positive influence that the new church is exerting on Brazilian society. The magazine *Veja* (7 February 1997) dedicated the front cover and the

53. The titles of two editorials of the *Jornal do Brasil,* in the same year, speak for themselves: "Million dollar worship services" (14 September 1990) and "Pastors of darkness" (8 November 1990).

54. The president of the Baptist Seminary of Rio de Janeiro, commenting on the "deviations" of the leaders of Universal, exalted the positive role of this church: it is awakening other churches, opening doors to opportunities that the older churches cannot offer, shaking the Catholic Church, and taking an aggressive stand against Macumba (*Religiao e Sociedade* 16.1-2 [1992]: 56).

cover story to Evangelicals, now seen in a more positive light in spite of all the ambiguities mentioned. "How religion is helping humble people to conquer the kingdom of earth" was the subtitle of the front cover, under a large yellow cross over a black background, surrounded by a big dollar sign (\$). The article has its ambiguities and gives special attention to the "theology of prosperity." But it emphasizes the benefits that several churches and Evangelical entities are providing for the poorest population: literacy training, liberation from addiction to drugs and alcohol, solidarity with the unemployed, support for agrarian reform, the use of artificial methods of birth control, and so forth. The article mentions the following Pentecostal churches: the Assembly of God, the Universal Church of the Reign of God, and Rebirth in Christ. It also mentions the Brazilian Evangelical Association (with a charismatic tendency, led by pastor Caio Fábio) and one historic church, the Baptist. It ends quoting Bishop Edir Macedo: "Money, health, and happiness are the proof of divine blessing."

5 *Only One Space of Life*

What happens inside a Pentecostal church seems to relativize the classic distinction between immanent and transcendent, sacred and profane space — a paradox, taking into account the apparent alienation of a doctrine that preaches separation from a lost world in subjection to sin and the demons.

Although the Pentecostal faithful are indoctrinated into a life predominantly *spiritual,* which in many churches is limited to the precinct of the church, the experience of conversion is extended into the world. And although this extension of witness is found in other currents of Protestantism (a remnant of the evangelistic fervor of the missionary era), I am referring here to the emphasis that the Pentecostal movement, since its origin, has given to personal evangelism.

I prefer, therefore, to speak of a continuum between the *internal* and the *external,* the first moment of which, announced incessantly from the pulpit, moves from the passivity of the church benches to the walk outside. It is necessary to enter into the world, to overcome the world, and to break the bonds that bind people to the forces of evil. In order for this to happen, one must live intensely in the world as if one were not in it and use all the moments of the daily routine to announce the will of God in the purification and transformation of human beings. With this conviction in mind, pastors, lay workers, and believers become missionaries in the midst of the day-to-day challenges, where everything seems to deny the "good news" announced in the preaching, songs, prayers, personal surrender, and the ecstasy manifested through the gifts of the Spirit — in short, at all those moments spent inside the church. "They are the ones, the faithful, the agents of Good, prepared to combat Evil by speaking of Jesus and binding the demons (agents of Evil), throughout the world in which both they and the demons are present. While moving about, they create a type of network for the symbolic extension of the Universal Church, seeking to increase the number of the faithful, that is, a network of those belonging to the Good."[1]

> In order for you to overcome him you have to have a lot of wisdom from God and a lot of patience, because they smoke, they shut the door in your face, drunks curse you, they turn up the radio so loud you can't talk, and they "raise the devil" with you. There are people that even smoke marijuana. All of this you have to endure with wisdom, with patience, and with love. You must forgive them and take the Word to them; and if they do not want to accept the Word at all, let it go. Leave it in God's hands, no? May Jesus bless you and that's it. Let's look for another person. We take the Word to another, we walk through places where no buses go. . . . That business of prisons is another thing. The pastors are working and getting many people out of jail. Because they go there to preach and baptize. Even in jail they baptize.[2]

This personal involvement, undoubtedly one of the strongest reasons for the growth of this new form of church, changes the nature of people, giving value to their presence wherever it may be, giving them courage to speak about their new life, to confess their past vices, and to suffer, many times, resistance from relatives or the ridicule of companions at work. What

1. Patricia Guimarães, "Ritos do reino de Deus: Pentecostalismo e invenção ritual" (master's thesis, University of Rio de Janeiro, 1997), pp. 92-93. The author adds: "to enter the Universal means to search for a new way of inserting oneself into the world, a way marked by rituals that guarantees the exclusion of evil and the inclusion of the good" (p. 77).

2. Interview with Juliana, IURD.

matters is to speak, not to be ashamed of, the gospel, as it says in Romans
1:16: "In truth, I am not ashamed of the gospel." This testimony outside
(the external space) is equally extended to the efficient use of the mass media, to social work, to participation in politics; and even to completely
worldly spaces. But all of this starts, or is renewed, inside the church, to be
prolonged in a pilgrimage with multiple spaces — or in one single space of
life.

The Inside Space: A Pilgrimage under Cover

The enormous size of the new churches that are constructed (or the
movie houses and theaters that are purchased) — with the certainty that
they will be filled — offers a first sign of a new relation between the *ad
intra* and the *ad extra,* a metaphor of other spaces. The inside, the hall
where the people meet, not only creates solidarity of a social group that
faces the same dilemmas and challenges, but also opens a symbolic horizon that extends itself far beyond an architectonic work, in general
stripped bare — a mere space of transition between the life of the world
and the life of the spirit.

The correlation antagonism-similarity between these two spheres of
existence, as was pointed out in chapter 1, is charged with personal and
institutional meanings. First of all, however, I would like to refer, although in a very succinct way, to the physical dimension, to the architecture of the churches built in the Pentecostal (and Neopentecostal) era as
an integrating element of the discourse, of the word that transforms and
calls to transformation. This relation, apparently uncommon, was sug-
gested to me by a free interpretation (on my part) of an article I read by
the architect Mark Wigley.[3] He reminds us of "the distinction between architecture as a matter of survival and architecture as something that goes
beyond survival"; that is, the radical opposition between "structure and
ornament." According to Wigley, people first of all build something sim-

3. Professor of architecture at Princeton University, Princeton, New Jersey. Lecture titled "The Deconstruction of Space," presented at the International Interdisciplinary Meeting on "New Paradigms, Culture and Subjectivity," held in Buenos Aires
(n.d.).

ple that will guarantee their survival, and later, little by little, they perfect and reinforce this structure, and decorate it. But this only happens when all the problems of survival have been overcome, when there are no more enemies, and when the world, I would add, is under the control of another power. Until this happens, churches do not give a prominent place to the ornamental. They are simply places of passage, of connection between ways of being and of living. We might say that these churches are "a kind of rhetorical figure, places around which (and by means of which) speech flows." Wigley speaks further of ornaments as "a linguistic system," a space "produced inside language." Perhaps this reference will allow us to observe other relations, maybe paradigmatic, which may contemplate form and content as objective and subjective expressions of the word (of discourse) in the simplicity of the atmosphere in which it is produced and in the sequence of its external effects.

The human gathering inside the churches, aesthetically closest to the poor classes, resembles the diversified composition of the profane world, including drunks, prostitutes, drug addicts, and homosexuals — who do not feel rejected in the *sacred space*. What could be totally strange and constraining in a traditional church (in many cases not even permitted) seems natural and welcome in a Pentecostal church. Several times we noticed the presence of those most marginalized and often excluded, more so in the churches of the Universal. In the church of Botafogo, in Rio, one woman dressed in very skimpy clothes and attracting the attention of those present was soon received with respect by a lay worker, who provided a large shawl to cover her. The IURD is without doubt much more tolerant than other Pentecostal churches concerning uses and customs, and thus they attract especially the younger people. The human movement, the entering and leaving, the circulation through the sacred precinct, also applies to personal behavior. "Christ is freedom" — said a woman we interviewed.

The dimensions of this internal space favor extensive movement inside the churches — a covered pilgrimage, without any distinction of persons. With a certain frequency the leaders invite the people to go up front. There are several appeals; the comings and the goings follow each other. There almost all fulfill their promises, be it through the tithe they deposit at the altar or the purchase of books, newspapers, objects — everything they can and cannot afford. There they must also receive the corresponding blessings or spectacular cures. There are several bridges or networks that are momentarily established in these physical acts of walking, kneeling, placing their hands on the head of the person beside them, crying with him or her, laughing at oneself, and leaving with a new hope of life.

Thus the internal walk creates a synthesis of this extremely diversified social, ecclesial, and religious universe. Those who gather in this large space unite the differences found not only in their life in the world but also in Protestantism and other religions This is something that has been studied very little and that raises another issue, that of syncretism, as another way of connecting inside and outside space.[4] The new converts carry the weight of their previous beliefs, which are added to their new religious perceptions. The Pentecostals then bet on the action of the Spirit as a mediator between the past and the new life, not worrying about what the convert was, but about what he or she will be from now on.

External Space: The Walk Continues

I believe that we can talk about a certain hierarchy of the spaces of action: inside (to sit, to gesture, to rise, to walk) and outside (to evangelize, to face the daily routine as heralds of a new reality). The external walk multiplies tremendously the space of internal experience, no longer confined to the church but open to the infinite spaces of the city and its different networks. In this new field of life, the faithful now have another vision of the world, an alternate, unconventional way of facing poverty, illness, unemployment, violence — theirs, their relatives', and their neighbors'. The experience of salvation has a continuity with the urban chaos, defined, with a bit of exaggeration, as "heaven in our daily hell" (Wilson Gomes). The relation with secular reality includes a unity between the spiritual life, acquired in the church, and society. In other words, personal testimony in all situations of life, so often a difficulty for traditional believers, is expressed naturally and with conviction by the converts to Pentecostal-

---

4. The New Birth research partially analyzed the religious transit between Evangelical churches, showing that among the many converts to Neopentecostalism a significant number return to their churches of origin.

ism. The believer is transformed into a new social actor "in a world marked by the complex cohabitation between domains and visions of the world, seen before as antagonic."[5] Many pastors and lay workers, from the IURD as well as from other Pentecostal currents (God is Love, for example), have established their presence in other countries, including those from which the first missionaries to Brazil came, a reverse movement of that historic missionary evangelization.

Their testimony is also manifested in social and beneficent work, expanding something more or less common to Protestant and Catholic churches. Our questionnaire did not explore directly this angle of the Pentecostal experience, which in the meantime appeared spontaneously in several interviews:

> I remember our sacrifice. There was a time when we made a campaign to take food to the northeast. We would stay there [in the church] until more or less midnight, filling that truck with food to take to the northeast. And it was during the time of Record, to buy Record.[6]

Without exhausting the full meaning of this secular dimension of the invasion of the external world into the interior of the churches, I would like to recall the use of public spaces, especially by the Universal Church. One reason for controversy in the press has been the purchase and transformation of movie houses and theaters by IURD into churches. (The Evangelical Community, another charismatic group, did the same in the southern part of Rio. It bought two large cinemas, with a large stage, and they have extremely well-attended services.) The Pentecostals still use open plazas and beaches and promote parades on the main streets of the city, but the public services that gather multitudes are in the football stadiums. In Rio de Janeiro, periodically, the Universal rents the Maracana stadium and is able to fill it with more than 100,000 people who praise God with hallelujahs. This initiative led the Catholic Church and the Protestant churches to do the same, but seldom with the same success.

Another sphere of external action is infiltration into totally secular structures. We attended a gathering of workers of Rede Globo Television

5. Guimarães, *Ritos do reino de Deus,* p. 164.
6. Interview with Rosa.

(the fourth largest TV network in the world), at the Evangelical Community of the Southern Zone (Rio, October 1995), and there it was said that "God is doing a great work at TV Globo." The whole, long service blended in the presentation of converted actors and singers and seemed to project the hope of these workers (who represented 400 Evangelicals that work at Globo) that an alliance with Globo TV (known by them as totally worldly) could be developed so that it could be transformed into a space that would serve the Evangelical cause. The speaker emphasized the fact that this broadcasting station had already made available a meeting room for Evangelicals. One of those we interviewed belonged to this network, which also publishes the newspaper *O Globo:*

> Look, there at the newspaper *O Globo* we have, for example, an hour for lunch, from eleven to twelve, and we have a worship service, you see? The place was made available to us, and so we preach the gospel. We preach the Word. Without mentioning name of denominations, we preach the genuine Word. And many there have accepted, do you understand? But there's a mixture, it's not only Assembly of God; there we have Baptist brothers and sisters, Presbyterian brothers and sisters, and brothers and sisters from the Universal Church. So our goal, in my case, is to preach the gospel without mentioning denominations.[7]

The fantastic penetration of the Pentecostals into the press and television proves its great success in the use of spaces of the media. The newspaper of IURD, *Folha Universal,* weekly prints around one million copies per edition. On the one hand, we still have no research concerning the nature and the role of the publications, records, cassettes, and CDs produced by the largest Pentecostal churches. On the other hand, the innumerable Evangelical radio and television programs have been analyzed by specialists.

The Political Space

In the circles outside the ecclesiastical structures of Pentecostalism, as in other expressions of the movement from the inside to the outside, is the

---

7. Interview with Aluizio, evangelist of the Assembly of God.

realm of politics — the most delicate and most complex space in the expansion of Pentecostal and other Evangelical churches into the secular world. Many see in direct political action (public office, election to Congress, one day maybe even the presidency of the Republic!)[8] another way, and perhaps the most efficient and practical way, of "giving Christian witness" and of transforming society. The political arena certainly is for Evangelicals the decisive social space, the ultimate expression of the power experienced in the ecclesiastical community. This is why they make increasingly greater efforts to elect their own candidates.

The results of this vision of the political space, including the concrete actions of Evangelical members of Congress, have been analyzed by several researchers. In many cases the projects or votes by these Evangelicals are opposed to a more progressive vision of Brazilian society. The majority of the Protestant representatives in the National Congress belong to parties that support those in power, whoever they may be.[9] A report in *Vinde* (January 1996) recalls that during the military regime the majority of them were in Arena, the party of the dictatorship. Of the thirty-two Evangelicals elected to the Constituent Assembly (1987-88), dispersed in several parties, only seven had an independent position and joined the opposition to the president (José Sarney, the extension of whose term from four to five years had the decisive support of the rest of the Evangelicals). In this period of political bargaining the "bancada evangélica"

---

8. A recent issue of the magazine *Vinde* (September 1997) informs that Baptist pastor Nilson do Amaral Fanini, president of the World Baptist Alliance, "would only wait for the results of a poll by Ibope in order to decide whether to become a candidate for the presidency in 1998"; and that he could already count on around six million votes from Evangelicals, just in the state of São Paulo. Brazil already had an Evangelical president, the Lutheran Ernesto Geisel, the third of four generals who took power in the period of military dictatorship in Brazil (1964-85). With Geisel, as a result of popular pressure and that of several churches and civic institutions, including the Evangelical Church of the Lutheran Confession in Brazil, the process of political openness began in the country.

9. Fernando Collor received a notable number of votes for president from Pentecostals, notably from the IURD. In Chile Pentecostals supported General Pinochet and had services of commemoration on the anniversaries of the military coup, with the presence of Pinochet himself. In Guatemala the Pentecostal vote was decisive in the election of another general, Rios Montt, whose government ended up being deposed. The same phenomenon was repeated in Peru, in the election of Fujimori.

[Evangelical Caucus] was formed. It was criticized by the press as a pressure group dedicated primarily to the defense of their personal interests and to the gaining of benefits for "Evangelical work."[10]

Here I am not interested in analyzing in depth the activity of Evangelicals (and mainly Pentecostals) in the political sphere; but rather in raising a fundamental issue about the expression of faith in this secular space: Will this type of relation with the social be liberating and understood as responsible participation in society and, in particular, in representative government? Or, is the political perspective restricted to the level of agreements and deals, looking toward returning to a *corpus christianum* inserted in modernity? The conservative Protestant ideology continues to affirm that if Brazil had an Evangelical majority, everything would be socially different. The participation of the Universal in politics is based on the same dichotomy of good and evil, God and the devil, a "holy war": "This election [1994] will be a battle between God's and the devil's candidates."[11]

In this sphere, however, Pentecostalism has gone through important changes. If we compare its political vision in the 70s, and what happened afterwards, especially since 1986, we can see a radical transformation. This is the terrain in which the word becomes extremely flexible, contradictory at times, but always conditioned by the orientation, according to them, of the Holy Spirit to the pastors (and leaders). "We do not use our pulpit to ask for votes for anyone, but we will make our opinion clear. The Holy Spirit, who speaks through the pastors, will explain what is happening."[12] This orientation, nevertheless, varies from church to church. In 1994, the General Convention of the Assembly of God, faced with the

---

10. There are numerous examples of negotiations with Evangelical voters for the purpose of acquiring financial resources: concession of channels for radio and television, charity work, and so forth, for churches or entities tied to them. One Evangelical Congressman, criticized for making deals of this nature, quoted Saint Francis of Assisi: "It is in giving that you receive."

11. Quoted by André Corten, *Le Pentecôtisme au Brésil: Émotion du pauvre et romantisme théologique* (Paris: Editions Karthala, 1995), p. 180.

12. Interview with preacher Orlando Leutério Torres, of the Assembly of God, speaking "for the church." On the same occasion the pastor declared that "God belongs to the right wing," because he does not want the earth to be invaded by anybody nor does he want the practice of violence or strikes. And Torres quoted Jesus' words: "My father works and I also work" (*Folha de São Paulo,* 2 November 1996).

scandals of the so-called "Evangelical Caucus" in the National Congress, preached a "holy war" in the choice of candidates for the presidency of the Republic and of the Congress: "This will be a battle between God's and the devil's candidates." The IURD also polarized the choices, giving the impression that the candidate of the devil was Lula (Partido dos Trabalhadores), in opposition to Fernando Henrique Cardoso (curiously, a declared atheist).

In more general terms, the first orientation was "a refusal of commitment," a "social strike" (expressions of André Corten), as if it were a commandment ("You shall not participate"). Then, in the mid-1980s "Evangelical candidates" arose under the strength of another order: "brother votes for brother." Finally, voters came to evaluate the candidates themselves, channeling votes even for non-Evangelical politicians when positions were still beyond the reach of believers — which seems to remain as a project of God himself, according to Congressperson Laprovita Vieira, of the IURD: "What we need the most today is a man of God, raised up by God himself to lead this nation. What Brazil needs is for the people of God to pray, to strive, to repent of its bad ways in order to raise up a 'David' from inside his own church to lead this nation. And, based on this purpose, we present our own candidates to prevent the people of God from sowing while the 'Amalekites' reap. . . . Evangelical Christians must occupy their space."[13] At any rate, according to this orientation, the larger the number of Evangelical politicians, the better it is for the country (and, of course, for the church). Including the candidates of the Assembly of God, the IURD, and the Baptist Church, the total number of Evangelical candidates for municipal and state offices in the state of Rio de Janeiro in the last elections (1996) was around one thousand, of whom the churches hoped to elect at least three hundred.[14] The IURD alone, according to the *Folha Universal* (11 August 1996), presented 160 candidates just in São Paulo. According to the New Birth research, the Universal Church, contrary to other denominations, prefers to concentrate their votes on their own candidates (56 percent of those interviewed).[15]

13. Alexandre Brasil Fonseca, "Surge uma nova torça política–A Igreja Universal do Reino de Deus nas eleições de 1994" (mimeo.), p. 19.

14. *Jornal do Brasil,* 8 August 1996.

15. Rubem César Fernandes, "Os evangélicos em casa, na igreja e na política," *Religião e Sociedade* 17.1-2 (August 1996).

Actually, in the 1994 elections, Evangelicals did not reach their electoral goals (certainly exaggerated), even though they elected about the same number of members of Congress as in previous elections. In addition, the significant modifications brought about by the growth of Pentecostalism and the new convictions about involvement in politics did not bring about a qualitative advancement or a greater social commitment. Quantitatively, as Paul Freston[16] points out, in the 1983-87 legislature, the Evangelical presence in Congress added up to seventeen members of Parliament (five being alternates), almost all of them belonging to the historic churches. In the elections for the 1987-91 term, the Evangelical representation increased to thirty-six (four alternates), the majority of them Pentecostals. In the 1991-95 legislature the number is drastically reduced, especially since of the thirty-five elected, only twenty-three were full members (twelve alternates). As regards the 1995 elections, we have two conflicting reports, both indicating, nevertheless, the growth of the number of Evangelical members of Parliament. Freston mentions thirty elected (four senators and twenty-six representatives), of whom nineteen are Pentecostal and eleven belong to the historic churches. Among the latter, the Baptists are in the lead with six members of Parliament (one senator). Of the Pentecostals elected, ten belong to the Assembly of God, including Senator Benedita da Silva representing the Workers' Party (PT), one of the two women elected (the other, Lidia Quinan, from Goiás, belongs to the Presbyterian Church of Brazil). The IURD elected six members of Congress, representing five different parties, while the ten members of Congress from the Assembly of God belong to six different parties. Another survey indicates forty elected (six senators and thirty-four representatives, adding up to 8 percent of the total number), seventeen of the representatives coming from the historic churches and nineteen from Pentecostal denominations (six from the IURD). The six senators are "historics."[17]

The Evangelicals' affiliation with several parties does not seem to mean there are ideological distinctions; indeed, even among the different

16. Articles in *Religião e Sociedade* 16.1-2 (November 1992) and 17.1-2 (August 1996).

17. Compare Paul Freston, "As Igrejas Protestantes nas eleições gerais brasileiras," *Religião e Sociedade* (ISER) 17.1-2 (August 1996): 160; and Jorge Antonio Barros, "Eles não gostam de oposição," *Vinde* 3 (January 1996).

parties now in existence in the country there seem to be few ideological distinctions, and almost all of them have the same discourse and promises. There also does not seem to exist any strategy for political action or for participation in the various political currents. Although much research is lacking concerning the relation of Evangelical candidates with political parties, I believe that in the majority of cases the party affiliation does not indicate an ideological position. A pragmatic attitude prevails — that of getting elected and then acting "as a Christian" in the political sphere.

Moreover, Evangelical candidates do not seem to want to play the political game of allying themselves with political bosses in order to more or less guarantee their election. Some, on the contrary, *pull* the votes they control in their communities toward supporting candidates outside the church. Nevertheless, it is interesting to point out that the Evangelical members of the 1995-98 Congress encompass the broad gamut of the Brazilian political spectrum, acting in seven different parties. The presence of nine denominations on the Brazilian electoral scene also seems to indicate a great mobilization of the Evangelical churches in politics. Churches with less numeric expression in general support candidates with the greatest potential for winning or those in whose political program they trust. The one exception is the Congregação Cristã do Brazil (a *historic* Pentecostal church), which condemns any political candidacy on the part of its members. At the municipal level the participation of the Evangelicals in politics has increased in each recent election. For example, 140 members of the Evangelical Church of the Lutheran Confession in Brazil (IECLB) were elected to office in fifty-three municipalities in the states of Santa Catarina and Paraná (South), among whom there were sixteen mayors.[18]

This still unclear relation of Evangelicals with the world of politics, complicated further by the competition between denominations, raises

---

18. *Evangélicos, Política e Sociedade* (Lima) 3 (June 1997). Evangelicals are occupying more than just a narrow political space. A report in the *Jornal do Brasil* (29 June 1997), under the title "Os evangélicos na polícia," registers the existence of an association of Evangelical police — the Union of Christian and Evangelical Military of Brazil — organized in 24 states. In the state of Minas Gerais, Evangelicals now make up 30 percent of the military police (more than 4,000 men), but the commanding officer has hopes that the number of Evangelicals in the military will reach 100 percent.

delicate issues concerning the occupation of a public space in which the Brazilian Protestant experience is in its early stages and theologically unprepared. In the panorama presented here, far from exhausting the issue, my intention was merely to indicate the space occupied by Evangelicals, emphasizing the Pentecostals, in the political sphere and to present the limitations of that sphere regarding a clearer commitment on the social issues of the country. There are not, on the part of the "Evangelical politicians," with few exceptions, relevant projects. A *spacial ideology* predominates at least for now, that is, the filling of one more space, which shows the growth of the Evangelical movements and gives testimony to issues of morality. There is unanimity in the vote against abortion (recently approved under certain circumstances), against the legalization of gambling, and against the use of drugs. These positions explain the strength of the Pentecostal vote for ex-president Fernando Collor, whose (demagogic) preaching against corruption led to the affirmation that this was a candidate who was "fearful of God." In the interviews we made there are references to the poor, to hunger, to illness, and even to criticism of the "selfishness" of those now in power and their lack of social sensitivity. Those interviewed, however, said nothing specifically about the activity of Evangelical candidates. Perhaps this reflects decisions made by the ecclesiastical authorities, apparently followed without discussion by the faithful.

At any rate, when studying the Pentecostal movement in Brazil, we can no longer ignore its penetration into the political space. According to the New Birth research, the civic and electoral participation of Evangelicals of Greater Rio has an expressive correlation with those believers who declared that they had the "gifts of the Holy Spirit": "Differing from what probably occurred in the past, Evangelicals and Pentecostals moved by the power of the Holy Spirit today have the tendency to extend their participatory efforts beyond the church halls."[19] For the moment it seems as if the Evangelical openness to the political space has pragmatic objectives, but this does not keep them from attempting to express their faith politically — and with it the possibility of expanding their democratic space, as well as bringing before their communities, in one way or another, the great national issues.

19. ISER, May 1996, p. 92.

The political participation of the Brazilian people in general grew 46 percent in ten years. Although education and culture have not developed in the same proportion as the growth of religiosity, the people are better informed and participate more. In the Pentecostal sphere, the growing relation with politics gives a new dimension to it as a religious entity, making more complex the sociological and theological realm in which it moves. This new space, with its more diverse motivations, certainly will become a key element in any effort to interpret, in a comprehensive way, the current reality of this movement. After all, politics and religion constitute one of the greatest sources of human passion, for the mobilization of action and the creation of a new culture.

6 *One Day, a Thousand Years*

The text of 2 Peter 3:8 is well known: "One day for the Lord is like a thousand years, and a thousand years like a day." In the chapter "Survival and Transcendence," I analyzed the implications of an attitude that makes it possible for believers to live through all the difficulties of their daily routine and go beyond them through the active presence of a personal God who is ready to attend to all the cries of those who surrender themselves to him without restrictions. Here we go further. I spoke earlier about the familiarity between the human and the divine, and of a correlation between spaces; I now refer to an interpenetration of times.

One of the characteristics of millenarian expectations is the decisive battle between good and evil, the defeat of the demonic forces, and the radical transformation of the whole world. Frequently, the proclamation includes the prediction of immediate, in general, catastrophic events. This is how it was in the beginning of the early church, although the expectation of the end of the world contained a certain contradiction between the conviction of the imminent coming of Christ and the preservation of community life. The new churches, even while aspiring to a dramatic turnaround *(apocalypsis)* in social and political reality, were spreading geographically and resisting any threat to their own institutional development. In other words, as Wayne Meeks shows us, what is traditional and radically new combine perfectly, favoring even a total transformation of worldview and ethos.[1] The dialectic between an organized community structure and an eschatological perspective, that is, the conviction of a new world about to break in, did not seem to shatter the institutional routine. On the contrary, the churches became self-supporting, establishing coherent links between the present and the future. The times would get blurred between the enthusiasm of the new faith and the certainty of the end.

In many ways the tension is maintained in the current growth and institutionalization of the Pentecostal movement, but the commitment to the daily routine has surpassed the expectation of the millennium — so dear to Fundamentalism — which in a certain way has lost its eschatological impact. An angel will bind the dragon, "which is the devil and Satan" for a thousand years, establishing the reign of Christ for the same period of time. The promise in Revelation 20:2, taken literally in some types of Pentecostalism, is simply reduced to the reality of the twenty-four hours of a day: Satan is bound daily, sometimes in several services, but above all reaching a climax on Friday nights at the Universal Church. As in a "first aid station for the spiritually wounded"[2] with people permanently on duty, the sinner can be freed from the devil at any time, remaining under the dominion of the reign of Jesus. It is not necessary to wait for the angel or for eternity. Even though the end is announced, however close it may be, it is possible to have a foretaste of the millennium and to renew life here and now. The time is now, determined by the word, whose power lies in "attending to the frequent and normal needs of daily life" (Weber). The devil — and Satan — is experienced more concretely in everyday life than in the millennium and must be tied up (eliminated) whenever he manifests himself.

This explicit designation of the forces of evil, identified with Satan

1. Wayne Meeks, *The First Urban Christians* (New Haven: Yale University Press, 1983), pp. 171-80. The author also points out the function of the "charismatic" leader, whose success builds community "in such a way that charisma and routinization — or, better, institutionalization — are not antithetical" (p. 173).

2. Bishop Edir Macedo, *A libertação da teologia,* 7th ed. (Rio: Editora Gráfica Universal, 1992), p. 21.

(and his angels), seems to correspond to an objective need of the human being, that illness, poverty, death itself, not remain in the terrain of subjectivity and conformity. Evil has a name, and it is called Satan, devil, and so forth.[3] Harvey Cox, a student of Paul Tillich, recalls that the professor was "brave enough to use the idea of 'the demonic' in his theology," concluding that "modern liberal theologians have too easily discarded the idea of *transpersonal forces* of Evil."[4] To accept the real contingency of this immense net of contradictions between good and evil seems to create a certain personal *harmony* and to favor a vivid relation with the transcendent.

The concept of the devil was very much present in the interviews and was a constant character in the life of those converted to Pentecostalism, as well as in the sermons and the prayers. One preacher said, defying sinners and the devil himself, before the "strong prayer," which generally comes at the end of the services:

> The devil is the cause of all evil. . . . The devil only acts in the life of a person empty of God. . . . The devil exists. He walks through arid places and returns, finding his house empty. . . . I didn't know what I was going to say today, but God is calling the attention of some of you here. . . . If you are not free from the devil the first time around, then

3. Compare Carlos R. Brandão, *Os deuses do povo. Um estudo sobre a religião popular* (São Paulo: Editora Brasiliense, 1980), p. 294. At times, the author says, "gods are everywhere"; it is necessary to call them by their names, to give a name to evil, in order for the abominable things of this world not to stay in the realm of philosophical abstraction. The theme has awakened the interest of other researchers, such as Cecília Mariz, "O Demônio e os Pentecostais no Brasil," in *O mal à brasileira,* ed. Patrícia Birman, Regina Novaes, and Samira Crespo (Rio de Janeiro: Editora UERJ, 1997). The author quotes other scholars and points out the importance of an understanding of the place of the devil in Pentecostal theology: "Thus conversion to Pentecostalism means not only a new way of knowing and relating to God, but also a redefinition of the devil and of his relation with the world" (p. 49). Curiously, Bishop Macedo *(A libertação da teologia)* and Bishop Roberto McAlister *(A esperiência Pentecostal — A base bíblica e teológica do Pentecostalismo* [Rio de Janeiro: Igreja da Nova Vida, 1977]) do not emphasize the role of the devil, at least in their respective presentations of the doctrine of their churches. McAlister, in a kind of Pentecostal creed, only affirms that "heaven is the destiny of the saved by faith in Jesus Christ and hell is the destiny of the unbeliever" (p. 11). The name of the devil does not appear.

4. Harvey Cox, *Fire from Heaven* (New York: Addison-Wesley, 1995), p. 286.

only a *prayer chain* can help. If the *pomba-gira* [female character in Afro-Brazilian witchcraft] made you a homosexual, start to speak deeper, to have *friends*. Leave the cigarette on the altar. If your lover is here with you, when you return to your place, tell him, "It's over!" Come out! Come out! If you are hiding around there, come! We are going to expel you![5]

The cure is always associated with the expulsion of demons. Another pastor, while preaching, ordered everyone to scare away their afflictions by shaking their hands and screaming "Xô! xô! xô!":

The evil that brought you here — some incurable illness that the doctors didn't give you any hope of overcoming — here and now people will leave the church knowing that a miracle occurred today in their life, in the life of the person that needs to be cured. . . . The thing is that this illness is the evil one that penetrates a person and takes the form of an illness and doesn't leave. But here today the people present in the church will say with authority that the evil one will leave your life; you will be cured.[6]

For two women interviewed, among others, Satan is a constant and very near presence:

The devil is always pursuing me. But you have to have faith and have to resist. . . . The devil is tied and chained in the name of Jesus. You cannot be afraid of Satan at all. You have to have strength and say that he is under my feet, Satan. The search for the Holy Spirit is a very serious thing, because sometimes you think that you are with the Holy Spirit, but it is not the Holy Spirit at all, it is the horned one. . . . Where doesn't this bad beast enter? Let us say, *cruz credo* [horrors], I am the one that is here with you — and he is here, look! He is here beside me. He doesn't let go of me. Eats with me, sleeps with me, wakes up with me. He doesn't let go of you at all. . . . Look, they call the Universal Church a "brain washing." But it isn't at all, because sometimes you are not freed, even if you've been there in the church for forty years. You continue with the demon. But as you go through this process, the

5. Sermon preached at the IURD of Abolição.
6. IURD of Princesa Isabel Avenue, Copacabana.

prayer chain of liberation, the devil is obliged to retreat and leave your body.[7]

This daily contact and familiarity with exorcism, with the explicit objective of expelling demons, can perhaps explain why the beginning of a new millennium has not been, at least until now, a central theme in the threatening sermons that always accompany this type of great expectation. In other religious movements, if one takes into account the acceleration of events in the spiritual realm, spectacular things are about to happen, especially in the innumerable currents that propagate the New Age. In the United States alone more than 1,100 groups awaited the end of the world in the year 2000, while three international megaprojects were being developed for this new time: Dawn, a New Pentecost, and a New Evangelization, the last two of Catholic origin, but only the third is approved by the Pope. Dawn has as its base the threat repeated in other historic moments: "The year one thousand passed; two thousand will not pass."[8]

It is very probable, however, that any millennial manifestations linked to Pentecostalism will barely emphasize what has constituted its ethos, its intense spiritual vibration that expands the hours in a day to a thousand years and anticipates someday the experience of the glorious promise of one thousand years of the full reign of good. As different spaces of life have been integrated into a new way of being, a new era makes the present and the future coexistent.

7. Interviews with Juliana and Rosa. Pastor Caio Fábio (in the interview referred to earlier) speaks of this "doctrine" of the devil as one of the "reductionisms" of the IURD, in which "all human unhappiness is the responsibility of the devil," reducing in this way individual responsibilities to a "minimum plane." "That is why there is no ethical appeal, because the devil is responsible for my ethical mistakes." The other reductionism is money, a "modern version of the Catholic indulgences." This theme also gave occasion for an article by Catholic Bishop Dom Bonaventura Kloppenburg, "A diafobia da Universal," *Jornal do Brasil* (21 January 1996). He says at the end: "To affirm an unlimited diabolical intervention in human life, with the power to cause illness or other evils, does not correspond to biblical revelation, is against the official doctrine of the Church, and would be a denial of the paternal divine providence over each one of us."

8. Compare Brother Nery, F.S.C., *Terceiro milênio e fé cristã* (Petrópolis: Editora Vozes, 1995).

The last years of the millennium, in spite of the anticipation of the end by some Pentecostal currents, promised an acceleration in the battle against the devil and the affirmation of a new world. Hope was always a central element in the passion for the millennium. The arrival of a new millennium was always marked by the multiplication of chiliastic movements, of the expectation announced among the early Christians and reclaimed periodically. In the thirteenth century the ardent preaching of Joaquim di Fiori proclaimed again the advent of the reign of God and God's absolute rule over the earth during one thousand years — a concept that could very well, in the current stage of universal religious expansion, penetrate secularity and modernity. Perhaps Christopher Columbus was infected by this vision when, on the eve of the sixteenth century, he declared: "God made me a messenger of a new earth." Pentecostalism goes beyond this and also predicts, above all, a new heaven.

7 Old Churches, New Church

The mass of those converted to Pentecostalism comes from other churches and religions, among them Afro-Brazilian cults and Spiritism, religions practically closed to evangelization (when it exists) by the historic churches and by Roman Catholicism. The era of Protestant controversy with Catholicism, Spiritism, and parareligious movements (Masonry, Positivism, and so forth) was limited to the early stages of the missionary movement and the first phase of Protestantism in Brazil. The arrival of Pentecostalism provoked in a certain way a return to the spirit of controversy in relation to the Protestant as well as the Catholic Church, producing new manifestations of antagonism and similitude between Pentecostalism and other Christian churches.

According to the New Birth research, 70 percent of Evangelicals in Greater Rio were neither born nor raised in an Evangelical home. They entered the church by a personal decision, breaking with their parents' religion. The faithful of the historic churches have greater temporal density — 52 percent of their members have grown up in the church — while in the Universal Church no more than 5 percent were reared in an Evangelical home. As we saw in the introduction, the majority of converts (in

Greater Rio) came from Catholicism (61 percent), followed by those coming from the Afro-Brazilian religions Umbanda and Candomblé (16 percent) and from Spiritism (6 percent). The charismatic churches are perhaps losing fewer members than the more traditional churches.

In one of the services of the Universal Church, the pastor asked how
many had been Catholic, and the great majority raised their hand. However, to a significant degree there also exists among Pentecostals a certain
amount of switching from one denomination to another, with a small
number of members returning to the historic churches. This switching
certainly reveals some type of dissatisfaction and/or a more radical search
starting from a new experience of faith. According to ISER, the medium
rate of movement among the various Evangelical denominations of
Greater Rio is 25 percent of the total membership. The Assembly of God
has a central place in these changes, with a greater volume of entries and
exits. Yet it maintains an equilibrium between the members it loses (24
percent) and those that it gains (24 percent) from other churches. The
historic churches lose more believers (38 percent) than they gain (26 percent), while the churches characterized as *renewed* (a subdivision of the
historic ones, in general charismatic) gain more (39 percent) than they
lose (17 percent). The IURD, which attracts members especially from the
other Pentecostal churches (excluding the Assembly of God), lost 18 percent of its believers and gained 27 percent. The motivations for these
changes vary from the simplest to the most profound.

> I believe that there are more Pentecostal churches because people leave
> one and look for another, also Pentecostal. All of a sudden people desire
> certain changes and cannot get them, so they solve their problem by
> leaving for another church, where they may be able to do something
> different. For example, here we do not usually clap hands, but there are
> some people who like it and so they go to a church where they can clap
> hands. They go looking for what they like, for what they want and
> don't have the freedom to practice where they are.
>
> What led me to accept Jesus? Look, I visited various churches. I vis-
> ited a Baptist Church frequently, then I went on to the Universal, but
> very few times. . . . I was between eighteen and nineteen years of age
> and I didn't know what I wanted. My conversion really was in the Bap-
> tist Church. There, when a pastor, today he is with the Lord, made an

invitation, I raised my hands and accepted the Lord. Time went by and I began to attend the Assembly of God . . . and I started to like the system. . . . What caught my attention were the Pentecostal services and the presence of the Holy Spirit. Far be it from me to put down my Baptist brothers and sisters, but what got my attention were the sermons and the lively services. I can even include here the noise, the noise, hallelujah. And there I was sealed with the Holy Spirit.[1]

The intense movement of the believers from one Evangelical church to another points to a central element in their relation to an ecclesiastical institution, an element that was being lost in the historic churches and in Catholicism. In Brazil, with a Catholic majority, there are not many who attend mass regularly. In some Protestant denominations, although on a smaller scale, many members attend only the services commemorating Easter or Christmas (besides ceremonies of confirmation, marriage, baptism, and the funeral of relatives). For Pentecostals, participation in worship services (daily or almost daily) is a fundamental part of their Christian living. More than this, the personal involvement is intense. Each moment of the service demands an untiring spiritual and corporal giving. The physical dynamics establishes a communion and vitality nonexistent in a traditional Protestant church. In the large, crowded hall of the IURD in Barra da Tijuca, all of a sudden everyone threw themselves to the floor for a moment of prayer. From the back of the hall I had the impression of a movie sequence, when an object suddenly disappears from a scene. The hall was now apparently empty. The believers expressed an act of humility, and a murmur echoed throughout the church. In many ways, the limited theological preparation of the pastors is compensated for not only by a message that speaks to the heart of the listeners, but by great gestures full of emotion — they must reach to the heavens.[2]

These characteristics, extremely well known, stand in the sharpest contrast to the simplified and informal style cultivated by popular Catholicism in the Christian base communities (CBC). While Pentecostalism

1. Interview with Janete.
2. Older Pentecostal movements, such as the Assembly of God, have programs and courses of preparation for their pastors and lay workers. The IURD had a seminary in São Paulo, closed by Bishop Macedo on the grounds that students there were wasting their time and that they should go out into the mission field and evangelize.

cultivates emotion, the CBCs emphasize the education of their members, giving priority to political issues and to human rights. This dimension, undoubtedly of great social import, seems to limit or hide a spiritual strength latent in popular religiosity. The forms of communication produced by Pentecostal fervor, including obviously speaking in strange tongues, seem to surpass the more traditional pedagogical processes. For Pierre Sanchis, Pentecostalism is a "challenge to a cultural tradition [of popular Catholicism] because it knows how to connect with some of its master lines." Pentecostalism enters the body and soul and the field of emotions, pointing out the symbolic strength of an apparent countersense of communication, as we saw in the chapter "Word and Reality."

The Pentecostal experience begins in the temple, through a simple liturgy, apparently improvised, under the strong leadership of pastors and lay workers. They and the temple serve as the mediators of the foundation of faith — which becomes concrete in day-to-day life, where a profession or a job are mere extensions of the testimony of a new life. The vitality of the Pentecostal experience manifests itself in this institutional and personal liberty, strengthened by opposition to the world, to the historic churches, and to other forms of religiosity, especially those of Afro-Brazilian origin. The aggressive character of their faith is part of a new sense of life, and this is sufficient for them. Everything seems to indicate that the numeric and institutional growth of Pentecostalism, alongside its doctrinal emphasis, leads it to surpass, ecclesiastically and sociologically, the historic churches, Afro-Brazilian religiosity, and worldly movements.

One must not forget, however, that the Catholic Church, contrary to Protestantism, has been aware of the importance of the popular religious phenomenon as a component of its own structure and unity. The Second Vatican Council and the Conference of Latin American Bishops in Medellín, signs of a new ecclesial era, recognized the possibility of a model of a church of the poor, a Catholicism of the poor, although this always existed in the context of its ecclesiastical history,[3] and in modern

3. "The Christian base communities were just beginning in 1968 to mature and multiply especially in some countries. In communion with their bishops and following the guidelines set by the Medellín Conference of Bishops, they became centers of evangelization and economic development" (Luiz Alberto Gómez de Souza, *Classes populares e igreja nos caminhos da história* [Petrópolis: Editora Vozes, 1982], p. 221).

times has taken form through the CBCs. This community experience, geographically dispersed, is consolidated through liberation theology, the fruit of a theory and of a new ecclesial practice in relation to the poor of Latin America. In this manner the CBCs would constitute one of the most significant ways of gathering the dispersed people in rural areas and in the peripheral zones of the urban centers. Contrary to Pentecostalism, which created innumerable new churches, the CBCs, even with official opposition, maintain themselves inside the universal structure of Catholicism. They represent a movement from bottom to top that the cupola of the Catholic Church still respects and prefers to preserve as an expression of its internal unity. The same, in a certain way, happens with the official tolerance of the charismatic movement or the progressive vanguard of the clergy. This capacity of the Catholic Church to articulate and make room for polarization and groups in opposition to each other, as is the case with the CBCs and the charismatic movement, also means that it recognizes the greater importance of the lay men and women in these movements — whose contributions in part diminish the impact that the lack of priests represents to Catholicism.[4] According to some analysts, Pentecostalism "attracts the masses much more than the 'liberation theologies' *[sic]*," since the "liberationists" have a "middle-class and radical intellectual accent foreign to the real needs of the poor." That is, their language does not touch on the real necessities of the poor, it only gives "idealized versions of these needs."[5] Nevertheless, the Catholic experience of internal tolerance could well make a very rich contribution to future efforts toward effective approximation of the historic churches to Pentecostalism. Because of their growth worldwide and in Latin America, in spite of their present limitations, Pentecostal movements in their different forms, especially those that are more open, must be taken into account. However, this does not imply, necessarily, a formal relation of an institutional nature with them by the historic churches.[6] This will be covered in the next chapter.

4. The last edition of *Annuarium Stasticum Ecclesiae,* published by the Secretary of State of the Holy See, registered in Brazil a total of 7,645 diocesan priests, 360 bishops, and 5 cardinals in 1994, while in the United States, less Catholic than Brazil, there are 394 bishops and 10 cardinals.

5. Compare Samuel Escobar, Estuardo McIntosh, and Juan Inocencio, *Historia y Misión: Revisión de perspectivas* (Lima, Peru: Ediciones Presencia, 1994), p. 51.

6. Conrad Raiser, the general-secretary of the World Council of Churches, dur-

The historic Protestant churches, partly as a result of their internal divisions, did not know how to or were unable to relate with so many and such varied forms of worship and spirituality of this movement. This indifference — or antagonism — can also be noticed in relation to the ecumenical movement, in spite of some more recent efforts to understand the Pentecostal phenomenon through studies[7] and pronouncements — some national Pentecostal churches have been accepted as members of the World Council of Churches. However, on the part of the WCC as well as the Pentecostal churches, there is a lack of mutual recognition of the global significance of the new force that both movements represent in contemporary Christianity. Therefore, an attitude of fear and concern with respect to the vitality of Pentecostalism prevails on the part of the ecumenical movement, historic Protestantism, and the Catholic Church. On the part of Pentecostalism, the great majority of its churches have rejected a greater contact with ecumenical institutions, on the international as well as the regional or national levels.[8]

Recent data from the secular press indicate a certain effervescence in the Christian churches, although it may not equal the strength of the Pentecostal revival, and seem to show that the vitality and freedom of Pentecostalism in the Brazilian experience may be stimulating a recovery of the missionary consciousness. The magazine *Veja* referred to the increasing importance of evangelization for the Catholic Church and some

---

ing the General Assembly of CLAI, the Conselho Latinoamericano de Igrejas, in 1995, "asked the churches of this continent to give attention to the phenomenon of Pentecostalism, more and more rooted in the Latin American and Caribbean culture. . . . Raiser added that the Pentecostal Evangelical communities are showing, little by little, a significant concern for the link between faith and the transformation of the marginalized social structures" (*A Cruz do Sul,* IECLB, March 1995).

7. The World Council of Churches, in 1966-67, sponsored the research of sociologist Christian Lalive D'Épinay on Pentecostalism and the history of religions in Latin America, especially Protestantism and Pentecostalism in Chile. From this research came the well-known book *O refúgio das massas [Haven of the Masses]* (Rio de Janeiro: Paz e Terra, 1970).

8. In 1986-87, at the request of Conselho Nacional de Igrejas Cristãs (CONIC), of which the Roman Catholic Church is an integral part, ISER carried out research on "religious diversity in Brazil," covering the main manifestations of Brazilian religiosity. The result of the research was published by ISER, in three volumes, under the title *Sinais dos tempos: Diversidade religiosa no Brasil* (1989).

Protestant churches: "Brazilian missionaries go throughout the world to propagate Christianity." According to *Veja,* 2,700 missionaries are preaching the gospel in more than eighty nations: "There are more than 1,000 Catholic priests, 1,200 Evangelical pastors and 500 lay workers of the Universal Church of Bishop Edir Macedo." The magazine's highlighting of IURD as a new missionary current alongside the traditional churches is curious and significant (we should not forget that this church is less than twenty years old). In the following week the same magazine dedicated four pages to speak about the vocations for the Catholic priesthood, that is, 7,000 seminarians "who renounce worldly pleasures in order to become priests."[9]

If these numbers represent reality, wouldn't the situation described here indicate the need for more creative initiatives and less criticism of Pentecostal movements on the part of the churches, above all the Protestant ones? If Pentecostalism is a popular expression of Protestantism, neither one nor the other can be fully studied or understood as autonomous religious entities. It is true that historically the Protestant churches always had difficulties coexisting with the *popular.* This is due not only to what they inherited theologically and ideologically from the missionaries, but also to the social and cultural complexity of popular culture. The constant transformations of this "undigested conglomerate of fragments"[10] surpass the generally restricted circles of ecclesiastical formation and structure.[11] The evangelization carried on by foreign missionaries transmitted a type of faith and culture that avoided — and even rejected — indigenous values. It took the converts out of their world and transformed them into beings disconnected from their origins. This type

9. *Veja,* 23 April 1997 and 30 April 1997. The first issue makes a comparison of the Catholic Church and the IURD. The comparison was continued in the second issue, ending with these words: "The Universal Church of the Reign of God, an institution of genuine Brazilian origin and present in approximately fifty countries, only begins a new work after mounting a structure that guarantees its economic viability. Before the arrival of the pastor with the gospel, a commission is sent ahead that studies the laws, establishes the church legally, and buys the building where it is going to function. Afterwards, it is the missionary's turn."

10. A. Gramsci, "Observações sobre o folklore," in *Literatura e vida nacional* (Rio de Janeiro: Editora Civilização Brasileira, 1938).

11. Compare Pedro Ribeiro Oliveira, *Concilium,* separata, November 1984: "Que significa analiticamente 'Pueblo' "? (p. 436).

of conversion ended up provoking, in different moments of the history of Protestantism, vigorous manifestations on the part of national pastors and Protestant intellectuals in favor of a more Brazilian church, of another type of theological formation and even, if possible, of a *"caboclo* (Brazilian mestizo) theology." In other words, while Protestantism exhibited for decades a certain cultural discontinuity and dependence on the outside world, Pentecostalism, with theological and financial autonomy, established itself in the context of the local culture. The forms of worship disseminated in Brazil by the historic churches can be understood as cause or effect of a theology peculiar to the missionary era, committed to an ideology of "manifest destiny."[12] The theologian José Miguez Bonino has described in his analysis of Latin American Protestantism the neocolonial character of the conditions that favored Protestantism's entry into the continent. A real "pact" guaranteed "the triumph of the modernizing elites over the traditional ones," leading Protestantism to favor the initiative and the objectives of its countries of origin instead of seeking its own dynamism.[13]

Pentecostalism, with its origins on this continent equally imported, adopted a simple style closer to the people, encouraged their participation, cultivated their rhythms, and turned the converts into new missionaries and preachers. Personal evangelism does not require great study or long theological preparation. It flows out of the power of a personal experience and decision. The message is easily grasped intellectually. It is those Evangelical doctrines less emphasized in the older churches that constitute the center of the faith of the simplest believers. Instead of the routine of a repetitive liturgy, the Pentecostal service goes from the trivial to the fantastic; it is not a static solemnity but an unexpected individual and collective happiness. As a religious experience, Pentecostalism "represents a *ritualized prolongation of the original Pentecostal event* (Acts 2:10, 19) that expresses the essence of Christianity with an intense spirituality that recalls the life of the early Christians. It serves as a foundational myth."[14]

---

12. I take this statement from Antônio G. Mendonça, in *Introdução ao protestantismo no Brasil,* ed. Antônio Gouvêa Mendonça and Prócoro Velasques Filho (São Paulo: Edições Loyola, 1990), p. 177.

13. Escobar, McIntosh, and Inocencio, *Historia y Misión,* p. 51.

14. Bernardo L. Campos M., "In the Power of the Spirit: Pentecostalism, Theology and Social Ethics," in *In the Power of the Spirit. Pentecostals in Latin America: A*

I believe that if things continue as they are, the historic churches are going to become a mere reference point for good behavior. That's all. . . . I see the historic Pentecostals [referring to the Assembly of God] almost as Pentecostal Protestants. And they are no longer growing as rapidly as before and are today very traditional. Now, it is a traditionalism that shouts "Hallelujah." It is a traditionalism animated by a band playing music. A lay traditionalism, less clerical. It is precisely because of this that they still have more mobility, more aggressiveness. It is a traditionalism that counts, theologically speaking, on the intervention of God with more intensity than Calvinist theology was ever able to produce.[15]

Of course, we have here different cultural values. I am not saying that Protestant worship should adopt (for us) a tame model of Pentecostal worship, but I do want to emphasize the great difference between a traditional type of religiosity and the novelty that emotion can bring as the result of a personal surrender — conversion — without restrictions. However, we must also ask ourselves if the historic churches do not have something to learn and cultivate from this new spiritual reality. In the emotion of the intense individual participation wouldn't a radical form of the "universal priesthood of all believers" be expressed? The historic churches should recognize in Pentecostalism its "singular essences" (an expression of Ricoeur) as alternative expressions of an Evangelical faith that is more adequate to the culture and the reality of the people; they should even rejoice in its "festive conviviality," capable of opening up to poor sectors of our population, rarely reached, the practice of a gospel for the daily routine.[16]

Challenge to the Historic Churches, ed. Benjamín F. Gutiérrez and Dennis A. Smith [Mexico City: AIPRAL, 1996], p. 50.

15. Interview with Caio Fábio.

16. See Helcion Ribeiro, *Religiosidade popular na teologia latino-americana* (São Paulo: Edições Paulinas, 1985), p. 162.

8 *Pentecostalism and Ecumenical Renewal*

Although the search for a new relation between Protestantism and Pentecostalism may be more feasible in the local sphere (between churches of the same neighborhood, for example), wouldn't it be more appropriate for the ecumenical movement to encourage cooperation and try to reduce the weight of denominational idiosyncrasies? Although the ecclesiastical and theological perspectives are the focus of the second part of this book, I would like to explore some practical aspects, as well as reactions of those interviewed. (As in the previous chapter, I am not referring separately to the historic churches and to the ecumenical movement, but relating them according to the diverse moments of research, of the interviews and observations in this sphere.)

First, through its international as well as regional or national structure, the ecumenical movement must mediate and encourage more pertinent studies and practices in reference to the similitude between doctrines and conduct common to the historic churches and to Pentecostalism, in the context of their own dynamics and cultural expressions. That is, ecumenism must take into account experiences of cooperation already in existence, from which new dimensions of Christian unity could emerge to stimulate and renew the churches and the ecumenical movement itself.[1] Is there unresolvable opposition among the various forms of ecclesial experience or can these differences be reduced to a few confessional elements? The theme is an old one. However, a new configuration of Christianity in our days, determined by the growth of Pentecostalism, should lead to a recapturing of what has been done until now in the ecumenical sphere and to a search for other possibilities of understanding that go beyond isolated moments of cooperation and mere academic studies. Cooperation is still minimal, and studies are generally limited to research that does not take into account the social and cultural dimension of the relations between the various Christian confessions. Social scientists will possibly have stronger reasons for not getting involved in the complexity of the ecclesial aspects of various Protestant denominations than theologians and pastors who study carefully the books, theses, and articles that the social scientists have produced recently.

Returning to the convergence of doctrines, perhaps we can say that the differences between historical Protestantism and Pentecostalism are manifested more in the doctrinal emphases attributed to them, or in their diverse ideological worldviews. However, the Pentecostal divisiveness, be it in the beginning of the movement or in its current multiplicity, still reflects the universal tendency toward division in Protestantism, due not infrequently to conflicts of leadership. We have outlined here what has developed historically in the Reformation, sometimes under dramatic conditions, later in the missionary era, and now with the ecumenical movement itself. The attempts to unite or to bring churches closer together, as a more visible and universal sign and testimony of Christian faith, have achieved significant results historically through the initiatives of the World Council of Churches and of regional and national ecumenical organizations. Nevertheless, these efforts have become more timid at the present time, above all in the presence of this new expression of a pop-

1. A commemorative ceremony of the Week of Prayer for Christian Unity, in Rio de Janeiro, in 1997, took place in a large Catholic parish of Copacabana, with a charismatic tendency, under the direction of the Cardinal-Archbishop of Rio de Janeiro (D. Eugênio Salles), and had the participation of pastors from Lutheran, Methodist, Anglican, Orthodox, and Assembly of God churches. The program, which takes place every year, always with the church crowded, was prepared by the Archdiocesan Commission for Ecumenism and Religious Dialogue of Rio de Janeiro.

ular Protestantism, which opens spaces in many respects closed to the historic churches. There are, however, indications of new ecumenical openings that indicate the possibility and urgency of new steps on the road toward unity and cooperation. The fact that, in its origin, Pentecostalism has cultivated the idea of a "community in the Spirit," that is, "a community that includes (not excludes) those that experience and speak about the Spirit in different ways," can be very meaningful for a badly needed renewal of the ecumenical movement itself. If it is a fact that, unfortunately, the ecumenical dimension of this original vision of Pentecostalism, without denominational distinctions, has been abandoned, it is also true that it can be rediscovered and practiced in our time.[2]

A more encompassing analysis of current Pentecostalism, in global terms, shows that the ecumenical dimension of Pentecostalism has been abandoned only in part, and that a certain ecumenical vitality, latent or effective, exists internal to the movement itself. The theme is exhaustively dealt with by Guillermo Cook in his essay "Interchurch Relations: Exclusion, Ecumenism, and the Poor."[3] Cook reminds us that, even a few years ago, the ecumenical issue would have been considered irrelevant, and it still is for many scholars of Pentecostalism. At the same time, the majority of Pentecostals maintain serious suspicions about the very term *ecumenism.* However, "the extent of their relationships with other Christians and, in some cases, non-Christians is remarkable."

Moreover, an ecumenical tendency in Pentecostalism, if it can be called such, can be found in earlier movements, in other circumstances. In the research about Chilean Pentecostalism done by Christian Lalive D'Épinay in 1965-66, the author observes "a certain consensus in which *the Protestant and Pentecostal denominations constitute the nucleus of the oikoumene.*" A Pentecostal pastor notes: "All denominations that affirm

2. Walter J. Hollenweger, "The Pentecostal Elites and the Pentecostal Poor — A Missed Dialogue?" in *Charismatic Christianity as a Global Culture,* ed. Karla Poewe (Columbia, S.C.: University of South Carolina Press, 1994), p. 206.

3. In *Power, Politics, and Pentecostals in Latin America,* ed. Edward L. Cleary and Hannah W. Stewart-Gambino (Boulder, Colo.: Westview Press, 1997), pp. 77-96. The quotes that follow, unless indicated otherwise, are from Guillermo Cook. Regarding Pentecostalism and ecumenism, see also Carmelo E. Álvarez, in *In the Power of the Spirit. Pentecostals in Latin America: A Challenge to the Historic Churches,* ed. Benjamín F. Gutiérrez and Dennis A. Smith [Mexico: AIPRAL, 1996], p. 46.

salvation only through Jesus Christ and are faithful to the Holy Scriptures, participate in the Body of Christ." In spite of greater reservations about certain confessions (such as the Anglican, "the ritual is extremely close to the Catholics"; and the Lutheran, "very materialistic"), the interviews indicated the existence of a "common conviction about their spiritual unity."[4] Pentecostal fundamentalism, as any other fundamentalism, which "identifies its own position in absolute terms and in this way absolutizes itself over against other theological and social positions," in the words of Heinrich Schäfer,[5] seems to be able to go beyond itself when confronted theologically with other types of churches and other spiritual and social realities. The study of Guillermo Cook, even though it recognizes in Pentecostal sectarianism a "necessary function of their search for identity," affirms, quoting David Martin, that the growth of Pentecostalism in numbers and in maturity has led it to become more aware of its social responsibilities. I believe that the same can be said about the relations of Pentecostalism to other ecclesiastical bodies, since "social involvement is one of the chief routes to ecumenical awareness." Julio de Santa Ana recalls: "As in the first century, we can observe that once again the poor are the point of union between the churches that have a tendency to divide or are already divided." He brings his affirmation up to date by saying that "the *ecumenical movement* in Latin America will only achieve its maturity when it enters into serious dialogue, on the basis of equality (consequently descending from its conquering and arrogant white horse), with the types of religiosity still in existence in those cultures."[6]

Cook gives several examples.[7] One of the most significant, I believe,

4. Christian Lalive D'Épinay, *O refúgio das massas [Haven of the Masses]* (Rio de Janeiro: Paz e Terra, 1970), p. 257 (italics by the author).

5. Compare "Fundamentalism: Power and the Absolute," mimeo., 1993, p. 11. In another article, "El fundamentalismo y los carismas: la reconquista del espacio vital en América Latina," Schäfer affirms that "spirituality of life also opens the possibility of a new way for an ecumenism of survival, an ecumenism of the oppressed" (mimeo., 1993/1995, p. 9).

6. Julio de Santa Ana, *Ecumenismo e Libertação* (Petrópolis: Editora Vozes, 1987), pp. 301-2.

7. Among other Latin American and Brazilian organizations with which Pentecostal churches have collaborated are the Evangelical Union of Latin America, the Latin American Council of Churches, the Ecumenical Center of Documentation and

is in the "Letter of Valencia" of the Venezuelan Evangelical Pentecostal Union, of 1987, in which this church justifies its option for the poor and its ecumenical practice. I reproduce a section quoted in the book:

> We do not deny our identity with these actions. But we affirm that we are not sectarian. Sects are hermetically closed and dogmatic groups that believe that they possess the absolute truth and are closed to dialogue. We believe in the ecumenical spirit that calls us to Christian fellowship and to interconfessional dialogue, and that impels us to accept each other as members of the same body — the Universal Church. . . . We shall continue to affirm our openness to dialogue . . . while maintaining our Pentecostal peculiarities.

Walter Hollenweger also emphasized this ecumenical awakening when pointing out five types of Pentecostalism: Black oral, Evangelical, Catholic, critical, and ecumenical. Only the last two, he says, are still in a process of study and discovery; but the characteristics of the first (among them orality, narrative theology and witness, maximum participation, prayer for the sick, and dreams and visions in both personal and public forms) made it possible to overcome racial, social, and linguistic barriers, contributing not only to the phenomenal growth of Pentecostalism in the Third World but to "an ecumenical holistic understanding of Pentecost as a 'body of Christ.' "[8]

The difficulties for an ecumenical turnaround of this nature are not a few and will continue to exist. But it is worth our while not to lose sight of the signs of unity that are appearing in the institutional sphere or are proclaimed by converts. The answer of one of the persons interviewed, a member of the Assembly of God Church, possibly reveals a position of his denomination. "How do you see the relation with other Evangelical churches?"

> Look, sister, it is very difficult. . . . I see that a lot is lacking there in the approach of Evangelicals to us. It is as it was said here by our evangelist: we, in terms of the Assembly of God, do not make distinctions, and

---

Information in Brazil, and the Brazilian Evangelical Association, with which some Pentecostal pastors and movements are affiliated.

8. Hollenweger, "The Pentecostal Elites and the Pentecostal Poor — A Missed Dialogue?" p. 201.

we do not practice favoritism about this, okay? Furthermore, on Sundays, our main church is visited a lot by Catholics, by Spiritists, by Presbyterians, by Baptists — and they are very well accepted in individual terms, in terms of the church, of the place, okay? Now, to speak like this in general terms, I think that a lot is missing for a more "reconciled" consensus.[9]

These examples seem to indicate with sharp clarity that the frustrations of the efforts for a wider Christian unity can be overcome. This leads me to recall two comments, one current and another historical, which illustrate what I am trying to say. While analyzing the role of Umbanda and Pentecostalism in their response to human afflictions, Peter Fry and G. N. Howe showed that although the religions arise out of different cultural contexts, in their practice they have reduced the significance of the persistence of traditional forms that shape them.[10] In addition, A. Gramsci's commentary, in his analysis of the differences between cultures of diverse origins, can help us to look again at objections of an elitist nature in the relations between Pentecostalism and Protestantism. The antagonisms between one and the other (more cultural and of social class than religious) do not necessarily represent an inferiority of the former in relation to the latter, as is sometimes insinuated as a justification to maintain distance or the current competition. The historical example leads us to the Reformation of the sixteenth century. The superior culture, produced subsequently by the Protestant Reformation, says Gramsci, had its origin in a vast popular-national movement in which Lutheranism and Calvinism spread widely. Gramsci recalls Erasmus, who considered Luther's Reformation a regression to barbarism; for Gramsci, however, "this apparent regression was a necessary condition for a superior culture."[11] A strong expression of the popular culture, a worldview, and identification between theory and practice constitute elements that he considered essential for the emergence and consolidation of a popular movement.

In this sense it is convenient not to forget another area, which is

9. Interview with Aloísio, Assembly of God.

10. "Duas respostas à aflição: umbanda e pentecostalismo em Campinas," *Debate e Crítica* 6 (July 1975).

11. Quoted by Maria-Antonieta Macciochi, *A favor de Gramsci* (Rio de Janeiro: Editora Paz e Terra, 1976), p. 21.

more ours and more current, which is pertinent to the objectives of our research,[12] and which situates the Pentecostal phenomenon in relation to certain forms of religiosity and of popular organization. It is not a matter of establishing parameters between religious movements and social organizations, but of searching in specific historical circumstances for elements that permit us to understand the emergence of popular religiosity and above all of the Pentecostal movement. I am referring to the new social force that emerged in Latin America with the organization of popular movements and the dynamism corresponding to nongovernmental institutions. These new social subjects, parallel to the Cuban and Nicaraguan revolutions — and to the expectations created by the populist governments — could not fail to reach the world of religion and the churches in particular. That is, popular religions, in their innumerable expressions, expanded in the context of a social, cultural, and religious awakening in which popular participation gained a strength until then practically unknown in Brazil and on the continent. This "awareness," to use the term of the times, contained the signs, explicit or latent, of the conquest of a more global liberation.

With all the frustrations and failures that took place, popular awareness was strengthened in the last decades, and significant segments of the people — of the "crowd" — stopped being mere spectators of what was happening, only passive and silent church-goers. Referring to the importance of the religious space in the effective organization of the people, Luiz Alberto Gómez de Souza points out the contribution of other groups, such as the labor movement or "the movement to reduce the cost of living," both closely linked to the pastoral work of the Catholic Church. Thus, "it is possible to also find a political dimension in this resistance," which unifies the spaces of life without establishing clear separations between the political, the religious, the social, and so

12. There is a great deal of literature, based on research, that deals with the Afro-Brazilian cults and their religious and cultural significance. See, for example, Yvonne Maggie, *Guerra de Orixás* (Rio de Janeiro: Zahar, 1975); Raimundo Cintra O.P., *Candomblé e Umbanda: O desafio brasileiro* (Rio de Janeiro: Editora Vozes, 1985); and Patrícia Birman, *O que é Umbanda* (Rio de Janeiro: Editora Brasiliense, 1983). The issue of *possession*, for example, as a "*radical change* which is processed in people through the mediation of a trance" has strong implications for a more comprehensive analysis of Pentecostal worship.

forth.[13] (The era of nongovernmental organizations — NGOs, fruit of the negligence of governments in relation to social problems — begins in the 1970s and exemplifies a new form of ecumenism, outside the ecclesiastical circle, but formed by persons of different Christian confessions and even of non-Christians.) Heinrich Schäfer, when referring to the new religious developments in Latin America, remarks that "Catholicism and various Protestant churches are beginning to overcome their deeply rooted confessional stances and are relating to each other in a different way around certain interests and social movements oriented toward concrete projects and with a variable theological impact."[14]

The differences, however, remain, some apparently irreconcilable. How can we face the growing obstacles of a social and confessional nature that seem to contradict the old ecumenical dream of a more just society? If on the one hand we have the concern of some ecclesiastical currents for a new social order, economic development, a healthy environment, and so forth, in the Pentecostal sphere on the other hand what prevails are the day-to-day issues — personal health, work, housing, a search for a place in society, migration, and survival. This does not mean that these latter problems are completely absent from the more socially privileged churches, or that the other issues are not incorporated, in one way or another, into the simplicity of a doctrine that emphasizes sanctification and spirituality. The difference — and perhaps also the convergence — is in the way in which the people, in their religious experience, deal with the afflictions of life and submit them to the same Lord of the church.

13. Luiz Alberto Gómez de Souza, *Classes populares e igreja nos caminhos da história* (Petrópolis: Editora Vozes, 1982), pp. 241-44. As a conclusion the author states: "What we have are concrete problems such as school, work, and land, integrated in a totality that constitutes the life of the people."

14. "El fundamentalismo y los carismas," p. 9. Schäfer adds, in the same article: "The ecumenical contacts between the Pentecostal movement and the Catholic charismatic movement are surprisingly close — taking into account the sharp lines drawn traditionally between Catholicism and Protestantism in Latin America — even though there may be a greater distancing in Neopentecostalism in relation to official Catholicism: 'I didn't want to sit down with a Catholic dignitary on the basis of equality, but certainly with any Catholic that has been born again, I would like to share and have relations.' . . . Due to the social positions of their members, for 'this ecumenism of expansion of power' there are more and more possibilities of exerting influence in politics, in the army, and in the economic life of the continent."

Peter Berger insists that theology today must be done in the context of an ecumenical conscience. Each day it is more and more difficult to remain *entre nous,* he says, since "all religious groups are constantly confronted by the massive presence of a secularized worldview in its multiform manifestations." It is not only Christians who run into people of other religions on each corner, he continues, as "the intra-protestant bumping process has attained almost orgiastic intensity." All of this, he adds, leads to an ecumenical awareness that can give fullness to the act of theologizing, taking into account this religious quest "that is probably unparalleled in the history of religion."[15]

How would all this — or even parts of this challenging *oikoumene* — work out in practice? How did the persons interviewed see an effective approach to other churches? The answer I presented above represents only one tendency, which is in contrast with others. A more representative picture of the Pentecostal ecumenical perspective in Brazil would depend, however, on more specific study, including that of ecclesiastical authorities of the main currents. (Naturally, the Afro-Brazilian cults and, even more, Spiritism, are unanimously rejected as demonic cults.) One pastor of the Assembly of God, in an important regional administrative position, was categorical:

> I am everybody's friend, up to a certain point. I do not raise questions about their way of life. . . . I get along with my Presbyterian brothers, I get along well with my Adventist brothers, personally. Doctrinally I don't agree with the Baptists . . . , I don't appreciate their baptism and if one of my members goes to their church, they baptize him again. . . . The Universal? I hate the way they use the Word of God. I don't mess with them. I don't trouble myself. It is not my problem; the problem is theirs and with God. The gospel is a pure thing. One cannot make a business of the gospel. Many people are fascinated with their growth. History shows: It is not quantity that God wants. God wants quality.[16]

The focus varies according to the different relations believers have with the denomination itself or with the mobilization between the churches. One woman interviewed praised the freedom in relation to

15. Peter Berger, *A Rumor of Angels* (New York: Anchor Books, 1990), p. 91.
16. Interview with Pastor Claudionor, Assembly of God.

"uses and customs" in the IURD, another limited herself to appreciation of their doctrine:

> I like short clothes; I can wear them at the Universal. In the Assembly of God we have to wear the skirt way down there and three blouses in order not to show anything: a little T-shirt, a blouse, and a dress on top. . . . Nothing that is forced is good, right?[17]

> It is very different because the preaching in the Baptist, the preaching they do, they keep talking and they don't think about the people at all. . . . They do not have this thing that they have at the Universal Church. I find it different. The God is Love Church is also good, but it is different.[18]

But aren't there Catholics who get converted, go through the Universal, and then go to other churches?

> This is something we are thankful for, because the person who goes through the Universal is prepared to take the word to all creatures, but nobody is obligated to remain at the Universal, you understand? But you went to the Universal, you didn't like their way of working, and you went to another denomination. Amen, thanks be to God, because you are getting to know the work of Jesus, the work of God alive through the Universal. Do you understand, my daughter? You don't have to stay there at all. Go to another church. You don't have to, but you were liberated.[19]

The observations of an evangelist of the Assembly of God reduced the importance of doctrinal issues and included what he called the "ethical aspect":

> No, the difference there is not even in the doctrinal aspect; it is more in the ethical aspect. Because in the doctrinal aspect it is very small; it hardly exists. Because the churches have the same biblical doctrinal vision. They do not diverge. For example, baptism. If one church baptizes by immersion, another baptizes by aspersion. But it believes it is a baptism too, and this is not a doctrinal difference. This is only a different way of baptizing. So the difference is more in the sense of custom and eth-

17. Interview with Leila.
18. Interview with Juliana.
19. Interview with Rosa.

ics. . . . The Evangelicals are the same. We preach in Baptist, Methodist, Wesleyan churches, and they preach in our church, too. There is an interchange. If they invite us, we go there, and if we invite them, they come, you understand? So it is necessary to work together; we are in this movement together, a crusade, a campaign. There is no division at all.[20]

Pastor Caio Fábio has achieved through the Brazilian Evangelical Association (AEVB), which he founded, an extremely eclectic ecumenical practice, bringing together not only Evangelical denominations but institutions and individuals, with different weight in the elections within the organization. There are historic Protestant churches, charismatic movements, Pentecostal churches constituting, until now, the widest range of cooperation or of collaboration among Evangelicals in Brazil. Among those not participating are the Pentecostal Congregação Cristã do Brasil ("they do not associate with any group that is not of their denomination. They have more than three million members, but they do not associate with anyone and do not participate in anything; they are the most closed group in the country," says Caio Fábio) and the Universal Church of the Reign of God. The ecumenism of the National Council of Christian Churches (CONIC), which includes among its members the Catholic Church, is criticized for this: "On the day that the AEVB would make this decision (to affiliate with CONIC), it would lose 80 percent of those associated with it. What do we have alongside the Catholic Church? Only a relation of informal dialogue."[21]

These few reactions indicate the difficulties that still exist — and that are growing as the churches divide and subdivide. But unexplored spaces prevail in this internal dialectic, as Ernst Troeltsch and Max Weber pointed out, between the institutional and the spontaneous, between conformity and protest. Only a more direct experience of the historic churches with the Pentecostal world, or vice-versa, could discover alternatives that might open new paths to Christian unity.

In spite of the difficulties that still exist ("Who could build a bridge over these troubled waters?" asks Walter Hollenweger),[22] I would men-

20. Interview with Josiel Matias, Assembly of God.
21. Interview with Richard Shaull, Waldo Cesar, and Clara Mafra.
22. Hollenweger, "The Pentecostal Elites and the Pentecostal Poor — A Missed Dialogue?" p. 209.

tion initially the importance of a more profound study, starting in theological seminaries, of the immense yet almost unknown world of Brazilian popular religiosity — an opening to a better understanding of the Pentecostal phenomenon. In this context, the issue of syncretism would certainly illuminate dimensions likewise little studied by Pentecostalism.[23] Nevertheless, there are simpler ways, directly linked to the day-to-day realities of religious developments that can no longer be omitted from the ecclesiastical agendas. Visits to Pentecostal churches, as some Catholic priests have made, would relativize the negative views that still prevail among the more traditional currents of Protestantism. "Priests learn with the Evangelicals" is a recent newspaper headline, with a more precise subtitle: "In order to face the challenge of evangelization, the CNBB [National Conference of Brazilian Bishops] adopts 'liturgy of the bishop.'" Part of the half-page article in this paper clarifies this: "Some priests that have attended churches of *bishop* Edir Macedo, leader of the Universal Church of the Reign of God, detected positive aspects, and are disposed to make use of them. The objective is to face the competition using, whenever possible, the same resources."[24]

The timid ecumenical expressions of our time mean very little in the presence of the great possibilities of an interconfessional practice that would explore the possibilities for a multi-confessional way of life. Such an openness, carried further, would correspond to another pole of relations in the international religious scene, that of "dialogue between faiths." The Catholic theologian Hans Kung, for example, defends relations without restrictions with Islam, model of life for almost one billion people. For him "Christian imperialism is over."[25]

The future of the Christian churches must therefore go along the difficult path of recognizing that a new form of church has emerged on

23. While characterizing Christianity as "a glorious syncretism," Leonardo Boff states: "Syncretism is not only inevitable but is positively the historical and concrete way in which God comes to people and saves them. The question is not whether or not there is syncretism in the Church. The problem is in the type of syncretism that exists at present and which one should be sought. Which syncretism truly translates the Christian message and which one destroys it?" (*Church, Charism and Power* [New York: Crossroad, 1985], p. 99).

24. *Jornal do Brasil,* 18 February 1996.

25. *Vermelho e Branco* (ISER) 9 (1990).

the international scene. It is no longer a matter, it is worth repeating, of an isolated, local parochial movement. It concerns a new dynamism of religious and spiritual life, a challenge to the older churches, their structures, and their relations with social reality. "What Pentecostals are offering to the ecumenical movement is a *spirituality* of ecumenism — a universal rediscovery of the Spirit for all Christian denominations."[26] Bishop Robert McAlister, of the New Life Pentecostal Church, tells an interesting experience. As secretary of the dialogue between Pentecostal leaders and the Secretariat for the Promotion of Christian Unity, of the Catholic Church, he was informed that a reform in Catholic liturgy would allow two pauses for "spontaneous praise" during the mass. McAlister, who interpreted this initiative as an influence from the Pentecostal movement, also had a meeting with the Pope, who greeted the Pentecostal Commission with hallelujahs.

The Pentecostal emphasis on the Holy Spirit, as is well known, definitely influenced the choice of the general theme of the Seventh Assembly of the World Council of Churches, in Canberra, Australia, in 1991: "Come Holy Spirit, renew all of your Creation." On that occasion, as Harvey Cox pointed out, it was evident that the Eastern Orthodox tradition as well as the new non-Western churches focused their attention more on the Holy Spirit than the majority of the Western churches, whether they were Catholic or Protestant. And although the Assembly followed its institutional routine, what had a marked influence on informal conversations and the reflections of the Council were the words of a Korean theologian, Hyun Kyun Chung, invoking the power of the Spirit not only over "the World Council of Churches but of Christianity itself."[27] In the midst of a beautiful choreographic spectacle, in which all were invited to take off their shoes in honor of the "holy ground" on which they were standing, according to Harvey Cox, "the World Council has never been quite the same since."

There may be some wishful thinking in what the theologian affirms, but there is evidence that the Spirit is mobilizing the church, with-

26. P. A. Hardiment, "Confessing the Apostolic Faith from the Perspective of the Pentecostal Churches," *One in Christ* 23.1-2 (1987): 67. Quoted by Cook, "Interchurch Relations: Exclusion, Ecumenism, and the Poor," p. 80.

27. Harvey Cox, *Fire from Heaven* (New York: Addison-Wesley, 1995), pp. 213-14.

out the distinctions so characteristic of our prejudices. The similitude, as can be seen, may overcome the antagonisms and open new perspectives for the future of the Christian churches — the renewal of its current forms and the discovery of a new matrix for its unity. If Pentecostalism has not found a space in the historic Protestant churches, it is certainly widening the space of Christian faith in society in our time. Openness to this religious diversity could mean a new era for the ecumenical movement and for the witness of the Christian churches.

Appendix:
Sociological and Theological Horizon

As was mentioned in the Introduction, we want to emphasize the contribution that a dialogue between sociology and theology can offer toward a more encompassing analysis of the phenomenon we are studying, in the expectation that this particular interdisciplinary dimension, not very common in studies of Pentecostalism, may open the way to a more comprehensive analysis of this religious phenomenon.

In Part I, while analyzing the effects of a radical spirituality on the lives of those who convert to Pentecostalism, we concluded that this task would be incomplete without the theological perspective — as an instrument to capture the deeper meaning of a new form of church and of Christian life. Starting from this vision common to the authors, what has been said here is not situated exclusively in the field of sociology, but pertains to theology and ecclesiology as well. Part II will present a more thorough analysis of the theological issues raised by the personal, social, and ecclesial impact of a new experience of faith. Here we must return to the proposal — perhaps pretentious (or excessively broad) — presented in the title of this book: What is the future of the Christian churches faced with a movement of universal dimensions, which not only encompasses sociological elements of major significance for the human sciences, but also reworks old concepts of a theology (or theologies and ecclesiologies) formulated throughout the history of the church, in many cases forgetting or ignoring the great doctrinal emphases of the early Christian communities?

There is no one answer to this big issue. Neither do we seek to solve the impasses — and the paradox — contained in the *promises, limitations, and challenges* to which the subtitle of the book refers. We are certain, however, that all of our work leads inevitably to the question about the future, especially in the perspective, indicated by Shaull in Part II, that the Spirit is present — as in the past — in the promises, limitations, and challenges of the Pentecostal movement.

Let us take up again an aspect that in many ways constituted the center of the research undertaken. When we say, for example, that the historic churches should review their forms of worship and religious experience, in a rereading of their faith and mission heritage, we also affirm that Neopentecostalism needs to deepen its reading of the Bible in terms of a vision that goes beyond a spirituality centered in the individualistic piety that has characterized it. Only in this way will it be able to face more adequately the challenges of the social structures that produce misery and poverty, complementing, for example, mere campaigns of distribution of food or a political participation limited to getting members elected to the National Congress. Although this does not exclusively characterize any one of the churches mentioned, it indicates a general tendency and offers one more example of an area in which theology and sociology can complement each other. This is because we consider the churches as possible *mediators* between human reality and "what might be called signs of transcendence in the sphere of an empirically given human situation."[1] In other words, what matters in the insertion of theological and sociological elements is capturing dimensions of transcendence in the institutional forms of the churches, as well as in the common life of common people.

There are sufficient indications that human commitments can be analyzed in the set of manifestations that surpass the visible phenomena, appearances, to arrive at the perception of their essence — or their transcendence. If at this point we have taken some ideas from Immanuel

1. Peter Berger, *A Rumor of Angels* (New York: Anchor Books, 1990), p. 91.

Kant, it is convenient to recall the perspective of analysis of religions in Émile Durkheim, when he referred to *permanent elements* in the base of all the systems of belief, constituting "what is eternal and human in religion."[2] If on the one hand Durkheim's idealism led him to affirm in the same work that "the idea constitutes reality itself," on the other hand Max Weber mentions the decisive contribution of *this-worldly asceticism,* religiously motivated, to social change.[3] This seems to indicate the importance of an interaction of the sciences of knowledge and, if that is the case, a certain limitation of the analysis based on only one discipline.

Here it is worthwhile to mention a good example of the possibilities and expectation generated by a more fruitful relation between sociology and theology, despite their conceptual and methodological differences. In the answer of sociologist Henry Desroche to a letter of theologian Harvey Cox, the former said that in the incidental encounters between their respective sciences there was "a decisive particularity": while one was anchored in some way in a heaven of notions (or ideas), the other "is built from the bottom up, rooted in a garden of phenomena," which does not prevent them from seeking each other, in spite of the fact that "analogous themes may be developed in different languages."[4] A similar issue is pointed out by Peter Berger. While mentioning the methodological impossibility of an "empirical theology," he insists on the value of attempting "a theology that seeks to establish a correlation step by step with what can be empirically said about humanity."[5]

Nevertheless, it is obvious that not even this *interdisciplinarity* can respond satisfactorily to certain issues raised in one or another sphere of the *logias* and of such specific languages. In the case of this book, it is less a matter of juxtaposition of procedures than of the encounter of reflections and experiences of students of Pentecostalism whose ideas and conclusions in many ways are close to each other as a result of many years of

2. Émile Durkheim, *Les formes élémentaires de la vie religieuse* (Paris: P.U.F., 1968), p. 11.

3. Max Weber, *Sociología de la comunidad religiosa,* Sociología de la religión (Mexico City: F.C.E., 1964).

4. Henry Desroche, *O homem e suas religiões: Ciências humanas e experiências religiosas* (São Paulo: Edições Paulinas, 1985), p. 104.

5. Peter Berger, *Para una teoría sociológica de la religión* (Barcelona: Editorial Kairós, 1971), p. 258.

work in common. This concrete fact is definitely reflected in this work as a whole, with possible interpenetrations and incidental repetitions in one chapter or another given the communion of ideas in the face of the Pentecostal phenomenon and other manifestations of Brazilian religiosity. However, without omitting the external and internal criticisms (many come from the faithful themselves), or what for us seems to provide evidence of the limitations of this movement, one common element is predominant: neither defense nor judgment of the conditions and directions that Pentecostalism (especially certain movements) has taken in Brazil; nor do we consider that the solutions offered by the Neopentecostal movement for each type of problem are totally defensible. In this perspective — if we are faithful to it — we hope to have gone beyond appearances and pointed out the values, explicit or not, that challenge not only the expressions of spirituality predominant in other churches and religious traditions, but also their institutional and personal relations with Brazilian society. In the wide individual and social range that day to day becomes wider in Pentecostalism, the "symbolic efficacy" that unites the protest of the oppressed to the utopia of a new reality is present.

PART II THE RECONSTRUCTION OF LIFE IN THE POWER OF THE SPIRIT

Richard Shaull

Introduction

I originally set out to examine theologically, from a Reformed perspective, what Pentecostals in Brazil are doing to respond to the needs of the poor and participate in their struggle for life. I ended up exploring, from a Pentecostal perspective, what Reformed and other mainline churches may be called to be and to do in order to respond to the needs and struggles of the poor.

I had been aware, for some time, of the surprising growth of Pentecostal movements among the poor and wanted to understand what they were offering. I was especially attracted to this project because it offered me an unusual opportunity to take part in an interdisciplinary study of this phenomenon. My major concern was to draw on the resources of sociological analysis as I reflected theologically on Pentecostalism and evaluated what these movements were doing. In the process, I expected to learn something for myself and my community, but my main object was to explore and raise critical questions about what *they* were doing.

As we proceeded with our research, however, an unexpected thing happened. I discovered that, in and through my involvement with them, *I* was being called into question. Whatever the nature of my reactions, positive and negative, to Pentecostals, I realized that they were raising new questions for me. My perspective was changing. A new response on my part was being called for.

The ensuing shift in my approach has set the terms for my theological reflections. But I realize that what I develop in these pages can make sense to anyone reading them only as you take into account some of the discoveries I have made along this road and the changes in my perspective that have occurred.

Before beginning this study, I was well aware of how the neoliberal economy of the global market was contributing to ever greater impoverishment and exclusion of masses of people. However, I had not perceived how radically this order was changing the life situation of vast numbers of these people, as well as the nature of their struggle for life.

With this global market economy, not only is the number of poor and abandoned people growing, but they are getting poorer as they are increasingly marginalized or excluded. In this situation, they are caught up in what is becoming an ever more desperate daily struggle for survival. As one Brazilian anthropologist put it recently: It is no longer a matter of people having certain preoccupations. Preoccupation with making it through each day has taken over their lives. At the same time, the most basic forms of life in the community — the family, local neighborhoods, social, economic, and political structures — are becoming unglued, leaving masses of poor people in both rural and peripheral urban areas without stable work, medical care, or opportunities for education, in a situation of almost total abandonment, without any supportive extended family or community.

I eventually realized that many people in this situation are searching for something very different from what was most important for them several decades ago. Now they are seeking for power to heal sick minds and bodies, to reorganize broken lives, to overcome addiction to alcohol or drugs, to give them a sense of their own identity and worth, and to help them overcome feelings of impotence, experience a taste of joy, and look to the future with hope. In other words, their supreme concern, though not expressed in these words, is for the *reconstruction of human life* beginning at the most basic level. The growing inability of our major institutions, together with social movements and political ideologies, to respond creatively to this situation points to a deepening crisis of civilization. A growing number of women and men of all social classes are facing a profound crisis of meaning and hope and often experiencing brokenness in their personal lives and communities similar in many ways to what is increasingly evident among marginal and excluded people.

Those engaged in this struggle for survival and for the reconstruction of life, individually and in community, may be as concerned about changing economic, social, and political structures as was a previous generation. But their priorities for this struggle have changed. And only as they find the power they need for the re-creation of life and community can they emerge as subjects with the drive and the vision necessary for such struggles.

Moreover, increasing numbers of people in this desperate situation seem less and less inclined to turn to or trust in ideologies or political movements for their liberation. In fact, they may have come to the conclusion that they cannot count on any merely human movement to rescue them; their only hope lies in a Power beyond themselves. In other words, they are turning more and more toward the religious realm. And as they do so, they find themselves connecting — or reconnecting — with something that has been at the core of their being, and so central to their cultural heritage that it determines their approach to life and the world.

Those of us whose concern for the poor has been motivated by our Christian faith should have every reason to rejoice in their growing interest in religion. However, I realize that neither I nor the churches with which I am associated are prepared to respond to this challenge.

We who belong to mainline churches are largely absent from the world of impoverished and broken people, far removed from their search for the power they need for the reconstruction of life. We have little or no contact with people in the poorest urban or rural neighborhoods, those living in areas of intense conflict and violence, those struggling to overcome addiction to drugs, or those in prison.

When we are in any way in touch with them, it is usually to offer them material aid or provide social services of one sort or another. Rarely are we present in their midst as witnesses to the gospel as the power of God for the reorganization of their broken lives or to equip them to face and overcome the demonic forces around them.

Even when we make an effort to relate to them from the center of our lives of faith, we soon face the fact that by and large their religious world is not ours. Especially for those of us, Catholic or Protestant, who in recent decades have experienced a conversion to the poor, and stand in solidarity with them in their struggle, it comes as quite a shock to realize that we may now be quite far removed from their struggle for life and may be in no position to help them find the spiritual resources for which they are searching.

This presents us with a difficult challenge, but it is something that our previous experience should prepare us to undertake. For many of us, our earlier contact with injustice and oppression led us to enter into the world of the poor and reread the Bible from their position and perspective. As we did this, our own faith was enriched and renewed, and we were often surprised by the new relationships that ensued. I see no reason why this cannot happen again, with similar results. But it can happen only as we make the effort to enter into the religious world of the poor.

The more aware I became of the nature of their search, the more I realized that Pentecostals are the ones who are now present among the poor and are responding to them. According to the testimonies of those we interviewed, this is where they have found new life. As I listened to them, I could not escape the conclusion that Pentecostals were offering them something I and my communities of faith did not have and thus could not offer.

From the beginning of our research, we perceived that the Pentecostal world was quite different from that in which those of us in the older and more traditional Protestant churches have been moving. Moreover, wherever we turned, we found what appeared to us as a strange mixture of diverse and frequently contradictory elements not only in the wide variety of Pentecostal movements but also within one or another Pentecostal denomination: a mixture of deep insights into the message of the gospel and what we considered to be serious distortions of it; open-ended reflection on the movement of the Spirit and rigid fundamentalism; serious biblical study and theological naivete; rich experiences of transforming spiritual power alongside exploitation of the desperate situation of lost souls; identification with the poorest and manipulation of them; participation in and support of the struggles of the poor and promotion of reactionary social and political programs; and support of powerful and even corrupt politicians in exchange for favors for the church and its leaders. All of this made it difficult if not impossible to identify, in any comprehensive way, what is most central in Pentecostal life and experience.

At the same time I realized that my own faith, as shaped by my Reformed heritage and by liberation theology, compelled me to see something more in the witness of those we interviewed. Whatever its limitations, the Pentecostal message and experience had radically transformed their understanding and experience of their world and enabled them to put together their broken lives and thus find new life and energy. Poor marginalized women and men had found the power they needed for physical, mental, and often material renewal and for a successful struggle to overcome the most destructive forces around them. They knew an ecstatic experience of the Spirit that filled their lives with joy and hope. Life in family and in community was being re-created. Some of those touched by the Spirit were responding dynamically to the most urgent needs of others and were involved in struggles for social transformation. And they enthusiastically witnessed to others about the new life they had found.

In the face of all this, I had to consider the possibility that, through the witness of Pentecostals, the Holy Spirit was present among the poor in a powerful way; and that, more than this, in and through them God might be doing a "new thing." If this is the case, then I, precisely because of my faith and commitment to the poor in their present struggle, would have to change the focus of what I was doing. While still concerned about understanding and assessing theologically what is happening in Pentecostal movements, my more important task, in my engagement with them, would be to discern what God is doing among the poorest and what response was being called for on my part in this situation. Whatever I might discover in these movements that was different from my own heritage and faith, and however critically I may view some of this, I would have to entertain the possibility that the presence and power of the Holy Spirit might be manifest precisely in the midst of those elements of faith that are foreign to me. In and through their witness, God may be addressing me and laying a claim on me, which is as important for me as for them.

Having arrived at this point, my own religious heritage challenged me to go one step further. I had to remind myself that a Reformed church is most faithful to its heritage when it is open, time and again, to reformation, an ecclesia reformata semper reformanda. This led me to conclude that we can respond to the suffering and struggle of the poor in today's world only as we perceive that God is indeed doing a new thing. We can respond only as we are

*open to a new understanding of Christian faith, which finds new expressions
in life, individually and in community. This calls for the articulation of a
new theological* paradigm, *which then makes possible the reinterpretation
and reworking of our biblical and theological heritage.*

For Pentecostals, the experience of the presence and power of the
Holy Spirit is much more important than the rational articulation of it in
theology, especially in systematic theology. But as we went about this
study, I began to perceive a number of elements in their interpretation
and expression of Christian faith that diverge significantly from what
emerged at the time of the Protestant Reformation and that, I believe,
point in the direction of a new theological paradigm. I have not found
them clearly articulated or neatly put together by anyone in the Pentecostal community, nor have I found any one Pentecostal church in which
such a new paradigm sets the terms for thought and action. What I have
found is that frequently the elements that might constitute a new paradigm are mixed with others that do not seem to fit with them or may ra-
tionally contradict them. Nevertheless, I'm convinced that, in the midst of
all this, Pentecostals are pushing us to move beyond the limitations of our
understanding and experience of our faith. In the pages that follow, I will
lay out what I perceive as some of the central elements in a new theological perspective that could open the way for a creative rereading of our biblical and theological heritage of particular relevance to the suffering and
struggles of impoverished and broken people at this time.

*If the movement of the Spirit in our time calls for a new theological
paradigm, then the development of it becomes the responsibility and calling of
all of us. No religious community, Pentecostal, traditional Protestant, or Roman Catholic, can claim ownership of it. As it takes shape, it will stand on its
own and make its own way. Each of these communities will be able to make
its own unique contribution, but only as it learns from and is changed by the
others. I would wager that those of us who are not Pentecostal will be prepared to make our contribution to this end* as we are transformed through
our interaction with them.

Wherever we may be situated ecclesiastically, if our primary commitment is to finding and living a new form of Christian faith and life
in response to the movement of the Spirit, we will recognize the importance of cultivating close and ongoing relationships between Pentecostals and mainline Christians. We will also discover that this requires a

type of relationship that will be different from any that we have experienced until now.

As Pentecostals captivated by this vision give greater importance to such relationships, they will perceive that they may be in a privileged position for the development of such a paradigm because of their awareness of the presence and power of the Spirit as well as their response to it. Consequently, they will be more inclined to emphasize and explore further what is unique in their history and experience, the special gift they bring to the Christian world, rather than trying to gain greater acceptance in the more established churches by emphasizing all that they may have in common with them. For it is this gift that they bring to all of us.

Those of us situated in the Roman Catholic and older Protestant churches have emphasized until now our rootedness in the riches of the history and heritage of faith from across the centuries. This, of course, provides us with a great resource for responding to the present human situation, a resource that may not be so easily available to movements without these strong historical connections. But we have not recognized that we will be able to bring these resources only as we are ourselves functioning within a new paradigm of faith and engaged in reworking and reinterpreting our heritage from that perspective. For only when we have arrived at this point, or at least are moving toward it, can we relate to Pentecostals in a way that will encourage them to move forward in response to the leading of the Spirit rather than to look backward.

One of the ways we can do this, perhaps the most important one at this time, is by entering into the experience and life of Pentecostals, allowing ourselves to be called into question by their witness, and thus transformed. They may not have articulated a new paradigm; they may never do so. But I cannot ignore the fact that I have arrived at the point I have as a consequence of my engagement with them, as a result of their witness to me through what they are experiencing and doing. I continue to need what they bring to me in order to explore further the new realm of faith and life they have helped me to envision and explore.

As we move forward along this path, we will be prepared to deal more creatively with the growing penetration of forms of Pentecostal worship and experience into our mainline churches. If we are attracted by what we see or experience in Pentecostal worship, we will realize that we can really understand and appreciate what it represents only as we per-

ceive what it means in the wider context of Pentecostal faith and life, not
as one element in isolation from that context. More than this, we will perceive that it might contribute something to us not when we import it but
when it challenges us to perceive and respond to the movement of the
Spirit in our situation. Its value is to be found in the change it may pro-
voke in us, through an authentic transformation of our experience and
life. But the end result may turn out to be quite different from what is
happening in Pentecostal communities. When we take over bits and
pieces of Pentecostal worship or experience, cut them off from their roots,
and try to fit them into what we now have, they may prove to be quite in-
effective. More than this, the end result may be the opposite of what is
called for from us at this time. It becomes a way by which we shore up and
hang on to a type of religiosity that has lost its creative power; thus we
avoid facing the need for fundamental transformation.

*From this perspective, what I originally set out to do, to understand
and reflect theologically on what is happening in some expressions of
Pentecostalism in Brazil, takes on even greater importance than I had imagined before. It is something that is as important for those who are Pentecostal
as it is for those of us who are not. But the nature of the task has been sharply
redefined.*

If the Holy Spirit is doing a new thing in our present situation, then
a crucial question for any Pentecostal movement is that of their faithfulness to this movement of the Spirit. Given their present dynamism and
growth, their faithfulness or unfaithfulness will affect all of us, as well as
the future of Christianity in general. Those of us in other faith communities, at the same time that we make every effort possible to discern the
movement of the Spirit in our midst and examine critically what we are
doing, have a responsibility to look critically at the response of Pentecostal
movements as well.

If there is any truth in what I have outlined above, I can no longer
make judgments about Pentecostal movements on the basis of what we
have been, or even who we now are. We can engage in constructive critical interaction only as we are being re-created on the frontiers of the action of the Spirit. This is something that I believe few of us in the more established churches are prepared to do. If we are concerned about what is
happening in Pentecostalism today and its future development, we must
first, in our interaction with them, explore the challenge they present to

us and allow ourselves to be changed. As we experience what they are doing to offer life to poor and broken people, we may find ourselves addressed in a new way and also transformed as we respond to a call from which we cannot escape.

At this point, the one thing I can do is to explore a number of areas of Christian thought and life in which, as the result of my engagement with Pentecostals, new perspectives have opened for me. In each of these areas my main objective is to identify and develop what I see emerging that is most compelling for me and that might speak to our churches. In doing this, I do not claim that I have captured the essence of Pentecostalism or tried to present an overall and balanced picture of Pentecostalism in Brazil. What I want to do here is to lay out some of the things I perceive as manifestations of the presence and action of the Holy Spirit that have opened new vistas and experiences of faith and life for me. I have come to them as a result of my participation in the life of Pentecostals, but they represent what I, as a Reformed theologian, perceive as worthy of further development. I have also indicated some critical questions that I want to raise for Pentecostals in each of the areas explored. But important as this may be, it is not my primary concern, although I hope that the perspective presented here will contribute, in some small way, to further self-examination among Pentecostals.

In the first four chapters, I deal with four major challenges that Pentecostalism presents to us:

- To accompany the movement of the Spirit in a church of the poor
- To discern new dimensions of the nature of God's redemptive action in the world
- To explore the meaning of salvation as a new *experience* of liberation for the poor
- And to recapture the power of the Spirit for the reconstruction of life here and now.

This is followed by a number of personal testimonies, from Brazil and elsewhere, to these dimensions of human transformation.

In a concluding section (chs. 6 to 10), I discuss briefly a number of issues that have emerged as a result of this study, which I believe merit serious consideration:

- The experience of the presence, here and now, of the resurrected Jesus through the Spirit
- The rediscovery of what Paul the Apostle calls the *charismata,* or gifts of the Spirit
- The potential for the participation of Pentecostals in efforts at social transformation
- One Pentecostal proposal for spiritual formation, which leads directly to action in community in the world
- And some very brief reflections on the foundation that the Pentecostal experience may provide for the creation of a new order of society.

I have done nothing more here than call attention to these issues, because I'm convinced that the exploration of them will be most creative when it is undertaken by Pentecostals and those of us rooted in other historical communities as we are willing to move into a new era in ecumenical relations.

1 The Movement of the Spirit in the Church of the Poor

*My friends, think what sort of people you are, whom God has
called. Few of you are wise by any human standard, few
powerful or of noble birth. Yet, to shame the wise, God has
chosen what the world counts folly, and to shame what is
strong, God has chosen what the world counts weakness. He has
chosen things without rank or standing in the world, mere
nothings, to overthrow the existing order. (1 Cor. 1:26-28, REB)*

When has it ever occurred to any of us that God's redemptive work
in the world might be following the same pattern today as is here
outlined so sharply by Paul the Apostle? When and where has the church,
with all its affirmations about the supreme authority of the Bible, dared to
struggle with what it might mean for us to take this word seriously?

Not only are our mainline churches made up primarily of those
who have "standing in the world," many of whom are powerful, wise, or
of noble birth, but rarely if ever does it occur to us that we might be called
by God to live our faith in community with those who are poor and marginal, much less that we should turn to them for help in understanding
what God is doing, to deepen our experience of the faith, or to learn what
it means to follow Christ. When we prepare women and men for lay leadership in the church or for ministry, we don't ask them to begin their
training by going to live with and learn from the poor. Nor do we consider
that, if we were to take seriously what Paul is saying here, we might be
compelled to restructure not only our programs of theological education
but our entire theological enterprise.

In recent decades, however, a number of factors have led many of us to look more critically at the assumptions behind our present practice and pay at least some attention to the witness of Paul. As we have become more aware of our own spiritual poverty and of the facile adaptation of our churches to the values of our society, we have often been amazed to discover the vitality of faith and its transformative power as manifested in faith communities of poor and marginal people. For some of us, the most decisive factor has been our contact with members of Christian base communities or struggling Protestant churches in Nicaragua, El Salvador, or elsewhere in Latin America. Others of us have had a similar experience in the United States, as we have related to faith communities of former addicts and other broken people who have amazed us by their depth of understanding of their faith as well as their experience of its power in their lives.

In addition to this, biblical scholars and theologians of liberation in Latin America have pointed out to us that the words of Paul in 1 Corinthians give expression to something that follows naturally from the overarching biblical witness to God's particular concern for and presence among the poor, and to the centrality of the liberation of the poor in God's redemptive action in history. If the God revealed in the Hebrew Scriptures is the God who acts dynamically to liberate slaves and the God of justice as portrayed by the prophets, who judges each nation in the light of what it does to the widow, the orphan, and the stranger; and if the message of Jesus of Nazareth is "good news" for the poor, then we can hardly escape two conclusions: (1) that the church can be the people of God only if the struggle of the poor for life is at the center of the faith and life of each Christian and each community. And (2) that the poor occupy a privileged position as interpreters of God's self-revelation.

For a few years, the faith and witness of the Christian base communities were such a compelling demonstration of this reality that many of us had to face and struggle with it. Now that these communities are less visible, it would be easy for us to continue on our former way, without being unduly disturbed, were it not for two new developments that are going to have a major influence on the future of our church and of the world: (1) the growing impoverishment and ever more desperate struggle for survival of vast millions of people suffering under the impact of the present global economy, and (2) the amazing and continuing growth of Pentecostal movements among the poor. They have become *the church of* the poor. Their leaders, both lay and pastoral, are largely from the ranks of the poor. In many countries of the Third World, they already make up the majority of the Christian population. And the faith, the vitality, and way of life of these churches as expressions of the religious life of the poor raise questions for those of us who are not poor, questions that we can no longer ignore.

The Pentecostal Presence among the Poor

David Barrett, well known for his work as editor of the *World Christian Encyclopedia* and for his careful studies of Pentecostal growth around the world, reports that half of all Pentecostals, approximately two hundred million persons, live in shantytowns in the depth of poverty. Of that number, nineteen million represent the poorest of the poor who, in the words of Jean-Jacques Suurmond, "have to scrape through the rubbish heaps each day in search of food."[1]

More than this, the Pentecostal churches have been able to continue to grow among the poorest at an amazing pace as they time and time again renew themselves from below. Protestantism emerged in sixteenth-century Europe as the result of a powerful movement of renovation, a movement that not only represented a re-formation of the church but that had as its slogan, *ecclesia reformata semper reformanda*. But the churches born in this renovative power of the Spirit rarely followed this norm. Pentecostal churches, however, have continued to grow and renew themselves for nearly a century through a constant process of formation of new movements. And as the great majority of these movements have come from below, Pentecostalism has continued to be identified, as a church, with poor and excluded people.

What is the theological significance of this? In other words, What is God saying to us in and through these developments? Commenting on this fact, Ricardo Gondim, pastor and theologian of the Assemblies of God, declares that "evangelization in Brazil has been carried out by the poor and for the poor. The major advances of the church in Brazil are oc-

1. *Word and Spirit at Play: Towards a Charismatic Theology* (Grand Rapids: Eerdmans, 1994), p. 18.

curring among the poor, among those most alienated, socially and cultur-
ally." And one of the reasons for this, according to Gondim, is that "while
in the First World the churches became victims of the dominant financial
system — churches with mortgages on imposing buildings, which must
be paid every month, and which are like a tourniquet on the souls of
churches — in Brazil we don't have mortgages because we work on a
'cash basis'. What comes in is what goes out. . . . This is a blessing. It
seems that the mark of the beast is not yet written on our foreheads. The
most successful churches are to be found in the *favelas,* and the pastor
lives in the neighborhood."[2]

In our interviews of lay women and men, we asked them if they believed that God was "the God of the poor." We were somewhat surprised to
find that no one connected positively with this phrase. Rather, their replies
were along this line: "God is concerned about the poor, the rich, the sick.
God has no preference for anyone." "Before God, all are equal." "God loves
everybody, the rich as well as the poor or the beggar. All are in the same position." In other words, such is their identification with the poor and their
experience of God in their midst that they have little interest in the question
about God's special concern for them. What they want to affirm to us is that
they, as poor persons, are as important before God as anyone else.

Immersed in the world of the poor and their experience of life, Pentecostals have developed their own perspective on the poor and the meaning of the gospel for them that is quite different from that of the traditional churches, both Roman Catholic and Protestant. André Corten, a
Belgian political scientist, author of an excellent study of Pentecostalism
in Brazil, compares their "discourse" with that of the Christian base communities and claims that Pentecostals have gone beyond the base communities in a number of ways: They have touched the lives of a much
larger number of poor people, especially those at the bottom. Their discourse, rather than being primarily rational, is an emotional discourse of
consolation. They do not celebrate the equality of the poor, which, in the
base communities, leads to new inequalities, but allow the poorest to
speak. Their discourse is not about the "option for the poor" but a dis-

2. Ricardo Gondim Rodrigues, "Evangelização Brasileira: patologias, potenciais, perspectivas," in *A Igreja Evangélica na Virada do Milenio,* ed. Rubem M. Amorese (Brasilia: Comunicarte, 1995), p. 94.

course of the poor that refuses to accept poverty. Instead of focusing on political liberation, Pentecostalism focuses on catastrophe, violence, and terror, the tribulations that precede the millennium.[3]

Does this imply that Pentecostals, who as poor people are reinterpreting the gospel and proclaiming it with fervor, may be opening our eyes to aspects of God's revelation that we have not yet perceived? Without answering the question at this point, I believe that we should at least consider seriously something that Latin American liberation theologians and biblical scholars have affirmed for some time: According to the Scriptures, *poor and marginal people are in a better position than others to hear, understand, and respond to God's revelation.*

The Hermeneutical Advantage of the Poor

Reading the Scriptures with an open mind, a mind not bound by our cultural conditioning, how can we overlook the fact that God revealed himself time and time again to those who were marginalized or excluded? We move through the Scriptures from slaves in Egypt, to the Hebrew prophets, to the shepherds to whom the birth of Jesus of Nazareth was first announced, to those whom Jesus chose to be his disciples, to the people who received the gift of the Holy Spirit at Pentecost and the majority of members of the earliest Christian communities.

This fact and the significance of it was put most radically by Paul in the text from 1 Corinthians we cited above. This should not surprise us if we make the effort to enter into the biblical world, especially the world portrayed in the Gospels. God chose to become incarnate in a poor man, Jesus of Nazareth, who belonged to a people who had lived for centuries under the domination of imperial powers. Jesus identified himself especially with the poor and the outcasts and spent his time healing the sick and the possessed. He was an itinerant prophet, who called men and women to leave everything and follow him. He ended up being crucified as a subversive by the political and religious powers of his time. Who is better prepared to grasp the meaning of these salvific events: the well-to-

---

3. André Corten, *Le Pentecôtisme au Brésil: Émotion du pauvre et romantisme théologique* (Paris: Éditions Karthala, 1995), p. 243.

do person seeking spiritual nourishment and orientation far removed from these struggles for life, or the person who is marginalized, rejected by society, struggling each day for the survival of her family, and facing death threats because she dares to protest, in the name of God, against this inhumanity? Does it not make sense to conclude that a church, the majority of whose members are living this reality daily, may be in a better position to understand and respond to a God who acts in history in this way in order to save us?

Moreover, this God is a gracious God, who offers us life as a gift. When we trust completely in this God, live by this gracious gift, and are open daily to the surprises coming from the future and expecting them, we are on the road to fullness of life. But this is exactly the opposite of what we usually are and do. Our fear of loss, of not being, drives us to seek salvation in secure relations, economic advancement, and power over others. If we are to see what we are doing to ourselves and to others and are to open our whole being to God's grace and live by it, we need the constant witness of those who are better prepared than we are to grasp and live this reality.

It is here that what the Scriptures say to us about the poor makes sense. Jean-Jacques Suurmond, a Pentecostal theologian who served for many years as a pastor with the Assemblies of God, declares that those who have nothing and no place in society and those who have been broken by it are in a privileged position when it comes to understanding and living this reality. "In the useless weak who cannot find any foothold in the dominant social order, God's grace emerges most strongly as the power that creates something out of nothing, life out of death."[4] Because of this, if we yearn to experience fully this quality of life, we need to turn to them expecting to receive something from them. In the words of Suurmond, "the poor, the handicapped, the unemployed, and others who have been cast aside by society have a power in their weakness to evoke gifts. Through their need they stimulate the functioning of giving and thus the encounter with God in Christ, so that the community is enriched."[5]

If we take into account the process of the destructuring of society and of social disintegration as it is being experienced by vast numbers of

4. *Word and Spirit at Play*, p. 53.
5. *Word and Spirit at Play*, p. 190.

people in Brazil at this time, we may perceive yet another advantage that the poor and excluded have in understanding and living the gospel. For most of us who are not poor, the existing social order remains more or less intact. We are an integral part of it; our values are shaped by it and our lives depend on it. We function within it even when we are striving to change it radically. However, as we have observed repeatedly earlier in this study, for large numbers of poor people in Brazil the whole social structure that people normally count on to sustain life has broken down. This leaves people without regular jobs, without decent housing, uncertain as to where the next meal for their children will come from, without medical care, and without any structure of community to which they belong — people who know only abandonment and brokenness in society, in their families, and in their personal lives.

Yet it is precisely in this situation that many are coming to know a richness of experience of the healing and saving presence of God that we cannot imagine. They not only understand the gospel stories of Jesus healing the sick and casting out demons, they also know them as part of their own experience. They understand and experience what Jesus taught about a God of compassion who binds up their wounds and becomes a source of life in the midst of death, of reconciliation in the midst of violence, and of joy in the midst of suffering, and who often inspires them to share the very little they have with others. Thus begins the reconstruction of broken personal lives, of broken families, and of wider human relationships, which could eventually provide the vision and energy needed for the development of new economic, social, and political structures from below.

Those of us who do not have this sort of experience have a hard time fathoming the depth of this social crisis or the radical nature of the social reconstruction that is being called for. And for most of us, this experience of the presence and power of God, to which those in this situation often witness is also beyond our grasp. Yet any concern on our part for the struggle of the poor and the future of our society now compels us to enter their world and to discern the changing nature of their struggles and the promise latent in them. If our reading of the current situation has any validity, because of the depth of the crisis of our society, the process of personal and social disintegration experienced by the poor is advancing and coming closer and closer to us.

As this progresses, we too will find ourselves facing the need for the reconstruction of life, personal and social, at an ever more elementary level. We too may find ourselves on a new spiritual journey, searching for an experience of the divine as real and as powerful as that to which poor people, especially in Pentecostal communities, witness. But on this journey we may discover that we must be open to learn from and be transformed by them. With them we can engage in a rereading of the Scriptures, and of the history of the church across the centuries, and be surprised by discoveries of how the Holy Spirit has been at work in the healing of broken lives and the reconstruction of human relationships in times when an old order is crumbling and a new order has not yet emerged.

Moving toward the Religious World of the Poor

What does all this mean for those of us in the historic churches, individually and as people called to live our faith in community? For me, one conclusion is inescapable: If we really want to grow in our experience of the riches of life in Christ and be faithful disciples, we must find concrete ways of sharing in the lives of broken people around us and living in solidarity with them. This includes living in communion with their religious experience and being open to learning from and being transformed by it. Given the present religious situation in Brazil and elsewhere, this may mean relating in some way to the Pentecostal community.

As we remarked earlier, in the Roman Catholic Church several decades ago, priests, women, religious and lay persons in many parts of Latin America took the extraordinary step of moving toward the poor and living and working in solidarity with them. We all know the results of their efforts in the reinterpretation and revitalization of our faith, in the creation of a new model of church among the poor, and in the support given to the poor in their struggle for liberation.

Is it too much to hope that something similar might happen in Protestant circles today? That a significant number of women and men would dare to respond to the call not only to explore new expressions of solidarity with those who are poor and excluded, but to learn with them what it means for the faith and community of our historic churches to be re-formed in their world and in the midst of their struggle.

There are courageous souls and communities who are already doing this, but I believe that something more is called for. Those who have already taken this step need to find ways to have more communication with each other, learn from each other as they identify and work on crucial issues they face, and challenge others in the Protestant community to commit themselves to this task and join with them. It was only as the Catholics who took this step earlier centered all their attention on this specific task and found ways to work together at it, that they eventually were able to envision and give shape to a new model of church among the poor. I believe that we will have to follow a similar process if we want to respond to the challenge facing us in the present situation.

At the same time, I find no reason to believe that the religious institutions of historical Protestantism will take any significant initiatives in moving toward the poor or entering their religious world in the foreseeable future. Whether we like it or not, the Christian message of "good news" to the poor, and its transforming power among them, is now being made available to the poor primarily by Pentecostals. Every indication is that this will continue to be the case in the years ahead.

Consequently, those of us who are committed to living in solidarity with the poor in their struggle and believe that the gospel is "good news" for the poor must at least consider that an essential step toward the fulfillment of our calling may involve seeking ways to relate to the Pentecostal community: to share in their life, to enter into their spiritual world and understand and experience it, to discover how to relate to initiatives they are taking with the poor, and to find new patterns of dialogue and collaboration with them.

I find this especially important at a time when so many people in our older, more established churches are being attracted by the charismatic movement. Our churches will not be revitalized, and much less reformed, if we simply appropriate some elements of Pentecostal worship and experience without subjecting our heritage and present existence to the sort of radical questioning that comes from a serious encounter with Pentecostalism. If in this encounter we limit ourselves to adding, to what we now have, some of the outward expressions of it without entering into the historical experience of suffering and struggle out of which it has evolved, and without seeking to understand what God is doing in the midst all this, we may create a bit of vitality to our superficial spirituality and sterile worship but will never open our whole being to God who can fill our lives with compassion. A satisfying emotional experience that does not flow out of the rejoicing of those who have nothing yet know that God is daily giving them life will do little more than help us to hang on to our present middle-class values and way of life at a time when the Spirit is challenging the church to be open to radical transformation.

New Ventures in Solidarity

For middle-class Christians in North America, new ventures in solidarity with poor communities in urban or rural centers near our churches, as well as those in other countries, must be created. Here I want to focus on one example of such a venture, from which we might gain clues for other similar efforts.

About ten years ago, Richard Fenske, a Lutheran pastor, and his wife Barbara, at that time a real estate agent, came in contact with a number of refugees from Central America and decided to spend several months living there. They were profoundly affected by what they saw: the suffering of the people, their struggle to change their society, and the role the United States was playing in preserving the established order. Knowing that they were called to do something about this, Richard gave up his parish, Barbara decided to become a nurse, and they went to live in a one-room apartment in one of the poorest neighborhoods of Guatemala City. Supported only by Richard's small retirement income, Barbara began to work as a nurse with the women in the neighborhood, and Richard developed SISTER PARISH, a program in which parishes in North America establish a relationship of solidarity with parishes in Guatemala. Over a three-year period, members of the parish in the United States visit regularly their sister parish, live with a family there, immerse themselves in the life of the parish and community, and work together with their host parish in a local church or community project. Likewise, representatives of the parish in Guatemala visit their sister parish in the United States.

In this way, a relationship of equality and of sharing is established, in which each partner both gives and receives, and people are transformed as they discover what it means to live in solidarity. One Guatemalan expressed what this has meant for them when she said: "We have been forgotten and ignored for so long. We feel we are being seen for the first time." On the one hand, out of this experience Guatemalans may gain new confidence in themselves and become more active in the struggle to transform their situation. North Americans, on the other hand, not only have an experience of the world of the poor, their suffering, their struggle, and the vitality of their faith, but also discover the structural causes of this poverty and realize the role that their own country is playing in maintaining these structures of oppression and exploitation. They may be able to look more critically at their own culture and its values from the perspective of their faith and, with a few others, seek ways to deepen their faith as they become more actively engaged in living out the implications of it in their communities and in the wider society.[6]

The Challenge Facing the Pentecostal Churches

If, as we have claimed here, the poor and excluded are in a privileged position for understanding the gospel and putting it into practice in life, and if, as a consequence of this, we in mainline churches are being challenged and possibly transformed by the witness of poor Pentecostals, we are, in turn, compelled to raise a further question: Do those in the churches of the poor, particularly in the Pentecostal Church, recognize the nature of this advantage they have and its implications for them? As they experience God's closeness to them, know in their daily life God's sustaining and healing power, and are enabled to live life as a gift, to what extent do they perceive the responsibility this places upon them to be ever sensitive to God's special relationship with them and the responsibility it places upon them to be faithful to it?

In 1 Corinthians Paul made it very clear that those who had nothing and occupied no position in society were in a privileged position to understand and respond to the gospel. But Paul also knew that God's revelation in Jesus Christ was very different from "knowledge of this world," and that life in the Spirit called for a radical transformation. Thus he struggled incessantly with the small congregations that he brought to-

6. See Richard Fenske, *En la Buena Lucha* (Shippensburg, Pa.: White Maine Publishers, 1996).

gether to keep before them the crucial issues of faith and of life, which they had to face daily, and to help them discern precisely where they were being led by the Spirit.

What evidence is there that Pentecostals are struggling to explore and be faithful to the understanding of the gospel and the nature of the fullness of the Christian life that they, as poor communities, may be in a privileged position to grasp and witness to? Or more specifically, as Pentecostal movements grow among the poorest people, those struggling daily for survival, to what extent are they looking critically at their preaching and teaching in order to be sure that they are faithful bearers of God's offer of life, healing, and hope?

If Pentecostal vitality is due to their response to the poor, and if their continued growth over nearly a century is due, in part at least, to the emergence in their midst of new movements from below, to what extent do they recognize this fact and reflect on its significance? When churches that began with the poorest people are no longer poor, what effort is made to live in dialogue with the history out of which they have come?

Do Pentecostals realize that much of the richness of their understanding of the gospel and their experience of God is the result of God's presence in their particular social situation and struggle? Do they realize that they have a special responsibility to name that experience and build theologically on it, rather than relying on imported fundamentalist theologies that are not capable of naming what God is doing in their midst?

To what extent do they realize that, in the present social crisis, God has given them an extraordinary opportunity and calling to participate not only in the reorganization of the lives of broken people but also in the reconstruction of community and society? To what extent do they realize that to be serious about refusing to accept poverty carries with it this responsibility?

What resources are Pentecostals — and especially their leaders — finding in their faith and experience to help them face the ever-present temptations, especially in our middle-class and materialistic society, to "conform to this world," to gain acceptance in it, and to use positions of power in the church for personal prestige and financial gain?

As I raise these questions, I realize that they apply to all of us, not just to Pentecostals, and that if some of them do not apply specifically to us, it is only because we are not even present in the struggles out of which they arise. Moreover, while these are questions that need to be answered, we who are not part of that religious world are hardly in a position to set the terms for the discussion or make judgments. What we can do is to strive for the cultivation of the quality of relationships between Pentecostal and mainline churches that will create conditions for a richer dialogue.

On the basis of our very limited research thus far, we can point to several lines that may be open for further exploration:

1. In various countries in Latin America, Pentecostal theologians are doing important work on some of these issues. Juan Sepulveda, a Chilean, has written a number of articles about the response of Pentecostal churches to the suffering of the poor, and a Peruvian, Bernardo Campos, has contributed an excellent chapter on "In the Power of the Spirit: Pentecostalism, Theology, and Social Ethics," to a volume on Pentecostalism in Latin America edited by Benjamín Gutiérrez and Dennis Smith.[7] In Brazil, theological reflection on the poor is increasingly evident in the writings of Pastor Ricardo Gondim, of the Assemblies of God. In a recent article in *Contexto Pastoral,* he declares that "the spirit of Jesus of Nazareth, in solidarity with the poor and the oppressed, needs to become incarnate with greater vigor in His church."[8]

2. In our interviews with church members, while there was little discussion of God's relation with the poor in theological terms, it was evident that this was often an important element in their faith. Lourdes, a young member of the Igreja Universal, insisted that God is equally concerned about all people, the rich, the poor, and the sick. At same time, she told us that when she was eighteen years old she became very upset when the elders of the Assemblies of God Church to which she had belonged since childhood failed to minister to those most in need. When they would not allow two drunken men, dressed in shabby clothes, to enter the church, she stopped attending it. Months later, she found another church that was especially open to such people and soon joined it. "I believe," she

7. Bernardo L. Campos M., "In the Power of the Spirit: Pentecostalism, Theology, and Social Ethics," in *In the Power of the Spirit. Pentecostals in Latin America: A Challenge to the Historic Churches,* ed. Benjamín F. Gutiérrez and Dennis A. Smith (Mexico City: AIPRAL, 1996).

8. *Contexto Pastoral* 1: 9-10.

said, "that suddenly, when a person is at the worst, that is when that person needs Jesus and seeks Him."

3. I believe that, for all of us, dialogue about the founding event of Pentecostalism, the coming of the Holy Spirit as portrayed in the book of Acts (ch. 2) and its significance in the life of the earliest Christian communities, is more important than abstract theological discussion. I consider this to be especially important taking into account the fact that this event, so central in the origin of the Christian church, has been practically ignored, for centuries, in many of our churches. Here I want only to call attention to what André Corten has to say about it. He speaks of the "schismatic impulse," which for him represents "the 'revolutionary' character of Pentecostalism," and affirms that the foundation of it is precisely this overwhelming experience on the day of Pentecost:

> If it is true that Christianity is a religion of the middle classes, it is equally true that across the centuries it has constantly manifested a tendency to religious rebellion. It always has to refer back to the primitive church, archetype of a communal church refusing to compromise with the world, archetype of the church of the poor. It is the image of new beginnings. The church of the poor is a constant protest, inspired by the primitive church, against the religious institution. It becomes respectable as it adapts to the dominant style, but it also rebels constantly in the face of this obligation.[9]

9. Corten, *Le Pentecôtisme au Brésil,* pp. 211-12.

2 *Retelling the Story of Salvation*

In our study of recent developments in Pentecostalism, we have discerned a major shift in evangelistic preaching. While still using much of the traditional language of evangelists about sin and salvation, they are now focusing more and more on the work of the Holy Spirit in this world, as the immediate presence and power of God in everyday life, bringing health and material well-being and a new quality of life here and now. This was highlighted for us when the founding pastor of a new Pentecostal denomination said that her pastors were giving so much attention to these day-to-day issues that she needed to instruct them to be sure to emphasize "salvation" in their preaching.

By making this shift, Pentecostals are clearly responding to the most urgent needs and deepest longings of the people, especially those who are poor and marginal. A recent study, carried out by the Institute for the Study of Religion in Rio de Janeiro, revealed that the majority of new converts in all Evangelical churches said that their conversion occurred at a time of crisis in their lives. But when asked about the nature of this crisis, the highest percentage spoke, first of all, of sickness (35 percent), followed by family conflicts (25 percent) and drinking problems (14 percent). Only 9 percent said that their conversion occurred in a time of "spiritual crisis."

We first became aware of this when, in interviews with members of the Universal Church of the Reign of God (IURD), each spoke in glowing terms about her experience of the transformative power of God and the Holy Spirit in her life, but always in terms of quite specific blessings related to everyday life: the healing of the body, the reorganization of a broken life, the solution of family conflicts, or the bettering of her economic situation. We soon realized that those in other disciplines who were engaged in research on Pentecostalism were finding the same thing. André Corten, who has studied the theological discourse of the Universal Church, has claimed that, in it, the term *solution* eclipses the term *salvation*.

As we have studied this development and tried to understand it theologically, we have come to the conclusion that it may represent a major reinterpretation of the nature and scope of God's redemptive activity, a paradigm shift that is leading to a rereading and reinterpretation of the biblical story of salvation, with implications for all aspects of Christian faith and life.

The significance of such a shift has become clearer for us as we have taken into account the fact that most of the major religions we know today are fundamentally religions that offer a path to salvation in situations of deep human crisis, situations in which people are obsessed with the problem of the meaning and direction of human life and history. Each religion offers an explanation of what has gone wrong in the human condition and a way of overcoming it. In the words of William James, we have, in each case, "an uneasiness and its solution."

In our Western world, Christianity became, early on, the dominant religion, with a particular story of salvation at the heart of it. In it, God created human beings in a state of goodness from which they fell. Responsible for this departure from God's plan, they stood guilty before God and under God's judgment, incapable of liberating themselves from this condition. But God acted to save us in and through Jesus Christ, especially through his death, in order to overcome sin and offer forgiveness and eternal life.

The Protestant Reformation not only preserved this overall perspective, it reinterpreted and gave new life to this paradigm through its rediscovery of the Pauline emphasis on God's gracious initiative in the justification of sinners, available to all through faith. This became the central message of the churches of the Reformation. From this center came a re-articulation of all aspects of Christian faith and life as well as a powerful experience of liberation that had a tremendous appeal to an emerging new social class in Western Europe and North America.

Since that time, this same paradigm has provided the foundation and set the terms for Evangelical preaching as well as for missionary out-reach. As it has found expression in evangelistic and renewal movements, its meaning has often been interpreted in a narrow and individualistic way. Yet centering as it has on the new birth in Christ and God's gift of eternal salvation, it has been a powerful force for the conversion of sinners. It has empowered converts to undergo a profound transformation in their lives, to recognize that God has a plan for them, and to give their lives in service to God and neighbor.

In fact, such has been the power of this paradigm to shape our understanding of redemption across the centuries, especially in the West, that we have only very slowly come to see some of the limitations of it. One of these is the fact that although it is a story of salvation offered to people within history, it is not integrally connected to the concrete realities of the historical process. God's redemptive action centering in Jesus Christ belongs to a special *holy* history. It is an event from outside history that breaks into it and has implications for it but is not really interwoven with the specific human struggles for life as they have taken shape in diverse cultures and historical epochs. God's free gift of salvation is offered essentially to individuals who receive this grace and eternal life quite independently of the concrete social, economic, and political realities and struggles around them.

During his last months in prison, Dietrich Bonhoeffer began to question the relevance, for mature people today, of this paradigm that compelled Christians to first convince people that they were sinners in order to bring them to faith in Christ. He also asked whether this particular story of redemption was faithful to the biblical message. "Redemptions in the Old Testament," he concluded, "are historical, i.e. on this side of death. Redemption now means redemption from cares, distress, fears, and belongings, from sin and death, in a better world beyond the grave, but is this really the essential character of the proclamation of Christ in the Gospel or by Paul? I should say it is not. . . . The Christian hope of resurrection . . . sends a man back to his life on earth in a wholly new way."[1]

Over the last several decades, the exegetical work done by Latin American theologians of liberation has pointed in this same direction. They affirm that, in the Scriptures, there is only "one history," the "history of salvation." God's salvific action is set in the center of human life and struggle in the world and has to do with the transformation of that history. More recently, a growing number of feminist theologians have declared that the traditional paradigm focusing on sin, the expiatory work of Christ, forgiveness, and the acceptance of God's grace may well connect with the experience of men belonging to the dominant classes, but it does not speak redemptively to the condition of many women. These scholars are making a major contribution to the reinterpretation of redemption from their situation and experience.[2]

On the one hand, we can find today, in Europe and North America, a number of biblical scholars and theologians who are raising basic questions about our traditional understanding of redemption, but thus far I have seen no evidence that this is becoming a major issue in the experience and thought of the general church membership. On the other hand, in Brazil the initiative for a radical reinterpretation of the Christian message of redemption is coming from the poorest people; it is arising out of their suffering and struggles in recent years.

In this, their struggle, three elements combine to reshape what they hope for and expect to find as they turn to religion. (1) There is growing impoverishment in the context of the crisis — and in many cases, the disintegration — of the social, economic, and political structures that normally support human life. As this happens, life becomes more and more an overwhelming struggle for survival. Around that horrendous reality all aspects of their daily life revolve. (2) There is an increasing awareness of this worldview at the heart of their cultural and religious heritage. In it, body and spirit are not sharply separated. Real-

---

1. Dietrich Bonhoeffer, *Letters and Papers from Prison* (New York: Macmillan, 1972), p. 336.
2. See Mary Grey, *Redeeming the Dream: Feminism, Redemption and Christian Tradition* (London: SPCK, 1989).

ity, as they know it, includes the realm of the Spirit, which they consider to be an integral part of their experience of life in this world. (3) There is the impact of constant exposure to the mass media, through which the acquisition of more and more material things is presented as the key to a full life. This daily bombardment by commercials on radio and television more firmly establishes this system of values of the consumer society at the same time as it intensifies the unfulfilled aspirations of those who are most deprived.

Given these developments, it is hardly surprising that, as people turn to religion, they demand of it primarily immediate solutions to the concrete problems that they are struggling with every day. This is well illustrated by research done by an anthropologist in a small rural village in northeast Brazil. In it, he found that the inhabitants of this village take for granted that religion offers the most effective means for the solution of their problems. "Many of them have the sense that they are living under such precarious conditions that their only hope is to throw themselves actively into the search for this salvation."[3]

For some time, there have been evidences, here and there among Pentecostals, that a significant change is taking place in their experience of the human situation and of the way God is working in the midst of it. In 1990, in a collection of essays, *Pentecostals from the Inside Out,* J. I. Packer remarked that many people in Pentecostal churches see themselves "less as guilty sinners than as moral, spiritual, and emotional cripples, scarred, soured, and desperately needing deliverance from bondages in their inner lives, and the structuring of counseling and prayer ministries to meet this need, thus viewed."[4]

Others have called attention to the fact that a significant number of Pentecostals no longer maintain a sharp separation, in their understanding of the nature of the gospel, between the spiritual and the material. The Chilean Pentecostal theologian, Juan Sepulveda, has put it this way: "Daily life has penetrated more and more into worship, at the same time that worship has become the sustaining force in a stubborn action in face

---

3. Allard Willemier Westra, "La conducta del consumidor en el Mercado Brasileño de salvación," in *Algo mas que opio,* ed. Barbara Boudewijnse, Andre Droogers, and Franz Kamsteeg (San José, Costa Rica: DEI, 1991), p. 118.

4. "Pentecostalism 'Reinvented': the Charismatic Renewal," in *Pentecostals from the Inside Out,* ed. Harold B. Smith (Wheaton, Ill.: Victor Books, 1990), p. 147.

of adversity. The struggle for life has been transformed into a place of encounter or reencounter between action and prayer."[5] In Brazil at the present moment, the IURD has presented a major challenge to all Pentecostal movements by the radicalness of its statement of this new salvation paradigm, even though it is often presented in a theological language that undercuts it.

We can best indicate the nature of this shift by juxtaposing two paradigms, focusing on the perspective offered by each on the nature of the human condition, the solution provided by the gospel, and the character of the human response to it.

The Drama of Redemption — according to Our Traditional Understanding

The Human Problem

Human beings have fallen from the state of goodness in which they and the world were created. They are now victims of original sin, guilty before God and under God's judgment. In this context, evil is largely internalized.

The Solution

God's free gift of forgiveness and justification of the sinner, made available through the expiatory work of Christ on the cross.

The Human Response

Faith as the acceptance of God's forgiveness and grace. Those persons who receive this unmerited gift offer their lives to God as an expression of their gratitude.

5. *Estandarte Evangelico* 3 (1991): 91.

The New Paradigm of Salvation Emerging from the Poor

The Human Problem

Human beings are poor, impotent, and condemned to insignificance. They are engaged in a desperate struggle for survival in a world falling apart around them. They and their world are "possessed," dominated by supernatural demonic forces who are agents of chaos and destruction. In their daily personal lives they are overwhelmed not primarily by the sense of sin and guilt but by the painful realities of the life of the poor. They experience evil primarily as something outside themselves that threatens them and their world.

The Solution

An experience of the presence and power of the resurrected Christ and of the Holy Spirit as the source of life and hope, the power to make it through each new day, and the guarantee of victory over demonic forces. Through the life, death, and resurrection of Jesus, and the gift of the Holy Spirit, God's saving work is manifest as an immediate response to suffering, pain, and brokenness, which makes possible a journey toward the fullness of life as health, material well-being, and happiness. The Holy Spirit is present with power in the midst of all that makes people cry and scream, love and hate, and feel hunger and abandonment. This presence carries with it the expectation of miracles, which bring immediate change, offering a solution to a very desperate situation and filling women and men with songs of praise.

All this is confirmed as the sick are healed, as family members experience reconciliation and new possibilities of life-giving relationships, as those who are impoverished discover new possibilities for improving their economic situation, and as those who have felt impotent in the face of evil are now empowered to confront and overcome the demons, manifested in hunger and sickness, prostitution and drugs, and social disintegration and violence.

Here, as in the Protestant Reformation in sixteenth-century Europe, the supreme reality is an overwhelming experience of the presence and power of God in the midst of life. But this captivating experience of

God is not centered in the announcement of forgiveness of sins and justification. God is experienced intimately and intensely as broken lives are reorganized, as those considered "worthless" and "insignificant" discover their worth before God, and as those who thought they could do nothing to change their situation or the world are empowered to act. This reality is communicated, not by a rational word or doctrinal exposition, but by a ritual of praise and worship. In the place of speech that was unintelligible and moralistic is speech with a supernatural character, made accessible through a sacred text, which generates emotion.

The Human Response

Faith that dares to start a new interaction with God and take possession of what has been lost. It means appropriation of the power made available by God now in order to take responsibility for one's life, live in community with others, and join in the struggle against demonic forces fully confident of the coming of the millennium.

In his study of the discourse of the IURD, André Corten has concluded that what it means to be saved is expressed, in the preaching of the pastors of this church, in an over-simplified way, by means of a set of contrasts. These sharply define the movement of the believer from one realm of reality into another: not primarily from sin to forgiveness, but rather from empty to full, from destroyed to prosperous, from humiliated to respected, from depressed to happy, from anguish to peace, and from loneliness to life in the community of the church. To this we would add: to be saved is to be called to participate in a struggle of global and eternal significance to extend the reign of God. This means, above all else, a total commitment to evangelism and, as now seems increasingly evident, a commitment to be involved in social and political struggles.

I know of no Pentecostal movement that has clearly articulated this paradigm as I have spelled it out. As we mentioned earlier, Pentecostals have not given much attention to theological reflection, and the doctrines of the longer-established churches are based primarily on theological language borrowed from North American fundamentalism and pietism. Thus, elements of this new approach are often blended with the more traditional language of salvation through the blood of Jesus. The IURD, which has gone the farthest in developing major elements of this new paradigm, has also combined them with perspectives and doctrines that contradict it. Its leaders have drawn heavily on a few North American theologians who at the very least are quite peripheral to the central Christian tradition.

Taking all of this into account, I'm convinced that a new paradigm of salvation may be emerging here. And if this is the case, those of us who perceive this possibility should be giving primary attention to reflection on the direction in which it is pointing us and to the responsibility we all share for contributing to its development in faithfulness to the gospel. This takes on special importance for me for several reasons: the evidence of its appeal to vast numbers of the poorest and most broken people, the fact that we can perceive signs of its penetration in a rather wide range of Pentecostal groups, and because of the important theological questions it raises for all of us about the nature of Christian redemption.

Bishop Macedo and the Universal Church: A New Paradigm Affirmed and Negated

The IURD has played the major role in this shift in interpretation of redemption, especially among the poor in Brazil, while at the same time its evangelists affirm many things that obscure or negate it. I think it important to look briefly at what the founder and leader of this church, Bishop Edir Macedo, has to say.

When I began to examine his writings, what first caught my attention was his reliance on much of the language of traditional revivalist preaching, his pervasive demonology, and his allegorical interpretations of many biblical texts, even those dealing with the most concrete historical realities. Accordingly, he declares that the lesson to be learned from the Exodus is about the power of God that liberates people from "spiritual Egypt," and Jesus' proclamation of the "acceptable year of the Lord" means that "all have the opportunity to attain the benefits of the sacrifice of the Lord Jesus."[6]

And yet, at the same time we find throughout his writings, right alongside of statements similar to the above, other affirmations that, if de-

6. Edir Macedo, *Aliança com Deus* (Rio de Janeiro: Editora Gráfica Universal, 1993), pp. 208, 329.

veloped consistently in openness to the work of biblical exegetes, would lead to dramatic changes in evangelistic preaching: "We have lived through the climate created by the Protestant preaching of Luther, and the revivalist preaching of Wesley, and now we have to leave behind the merely charismatic preaching, which is now in style, for 'full preaching.'" This means that, "above all else, Jesus Christ liberates persons who are oppressed by the devil and his angels."[7]

In his book *Aliança com Deus,* in the midst of long expositions of the meaning of this covenant with God written in the most traditional evangelical terms, we also have statements like the following. Speaking of the situation of Jacob before his reconciliation with Esau, he declares:

> This situation was similar to that of Isaac, in the land of the Philistines, and is the same situation of billions of persons in the whole world, driven to desperation by sickness and disease, fugitives from the state of misery and hunger, with no hope for the future, and worse, ignorant with respect to a living God, great and powerful, capable of giving them, gratuitously, a new and blessed life.[8]

God's promise to Abraham is that of "a nation blessed in every sense, without misery or hunger, without sickness or diseases. A just nation filled with peace, whose citizens would be ruled by the law of love and mutual respect."[9] Regarding the "good news" of the gospel, he notes: "We say that Jesus died on the cross to forgive our sins and give us eternal life — but is that all the 'good news' we should announce? The 'good news' that Jesus ordered us to preach includes all kinds of blessings for people: spiritual, physical, and financial. Certainly it guarantees the healing of our sickness, complete liberation from the dominion of Satan, and the help we need for the solution of our problems."[10]

The writings of Bishop Macedo on this theme reveal the severe limitations of his theology as well as the many contradictions running through it. I can find no evidence in his most recent writings to suggest

---

7. Edir Macedo, *A liberação da teologia* (Rio de Janeiro: Coleção Reino de Deus, 1992), p. 118.
8. Macedo, *Aliança com Deus,* pp. 167-68.
9. Macedo, *Aliança com Deus,* p. 87.
10. Macedo, *A liberação da teologia,* p. 138.

that his theological reflection will evolve beyond the lines he has already marked out. But then, what he does or does not do theologically may have little to do with the articulation and development of a different paradigm of redemption. As the result of what Macedo has done and what is happening in the lives of people in the IURD, a major shift in our understanding of the nature of salvation is taking place. It is being experienced and lived out by many, whatever its limitations. The crucial issue for the future is whether we who cannot avoid reexamining this issue, whatever our present theological and ecclesiastical positions, are willing to explore and develop it further in dialogue with the biblical witness and the experience of the poor.

3 *Salvation: A New* Experience *of Liberation for the Poor*

The reinterpretation of the nature of salvation we have just described represents a fundamental shift in our understanding of the gospel, which could have radical consequences for Christian faith and life. Especially because what we have here is not just a rational statement about the meaning of the gospel but a perspective that finds expression in a *compelling new experience.* It is this focus on experience, as well as the nature of it, that we must take into account in any theological reflection on the reinterpretation of salvation now occurring in some Pentecostal movements.

A half century of theological and biblical scholarship has centered on the definition and exposition of the New Testament *kerygma* as the declaration of the greatness of God's redemptive work in the world. This lays before us what God has done for our salvation, the offer of forgiveness and grace, to which we are called to respond. Yet for many of us this has meant primarily the rational articulation of the essence of Christian faith, which we may accept, and from which we may benefit, but which has rarely turned our world or our lives upside down.

For Pentecostals, however, the saving action of God, centering on the resurrection of Jesus and the presence of the Holy Spirit, is first of all an experience of something happening daily in their lives and in the world around them, in which they are caught up. Moreover, it is a unique type of experience that transforms their perception of the nature of the world and of what life is all about. Christ conquered death, and the resurrected Christ is present and at work now with the power to do what he did during his earthly ministry. In the words of Bishop Macedo, "If the Lord Jesus conquered death, what sickness, or disease, or vice, or misfortune can resist His great power?"[1]

This interpretation of the nature of God's redemptive action expresses itself in an experience that is a powerful force in the lives of the poor. But it is an experience of salvation that differs in a number of ways from what we in mainline Protestant churches have taken for granted over the centuries.

(1) As we indicated in the last chapter, this experience is something quite immediate and concrete, related to the daily struggle of the poorest and most afflicted people. A gracious and forgiving God, whose redemptive action aims at the transformation of the world into the reign of God, has created human beings for a divine destiny. They are destined to have all that is necessary for a full and happy life. Anything that denies this to people — to be unemployed or without material resources for other reasons, to be sick, to be deprived of decent housing, or to suffer because of family conflicts — is directly opposed to what God has willed for us. For people not to have these things most essential for a full life means the rupture of the cosmic order.

Especially in the IURD, the main obstacle to the fulfillment of this divine destiny is the devil. The world and human life are filled with demons, but these demons can be localized, named, and cast out. While I react negatively to the exaggerated emphasis on this in the IURD and see it as something that can easily be used to deceive and exploit people, I recognize that it also has some very positive effects: the expulsion of demons is a powerful demonstration of God's action among people who see themselves and their world as "possessed" by supernatural forces of evil. When the most broken people are able to see the evil around them as something primarily external to them, they are relieved of one burden that increases their suffering, that of feeling guilty or blaming themselves for their desperate plight. People

---

1. Edir Macedo, *Aliança com Deus* (Rio de Janeiro: Editora Gráfica Universal, 1993), p. 328.

who have little or no sense of their own worth get a new sense of who they are as human beings when they perceive that their well-being is at the center of a tremendous struggle between God and the demons.

Just as in the Reformation, God's grace breaks into the center of the life of women and men with no need of any intermediary. But it is known as an immediate experience of the divine, especially among the poor, an experience not primarily of sinners being forgiven and justified, but of sick persons being healed, of broken lives being reintegrated and restored, and of those abandoned finding what they need to live.

(2) It is this gradual change in the understanding and experience of salvation that is leading Pentecostal preachers to reaffirm something that was present in the origin of this movement but was not developed in the United States due, I believe, to the impact of Evangelical revivalism on Pentecostalism during the twentieth century. From the beginning, Pentecostals expected the power of God to be manifest not just in tongues or an experience of ecstasy but also in the healing of the body. Yet, if the saving power of God is expressed in the healing of the body, people who are not part of a culture that separates material and spiritual realities will not for long limit God's salvific work to this one aspect of bodily existence. Sooner or later, they will see that Jesus also fed the hungry, lived with the outcasts, defended the poor, and identified himself with the full life of the people of his time. Their faith assures them that the Holy Spirit, as the Spirit of Jesus, continues this same work.

It is thus not surprising that, in much Pentecostal worship, God's salvific work is being connected more and more with the fullness of bodily life. Jaci Maraschin, an Episcopal priest, perceived what this means for the tired and broken bodies of the poor when he wrote in 1985 that the people of God "meet for the liturgy as special bodies, and bodies enter the 'liturgical space' led by their feet. These feet walk the roads and the streets, they ascend and descend steps and mountains, and they walk across hallways and through rooms." "They walk on what we might call the 'space of life'. In this space, there is pain and exhaustion. These feet carry the dust of these roads into the liturgical space, and the liturgical space becomes the space of these feet with their sweat and their exhaustion, and thus the space of bodies."[2]

2. Jaci Maraschin, "O Espaço da Liturgia," *Estudos da Religião* 2, p. 162.

(3) In many circles in which I move today, both in Latin America
and the United States, we often find ourselves engaged in an agonizing
discussion about the future, how to keep hope alive in a time of messianic
drought. Among poor Neopentecostals, however, I don't find many people struggling with this problem of keeping hope alive. In the past, in
many fundamentalist and Pentecostal circles, hope for the future was
bound up with a premillennial theology and the belief that Christ was returning soon to establish his kingdom, but I find very little emphasis on
this in Brazilian Neopentecostalism.

I'm convinced that the reason for this is to be found in what Waldo
Cesar has emphasized earlier (see Part I, ch. 6). People for whom the
world has been a prison, many of whom are living, in a sense, on their
own "death row," facing total deprivation and abandonment, enter,
through the Spirit, into another realm. They find themselves in another
world, an open world, in which the gates of their prison have been un-
locked. It is a world in which the sick are being healed, broken families
restored, broken lives put together again, and desperate economic situations often changed. All of these things confirm the claim made by Bishop
Macedo that "God always has been ready to make possible the impossible
things in life."[3] They attend services several times a week, in which they
experience something new stirring within them, and see the "impossible"
happening before their eyes. Their pastors assure them that these things,
in addition to the action of the church in responding to basic needs of
hungry people, drug addicts, and prisoners, as well as actions of the
church in the political realm, are all signs that Satan is being overcome.
They are concrete indications that the reign of God is already breaking
into the present. For those who live this reality, who experience the world
in this way, hope is very much alive and is nourished and often sustained
even in the most devastating circumstances. In this context, the theology
of the millennium and repeated references to the second coming of
Christ, while not absent from some evangelistic preaching, do not have a
central place.

Those of us who function out of the Reformation heritage can find
many reasons to criticize this theology, but I believe that our theological
insights will be heard only when we have experienced the renewal of

3. Macedo, *Aliança com Deus,* p. 67.

hope that comes through living in the realm of the Spirit and participate in communities of faith in which signs of the coming reign of God are evident to us as well as to those who are struggling daily for survival.

(4) In their most radical departure from the heritage of the Reformation, some Neopentecostals, while continuing to affirm the centrality of the divine initiative in the forgiveness and justification of sinners, are also emphasizing the vital importance of human initiative and responsibility in this process. Before we reject categorically this departure from what has been at the very core of our faith, we would do well to consider what it may represent as a response in faith to a very different human and historical situation.

The Reformers were addressing the situation of proud men, who were struggling for the creation of a new world with great confidence in themselves and their abilities. Pentecostals today are preaching to poor and excluded people, humiliated and broken under the overwhelming power of oppression. Their experience is that of impotence and lack of worth. They have no clearly defined identity nor are they fully recognized as human beings. They are convinced that they can do nothing to change their lives or their situation and everything around them in the dominant society contributes to convince them that they really are like that.

In this situation, Neopentecostals proclaim the love of a gracious God, who wants them to have a full life here and now, and the presence of the Holy Spirit with power to give life to those to whom it has been denied. Yet they cannot expect to receive these gifts if they continue to believe that they are nothing and can do nothing and thus remain passive. They need to hear the "good news" that they not only occupy a privileged position before God but also that they have a right to well-being because that is God's will for them. Having this right, they can and should stand before God, pray fervently with confidence and daring, and even demand of God the fulfillment of the promise he has made to them.

In the IURD, this daring initiative takes the form of an offering made to God, often an offering of everything that one has — or even of what one does not have — which will prove the faith of the believer, put that faith into action, and oblige God to respond. In this way, a new interaction with God is set in motion. We give God what we have, and God is then obliged to give us what he has.

I consider this to be a very serious distortion of the nature of the divine-human interaction as presented in the New Testament. Moreover, it is not at all surprising that those who preach it can so easily be corrupted by it. The offering required to prove one's faith is made to God but goes into the coffers of the church — and into the hands of its leaders.

At the same time, I have to admit that it is only as I have been confronted by the appeal and power of this approach that I have been compelled to raise questions I should have raised long ago about the limitations of our traditional reading of the Pauline message, about the extent to which that reading has been shaped by a particular cultural and historical situation, or about how this has kept us from understanding the meaning of the gospel as "good news" for poor and broken people.

Whatever the distortions here present, many hear a message which leads them to risk taking initiatives toward changing their situation for the first time in their lives, confident that God will support them as they do so. In community with others whose lives have been changed, they learn to pray fervently, having been convinced that God will not be moved by the prayer of anyone who starts out already feeling defeated. And in a community in which women and men firmly believe that God will change their life and their world if only they ask in faith, such prayer can become, as one pastor put it, the first step toward victory. In this context, those who are ill dare to say: "I refuse to accept this sickness." Those who were convinced that they were impotent, now know they have power. One woman, who had a crippled child, prayed for him, and when he was cured, she could say: "I didn't know that I had such power before God."

The Disturbing Challenge of a New Paradigm

Those of us who feel at home and secure within the traditional paradigm of redemption will be able to find many good theological reasons for rejecting what may be emerging in Pentecostalism. However, I'm convinced that something is taking shape here that is making the gospel a dynamic and transformative force in the lives of millions of people. If the present crisis continues to deepen and becomes more destructive of human life, the appeal and power of this message will continue to grow. And if, in this process of growth, it is constantly being enriched by the biblical witness, it could lead to a new era in Christian history comparable, in its vitality and impact, to the Protestant Reformation.

Whether or not that happens may depend, to no small degree, on the willingness of those rooted in the Reformation heritage to explore this new paradigm of salvation as they situate themselves on the frontier of the encounter of their heritage of faith with the movement of the Spirit today in Pentecostalism. This calls for an ongoing theological effort of many different communities who are willing to embark on this journey without knowing where they will come out. In fact, such a journey may lead to quite different conclusions than those I perceive to be taking shape in some Pentecostal circles. At the same time, I am discovering that a growing number of Pentecostal theologians have begun to articulate some element of what I have called the new paradigm. I believe that their reflection, in the context of the Pentecostal experience, can help us not only to focus our attention on some of the important issues but also to find our own way.

Here I want to mention only two comments by a theologian I referred to earlier, Jean-Jacques Suurmond. In his development of a Pentecostal theology, *Word and Spirit at Play,* he calls our attention to the fact that, for Pentecostals, the story of salvation centers not only on the cross, the sacrifice of Jesus, and the gift of forgiveness and justification, but also on the life, death, and resurrection of Jesus culminating in Pentecost. Pentecost is "the consummation and the crown of the events of Christmas and Easter. The end is more than the beginning. The birth, death, and resurrection of Jesus have made possible the 'outpouring' of Christ's Word and Spirit on all that lives, so that the purifying fire of God's love can now be kindled all over the earth."[4] He adds that all the elements of "good news" — including health, well-being, and liberation from demons — are related not only to the full bodily life of the individual person but also to all parts of the body of the suffering world. To the extent that Pentecostalism recovers the worldview of William Seymour and African-American spirituality, which does not function in terms of the sharp separation of the spiritual and the earthly-physical worlds, it may well articulate this perspective much more clearly.

4. Jean-Jacques Suurmond, *Word and Spirit at Play: Towards a Charismatic Theology* (Grand Rapids: Eerdmans, 1994), p. 139.

From this perspective, Suurmond contends that faith centering on the experience of the Holy Spirit compels us to enter fully into historical reality and be concerned about its transformation. But this, he reminds us, will not be easy because our distortion of the Christian message of redemption can be traced back as far as the Councils of Nicea (325) and Chalcedon (451). He calls our attention to the fact that in the definitions of the faith proceeding from Chalcedon, neither the Spirit nor Jesus' life and work are discussed. Even the resurrection is not mentioned. Furthermore, "the person of Jesus is reduced to a static and bloodless formula remote from the lively person who according to the Gospels roamed through the streets, sorrowing with the sorrowful and rejoicing with the happy."[5] In this context, and with the ongoing influence of Neoplatonic thought, "the Christ of faith, justification by grace, and the church as the body of Christ were taken out of history and became irrelevant to this world. On the other hand the concrete life of the historical Jesus, the struggle for the liberation of the world and the church as an institution were secularized."[6] In the churches of the Reformation, justification by faith was largely objectified and represented by the Word and sacraments of the church.

The Challenge to Pentecostals: To Develop a New Paradigm in Faithfulness to the Biblical Witness

We have dared to affirm that we are dealing here with a new paradigm of redemption, which, if developed biblically, could become the foundation for the spread of Christian faith as "good news" among those most hungering for salvation and at the same time compel those of us who are not Pentecostal to reexamine our most fundamental doctrines in the light of a new reading of the Bible.

But what we see happening in movements such as the IURD raises serious questions about their ability to meet this challenge:

- Their evident lack of interest in serious biblical studies or theological reflection, in general and on this particular issue.

5. Suurmond, *Word and Spirit at Play,* p. 44.
6. Suurmond, *Word and Spirit at Play,* p. 64.

- The fact that Bishop Macedo and other leaders mix together the new insights we have mentioned with sterile traditional fundamentalist theology, often producing contradictory affirmations of which they seem to be unaware.
- The fact that, when they are attacked by conservative Evangelicals and leaders of mainline churches, they tend to defend themselves by declaring that they are completely in line with traditional conservative Protestant teaching. For example, *A Manifesto to the Evangelical People of Brazil* (13 September 1991), initiated primarily by IURD pastors, starts out by affirming that the IURD accepts the teaching common to all Evangelical churches in Brazil: faith in Jesus Christ as the only Savior, belief in the Trinity, belief in heaven and hell and the final judgment, belief in the Bible as the only and inerrant Word of God. In that climate, there is no space for even suggesting that a new perspective might be emerging, or for developing it further.

At the same time,

- Pentecostalism has demonstrated, throughout its history, a flexibility and openness to change that could well occur again as the situation of people becomes even more desperate.
- What we have outlined here is not just limited to Brazil. It is evident, in different forms perhaps, in other countries and movements. With the present means of worldwide communication, increasing interaction among those searching for and attempting to articulate a new paradigm could well lead to unexpected developments in this area.
- If this paradigm shift is being driven by response to the changing spiritual concerns of a widening circle of people, we can expect that some of a new generation, who are committed to serious theological reflection, will recognize the significance of the breakthrough of which they are a part, will see no reason to defend themselves over against those who would bind them to the past, and will give greater priority to biblical studies. As they do this, they may discover resources they have not been previously aware of and may be able to develop and rework their paradigm in ways that none of us can now foresee.

As they do this, they may discover that a number of biblical scholars are already doing a great deal of work that could provide valuable resources for them. At the same time, they may realize that their Pentecostal heritage has prepared them to make their own unique contribution to these discussions, whether it be in relation to our interpretation of the meaning of the death of Jesus, of the nature of the presence and power of the Holy Spirit, or of the relation between God's initiative and human initiative and responsibility in the process of salvation and sanctification.

Such reflection is not likely to be eagerly accepted by those now in power in Neopentecostal movements, but it will provide many in those movements with the means for orienting their experience of the Spirit as well as for taking a critical stance that may contribute to ongoing change. One thing that became clear in our interviews over the last two years is that Neopentecostalism is not producing a generation of people who blindly accept whatever their pastors tell them. Their experience of the presence of the Spirit in their midst often gives them a spirit of confidence that frees them to judge for themselves what is and is not authentic in the teaching they receive. This spirit of openness holds hope for the future. It also makes more urgent our responsibility to be engaged in constant interaction with these communities as we, together with them, seek to be ever more faithful to the biblical witness as we live in a dynamic and rapidly changing world.

4 *In the Realm of the Spirit: Power for Living Here and Now*

Early on, as we participated in services in the IURD, we became aware of the shift in evangelistic preaching we have just described, which indicates a radical reinterpretation of the story of salvation. As Waldo Cesar has described it, what we have here is a religious experience that deals with the most immediate and concrete day-to-day realities of life in the daily struggle for survival. A movement in which the four services held each day of each week focus on family problems, spiritual healing, economic difficulties, and the overcoming of demonic forces in personal life and society.

But what perplexed us was the realization that, with all their emphasis on the problems of daily existence, they did not deal with them in any way that made sense to us. They gave little or no attention to the analysis of what was happening in the world around them, the social, economic, and political realities causing this destruction of life. Nor did they seem to encourage people to struggle to find what we considered to be solutions to these concrete problems. Here are women and men faced with issues in all these areas that are pushing them to the boundaries of life and death, where their very survival is at stake. Yet, they seemed to have little interest in using the resources now available for understanding or dealing with these threats.

Gradually, we had a revelation. The IURD and other Pentecostal movements can be faulted for the superficial way in which they deal with these issues, but this does not necessarily mean that they are less concerned about them than we are. They simply approach them in a very different way. In his chapter on "Survival and Transcendence," Waldo Cesar has undertaken a careful sociological analysis of this different way. As a theologian, I have attempted to understand this difference by taking into account their religious worldview as I have come to understand it.

What this has meant is, first of all, a recognition of the way that people who have not been immersed in our Western culture and the scientific worldview of modernity face these daily issues of life and death. They naturally seem to turn toward that which is taken for granted as most fundamental in their heritage and experience: They assume that their lives and their world are set in the context of the divine. Reality, as they know it, is not a realm in which there is a sharp distinction between spiritual and earthly reality. In fact, their world is one in which this spiritual reality is not only present but also constitutes the center around which all their life revolves; it is the point at which they experience most profoundly the mysteries of life and the world. For them, nothing could make more sense than turning to this realm for the solution of the problems of their day-to-day existence.

For nearly one hundred years Pentecostalism has made an immediate connection with those holding this worldview, especially the poor in cultures not integrated so completely into our Western modern world. It affirms their perception of reality, in which human beings are integrally related to others, to nature, and to the divine. It also proclaims and demonstrates that this divine reality is present with power in the midst of all that they are suffering. The Holy Spirit is active now in their world and their lives and is changing their daily lives and their situation, often dramatically. It is from this perspective, with confidence in this divine presence and power, that they are able to receive what they most desperately need and are thus equipped to face and overcome everything that threatens to destroy them.

This was the overwhelming testimony of those whom we interviewed. They spoke time and time again of their problems of daily survival, their broken families, their material deprivation, or their daily struggles with addiction to drugs or alcohol, but what had changed everything for them was what Pentecostalism offered them: an experience of the presence and power of God who had performed miracles in their midst, and thus provided them with a resource, unknown to them before, for finding solutions to their problems.

As they have responded, they have experienced the reality of the Holy Spirit that penetrates, permeates, and encompasses reality as they know it and is dynamically present in all aspects of it. As they have opened their lives to this presence and live in this realm of the Spirit, oriented and empowered by it, everything around them is seen and experienced in a radically different way:

- They see the world and human life infested with demons. At the same time, they firmly believe that their lives and their world are in the hands of God, who acts to overcome these demonic forces.

- As they live out of this realm of the Spirit, in the midst of all the forces of destruction and death around them, their lives are centered in an experience of God who is very close to them, a God who is gracious and compassionate. To the degree that they live this reality, women and men overwhelmed by utter deprivation experience ecstasy and joy.

- For persons caught in impossible situations, the impossible becomes possible time and again. In their lives, miracles are happening and are expected to happen. Family relationships are transformed; alcoholics and those on drugs break their addiction; broken bodies and disturbed minds are healed; and those who had no worth and no place in society discover their worth before God and feel empowered. Many thus transformed find new openings for richer human relationships, the restructuring of life in community, and the improvement of their economic situation.

- Those who, connected vitally with the realm of the Spirit, experience miracles begin to perceive the world in a different way. With all the threats of demonic forces around them, they experience something even greater: the presence and power of the Spirit. As this becomes a reality for them — and their perception is not blocked by imported fundamentalist and millenarian theologies — the world is open and life is oriented toward a new future, the coming reign of

God. Thus they are enabled to trust their lives into God's hands in the midst of change and insecurity. Their lives are focused on God's call to them to join in his struggle, and on the promise of God's continued guidance. Having experienced the impossible, they are energized for the struggles of daily life. They see all that they do as related to and sustained by the God who is in the process of establishing his reign as they engage in evangelism and, in many instances, take their place in the struggle for social transformation. Conscious as they are of the reality of this presence and power, they realize that they participate in it as their lives are centered in surrender, prayer, and expectation.

From this perspective, those who have known God's call realize that what is most important in their preparation to fulfill it — whether as clergy or lay persons — is not primarily instruction in doctrine and in the understanding of society but rather a process of training that teaches and disciplines them to enter into a fullness of relationship with the Spirit. As they live in this realm and thus become empowered, they can draw daily on this experience of life and power to be effective ministers of healing and of transformation in the midst of all the brokenness and suffering around them.

I confess that I have not found this perspective articulated in just this way in any Pentecostal preaching or writings. Moreover, all the dimensions of the experience I have described here, and its implications, may find expression at this moment in a relatively small number of Pentecostal communities. However, this does not negate what I have outlined or the possibility that it is pointing toward a new interpretation of Christian faith and life that all of us, whether traditional Protestants, Catholics, or Pentecostals, would do well to take into account. We should not overlook the fact that many breakthroughs in Christian life and thought in the past, including Latin American liberation theology, began with the often limited vision and confused and even conflicting insights of very small communities, which nevertheless laid the foundation for a new paradigm — the reinterpretation of our heritage of faith and the reformation of the church in response to a new and compelling human situation or crisis.

This promise indicates the new direction in which we — especially those of us whose consciences have been awakened in the face of the suffering and exploitation of the poor — may find ourselves being led by the Spirit at the present time. Dennis Smith, who has also been struggling for several years with the challenge presented by Pentecostalism in Central America, hints at what this might mean for us in a recent paper entitled "Reflections of a Disenchanted and Progressive Evangelical in the Face of the Pentecostal Phenomenon."[1]

He speaks of those of us who, in the last twenty years, have become aware of the social, political, and cultural processes that produce the marginalization and death of the majorities in Latin America and who have struggled to "build an alternative in solidarity with them, which is just and in favor of life, starting from secular political categories." This effort, he concludes, is still urgently needed but without limiting ourselves to secular options in "reenchanted" societies and without losing the capacity to "be astonished in the face of the wild mystery of God." Along this road we may be enabled to develop "prophetic communities capable of speaking words of truth and justice to those in positions of power, in favor of the excluded majorities; communities that celebrate the presence of the divine in their culture, their music, their poetry, and in all the creative expressions of the human spirit; communities that find, in the Eucharist, a mystery of life that leads them to serve others."

From Whence Our Reluctance to Respond to This Witness?

We can easily see the limitations of these movements. We can and should raise critical questions about much in their doctrine and practice. But if we are passionately concerned about the suffering of the poor and are in solidarity with them in their struggle for life, and if we are committed to the transformation of our world in the direction of God's reign, then I believe that we should rejoice in this manifestation of new life and power and seize the opportunity it offers us to carry forward the struggle that has claimed our lives and energies in recent years. If this is not our response, we should ask ourselves what it is in us that keeps us from doing so.

1. Unpublished paper: "Reflexiones de un evangélico desencantado y progresista frente al fenomeno pentecostal."

For some of us, the major obstacle may be found in our justly negative reaction to our past religious experience. Many of us have been brought up religiously on a type of fundamentalist doctrine that we eventually came to reject as we became aware of a richness of thought and dimensions of human experience that exposed the rigidity and sterility of it. For some of us this has been accompanied by a type of religious experience that at one time appealed to us and gave meaning and direction to our lives but that, we later perceived, was highly individualistic, limited to a narrow "spiritual" realm, and combined with a rigid legalistic moralism. Eventually our own spiritual development led us to reject this interpretation of Christian faith as an obstacle to our spiritual growth rather than a resource for it. As our consciences were perturbed by our growing awareness of the human suffering caused by exploitation and injustice, we rejected any interpretation of Christianity that did not take into account the social dimensions of the gospel. However, it often happened that our rejection of this sort of piety, with its limited understanding and experience of the transcendent, led us to concern ourselves less and less with the cultivation of those spiritual disciplines that, earlier on, had been so important in shaping our lives.

For the majority of us, the reason for our reluctance to follow the path indicated above is a quite different one. We may believe in God but we live our lives in a realm, the visible and material realm, from which God is largely absent. It is essentially a one-dimensional world, a world closed in upon itself. In it, we go about our daily round of activities — in family, work, recreation — without assuming that in all of these areas we are meeting and interacting with a transcendent reality present in our midst. Much less are we inclined to have our lives centered in this realm of the Spirit, as the context in which we think and live, or to assume that it is in this realm that we might find the orientation and power we desperately need for the struggles to which we are committed.

Recovering Our Biblical Heritage

If we hope to free ourselves from this closed-in world, we will have to take much more seriously than we have until now, the religious worldview at the center of almost all cultures except our own, which does assume the existence of this realm of the Spirit and functions in relation to it. It is, moreover, the worldview of the biblical writers, both Hebrew and Christian.

In recent theological discourse, such a perspective has not been a popular one. In fact, following on the emphasis placed by Karl Barth and other neoorthodox theologians on the radical difference between religion and Christian revelation, many theologians have tended to dismiss all religions as expressions of idolatrous human efforts to reach God. Whatever the value of this approach has been in establishing the centrality and distinctiveness of God's self-revelation and God's gracious initiative, it has also closed our eyes to a most essential dimension of biblical faith. Consequently, we have not perceived the way in which our own rational, scientific, theological constructs — claiming to be instruments for communicating God's self-revelation — have limited our knowledge and experience of God and produced theological formulations and forms of worship that have little connection with the presence and work of God among vast numbers of people, especially the poor and marginal of other cultures than our own. Rather than helping us to perceive and respond to new manifestations of the Holy Spirit in our midst, it has blocked our critical examination of the limitations of our modern worldview.

If we realize this fact and allow ourselves to experience the presence of God among the poor and the vitality and depth of their faith, we may be disposed to question our own logic rather than to judge so quickly the religious experience of others. It may well be that those of us who have been shaped by our Western rationality and modern scientific worldview are less prepared to perceive and respond to God's self-revelation than many whose whole approach to life and the world flows out of their grounding in the realm of the Spirit.

If we are open to this perspective and are willing to expose ourselves to the Pentecostal experience of the poor, we may be compelled to engage in a new rereading of the Scriptures. If we do this, we may have to ask ourselves, How is it that we have spent so many years reading the Bible and have not perceived something that stands out so clearly as central to the biblical story from beginning to end? Whether we focus our attention on Moses or the prophets, Jesus or Paul, we cannot escape the fact that they are all persons who are vitally connected with the realm of the Spirit and who find in it the source of their life and power.

These manifestations of divine power are experienced as manifestations of the closeness of a God who is gracious and compassionate and who hears the cry of a slave people and acts to liberate them. The prophets, who had ecstatic visions and lived in communion with this realm of the Spirit, were driven by this experience to confront those in power, denounce all forms of injustice, and declare that to know God is to do justice. This same extraordinary combination — life grounded in and empowered by the presence and power of a compassionate God, which leads inescapably to total commitment to the struggle of the poor — is at the very center of the life of Jesus of Nazareth.

According to one New Testament scholar, Marcus Borg, Jesus had an intensely vivid relationship to the world of the Spirit. His ministry "was dominated throughout by intercourse with the other world" and "that relationship was the source of his power and teaching, his freedom, courage, and compassion, and of his urgent mission to the culture of his day."[2] It is precisely out of this sustained intercourse with the other world that he could declare that the Spirit of God was upon him, leading him to announce "good news" to the poor, to proclaim release for prisoners and recovery of sight for the blind, to let the broken victims go free, and to announce the proximity of a radically new order of human life (Luke 4:18-19). Living in the realm of the Spirit and in communion with a compassionate God who responds to the cry of the poor, Jesus saw the world that was about to crucify him as a world moving in the direction of God's reign of justice and peace, and thus a world open and unfolding, the context for ongoing struggle for the creation of a new future.

With the coming of the Holy Spirit on the day of Pentecost, the lives of a little band of marginal people are overwhelmed by their experience of this reality of the Spirit in their midst, and they experience signs and wonders, joy and ecstasy. This presence and power creates a new quality of life in relationship, even to the sharing of all their possessions, and carries people out into the world to proclaim this message.

Saul of Tarsus, engaged in a zealous struggle to defend the existing religious order, had such an overwhelming encounter with the risen Christ on the road to Damascus that his whole life was turned completely around. As a result, he was led to abandon the struggle in which he was

2. *Jesus: A New Vision* (San Francisco: Harper and Row, 1987), pp. 42, 15.

engaged, to identify himself with a small community of unknown poor and marginal people who were risking their lives proclaiming that the crucified Jesus of Nazareth had risen, and to declare that in Christ "there is neither Jew nor Greek, there is neither slave nor free, there is neither male nor female" (Gal. 3:28).

If all this is so central in the experience of biblical people and at the heart of the Pentecostal experience but so foreign to the worldview of many of us, we would do well to ask ourselves if perhaps we have departed from it because we have allowed ourselves, much too easily, to feel at home in our modern Western world. To the extent that this world in which we feel at home is now not only becoming so destructive of human life but also entering into an ever more profound crisis that it cannot resolve, this question becomes a life and death issue for Christian faith as well.

Facing and Overcoming Theological Obstacles to the Recovery of This Heritage

If we hope to understand how it is that we have become so alienated from — and so unable to engage ourselves seriously with — the biblical witness to the realm of the Spirit, we will have to look more critically at two factors that, combined with each other, have brought us to this point.

(1) At this point in our Western history, we hardly need to be reminded of the way in which our modern scientific worldview, so closely associated with the mentality of the Enlightenment, has set the terms for our perception of reality. The radical distinction between matter and spirit, as spelled out by Descartes, led to conceiving of reality as it could be known and measured objectively. The appeal and power of the scientific method, which was able to function so effectively in mastering and harnessing this reality and facilitating amazing progress in many areas, led those who used it to near obsession with the pursuit of this and with all the progress and novelty that came by this route. The men of the Enlightenment, increasingly confident of their own powers as witnessed by their amazing advances in knowledge and in shaping society, created a situation in which God had no place and was not needed. Belief in this God was perceived as a major obstacle to human freedom and creativity.

This God was not only absent from the world; those who persisted in affirming God's existence had to struggle to bring God in from outside, and belief in God could only be seen as the cause of radical alienation. In this situation, theologians found themselves fighting an uphill battle. But the appeal of this worldview was so strong in Europe that it had a profound influence over theology. The Belgian-Brazilian theologian Jose Comblin goes so far as to claim that by the nineteenth century even philosophers and theologians such as Hegel and Schleiermacher "knew that traditional Western Christian theology led inevitably to atheism."[3]

(2) This capitulation of theology in the face of these developments was greatly aided from within by what William C. Placher has called "the domestication of transcendence" that occurred as the theology of the Reformers was reinterpreted in the seventeenth century. According to his reading of Luther and Calvin, for them God was not intellectualized and thus confined to logical limits. Central for them was the realm of transcendence as "mystery," God as a reality not to be defined or enclosed in their concepts but rather to be known and responded to in a vital relationship. Consequently, for Calvin, the primary goal was "not to provide a set of propositions to believe, but to evoke feelings and behaviors."[4]

But in the seventeenth century, these dimensions of transcendence and this emphasis on a personal relationship with God were largely lost. The dominance of the rational in secular thought had a profound influence on theology, narrowing the limits and setting the terms for thought about God. As this happened, people who were caught up in the excitement of dealing with the concrete realities of this world as defined and limited by science had less and less time for or interest in a wider realm of reality. At the same time, as people gained more and more confidence in their own capacities and their ability to create and shape the future, the God already diminished and transformed by the categories of limited rational thought was removed farther and farther from the created world and was neither needed or wanted. According to Placher, this "combination of a kind of confidence in human abilities and constricting definitions of acceptable reasoning led theology astray."[5] The efforts of Pietistic

---

3. *The Holy Spirit and Liberation* (Maryknoll, N.Y.: Orbis Books, 1989), p. 17.

4. William C. Placher, *The Domestication of Transcendence* (Louisville: Westminster/John Knox Press, 1996), p. 58.

5. Placher, *The Domestication of Transcendence,* p. 3.

movements to remedy this situation through an emphasis on experience, without challenging the fundamental capitulation of theology or undertaking the task of theological reconstruction carrying forward the work of the Reformers, led to the domestication of grace. It also failed to offer an alternative to the growing intellectualization of Christianity in the modern age. As the spirit of the Academy had its impact on theologians trained in that same intellectual milieu, thought about God in the context of mystery and vital experience gave way to academic thinking about God as one thinks about other things in the world.

This transformation of theology in line with our modern Western worldview might not have been so easy had it not been for the influence on theology of the rational thought of the Greeks that began as early as the second century: the tendency to have our thinking about God start with God the Creator, that is, a rational God; the way in which this type of rational thought has led to the formulation of doctrines about God, justification, or Christology, all divorced from history; and the ease with which we identify faith with the right logical thinking about God and God's gracious gifts to us.

As a result of all this we have practically lost the ability to connect with, enter into, and live out of the realm of the Spirit so central to the biblical witness. At best we cultivate "right thinking" about God rather than a radical experience of a vital relationship with God. And even this thinking about God is so intellectualized, so dominated by a particular type of Western male rationality, that it does little to help us enter more deeply into, organize, and orient our own experience in the richness of life in the Spirit. It also produces a language about God and forms of worship that cut us off from contact with the vast numbers of poor and marginal people who are not part of our conceptual world as well as with a new generation of "postmodern" women and men who live a quite different reality and are searching for spiritual resources capable of ordering their lives and providing them with meaning and hope in their existential situation.

In the light of this, we may be called to engage in much more radical theological reconstruction than those of us who have been so thoroughly immersed in the conceptual world of our theological academies will be willing to undertake. My wager is that it is not enough for us to continue to function within the categories provided by our Western theological rationality and from this to explore critically the way in which seventeenth-century theologians domesticated transcendence, or now to give priority to theological reflection on the doctrine of the Holy Spirit while preserving the same type of rationality we have been using.

If we are committed to the struggle of the poor for life and recognize how far our theological conceptualization has departed from the biblical witness to the realm of the Spirit, we can go forward only as we undergo a much more radical process of unlearning, of "self-emptying," which will prepare us to perceive dimensions and realities of faith that have thus far been closed to us. To do this I believe that nothing short of immersion in Pentecostal and other popular religious movements, and openness to the experience of those being transformed by them, will enable us to perceive and respond to the moving of the Spirit, to be free to reread the Bible, and to engage in an ongoing task of theological re-creation in dialogue with such grassroots communities. As we do this, we may find ourselves embarking on a new journey of faith and participating in the formation and development of communities of faith living and struggling in solidarity with the poor.

5 *Personal Testimonies*

I n the previous chapter, we focused on what has emerged as most significant from our study of Pentecostal movements: These movements make it possible for those who are most burdened by the suffering resulting from impoverishment and exclusion to open their whole being to the overarching reality of the realm of the Spirit in which their lives are set. They entrust their lives, with all their burdens, to the God they encounter at the heart of this realm. As they do this, they experience the presence of a gracious God who takes possession of and fills their lives. They find themselves connected with a power that gives them new life, transforms and empowers them, and fills them with new energy and hope.

Confronted by their witness, we have come to the conclusion that, through them, we are being called to the rediscovery of a lost heritage, which could have revolutionary consequences in our lives and in our churches. Their witness challenges us to live more fully in the realm of the Spirit, to be more attuned to the presence of God in the midst of our daily lives, to trust more completely in and follow the guidance of the Spirit, and to expect that God's Spirit will be present with greater power in our struggles for life and for justice.

Yet how many of us are convinced that it is important for us to make this effort to enter into dialogue with those who live out of an experience of faith so different from our own? Especially if it involves relating to individuals and faith communities in which we may not feel at home, communities with doctrines and spiritual experiences some of which may seem not only exotic but contrary to what has been central in our own interpretation of Christian faith?

Many of us may not be inclined to take that step at the present time, but there is one step we can take that could prepare us for this engagement and open new horizons for us. As I was struggling to relate to Pentecostal churches in Brazil after my first contacts with them, one of the things that was most helpful to me was to listen to the stories of women and men whose lives had been changed by the spiritual experience we have here described. This led me to become aware of the witness to similar experiences on the part of other people in the United States, not all of whom were Pentecostal. As I read their stories, the shift in Christian thought and experience I had first perceived in Pentecostal communities in Brazil was set in a broader context in which it took on new importance and meaning.

In this chapter, we will present a number of testimonies of women and men whose lives are centered in the realm of the Spirit and witness to what this has meant for them. Given the fact that this radical change in religious perception and action has been examined from diverse angles throughout the first part of this book, we will present only one brief story from our interviews with Brazilian Pentecostals, which brings together a number of the central elements in their experience.

This will be followed by

- A brief report on what is happening at Old Bethel African Methodist Episcopal Church in inner city Baltimore, where dramatic experiences of life in the Spirit are making a profound impact in the lives of African Americans in this country.
- The witness of Dennis Covington, a journalist and college teacher, to his spiritual transformation as a result of his life with Pentecostal snake handlers in Appalachia.
- And the unusual story of the spiritual journey of Joseph Jaworski, which suggests to us that what Pentecostals witness to not only connects with those who have not been part of our modern Western

world of the Enlightenment but also has parallels in the experience of some who are trying to move beyond the limitations of our modern worldview.

The Empowerment of a Brazilian Peasant Woman

Dona Juliana is from a peasant family in a poor and isolated region of the state of Bahia. Now in her late sixties, she served as an obreira (lay worker) in the IURD for more than thirteen years in Bahia and in Rio de Janeiro. On the basis of a two-hour interview she gave to Clara Mafra, I have attempted to present the story of her faith journey as she told it. I have used her own words in order to allow her to tell her own story, but I have taken the liberty of presenting here a shortened version of it. I have rearranged some of her comments in order to present a more coherent picture, while avoiding taking her words out of context.

I'm a peasant woman from an isolated rural area in the state of Bahia. I never went to school. My parents didn't want girls to study but to work cultivating the land. Besides, since I was the oldest girl in the family, I had to take care of my younger brothers and sisters — eight of them — as well as the children of our neighbors. And in between the things I did for them, I also picked coffee.

I married very early and had seven children. I took care of them along with my younger brothers and sisters. I worked as a day laborer on *fazendas,* which meant moving around a lot. When my husband left me, I had full responsibility for my children. One is now a mason, another a painter, others are rural workers.

While I was still living in Bahia, a young woman evangelized me and took me to a Pentecostal church. There I gave myself to Jesus, was baptized, and a few days later, was baptized with the Holy Spirit. I wanted this, I wanted it very, very badly. One night I felt this noise like a wind and I felt my tongue starting to move, but I didn't know what I was saying. I was seeking this, seeking for it. I cried a lot. I felt wonderful. Sometimes I would speak in tongues. I began to attend regularly the services dedicated to the Holy Spirit.

After I was baptized, I bought a Bible. I don't know how to read, but many other members read it to me. I began to attend the youth group, even though I then had grown children, and I started evangelizing. Before long, I was asked to become an *obreira*. I got people together and took them to church and to take part in vigils. To be an *obreira* you must have the Holy Spirit, be baptized by the Spirit, and be moved to help other people: to visit them in their homes, care for the sick, visit hospitals, visit people in prison, and evangelize in poor neighborhoods. This is hard. It takes much wisdom from God, much patience. People shut the door in your face, drunks curse you, others turn up the radio so loud you can't talk or make fun of you, and others even smoke marijuana when you're trying to evangelize them. But you learn to forgive them and offer them the Word.

Obreiras are scheduled to give two or three days each week to this work, in the church services and in the other activities (without pay). To be an *obreira,* you must try to be aware of your sins and have God's forgiveness. You cannot lie, deceive others, or owe anything to other people. Also my group took food and clothes to the poorest people in the farthest neighborhoods, far beyond the end of the bus line, because they are the poorest. I often made clothes for the small children. I visited families, prayed with them, anointed them with oil.

In the homes where I worked, I always asked for clothes to take to the poorest. I never asked for anything for me; I often took my own clothes and gave them away. I give everything to others, to the church. Why should I keep storing up clothes for myself? When I'm gone, nobody will want what I have stored up. So I collect all I can and give it away. I felt sorry for those who were so poor, and I could see their happiness. All this time, I washed clothes to feed my family, but I would get up and do this early so that I would be free to do my part as an *obreira* with the church.

I visited other churches, more traditional ones, but they're different. The pastors speak a lot, but they don't think about the people. In my church, the pastors speak with the people. And many times you go to church with a serious problem in your life, and the preacher speaks directly to your problem. You listen to him and you say, this problem is happening with me. This has happened with many people. Jesus gives that gift to them, to preach that touches your own problem and you say: this is what is happening with me.

There's much emphasis on fasting. Lay workers fast three times a week from midnight to noon of the next day. We also have many vigils, a beautiful experience. We go to church in the evening, stay there until 11:00, and then people from several churches gather and begin the vigil in the church, or on the beach, or maybe at the foot of a mountain. We spend the whole night singing, praying, seeking the Holy Spirit. We take food and eat together, until 4:00 A.M., when it's over.

The world is evil in the time before the return of Jesus. No love, people killing each other, or on drugs. The IURD is growing rapidly, working very hard to free people from all this. Working very hard in prisons, where there are many people who have done nothing wrong but can't protest because they might get killed. Pastors and lay workers are working hard there, preaching and baptizing. Many people are being saved, and pastors help many to be released. The believer, especially the lay worker, is in constant confrontation with the devil. The devil is very powerful, but we have the power to bind and expel these demons.

One night I was returning home from church, full of faith in Jesus and of the Holy Spirit. I had a neighbor who was always fighting with his wife. Just as I was arriving home, I saw the fight, heard the shouting, and saw many people standing around watching it. I looked to see what was happening, and saw that he was vicious and ready to physically attack his wife. As I was approaching the door of my house, I cried out: "The blood of Jesus has power, soften this man, my God." In that very moment, he calmed down, and the fight stopped.

Many such things happen, and I pray to God. But I never ask him to do anything evil, only good. To be a faithful worker I need to have a good heart, the heart of a child, always do the right thing, and not continue to be angry with anyone. Because if a lay worker does not live this way, how can she pray that the devil leave a person? As long as we do the will of the devil, how can I expel the devil? Whoever has faith in Jesus, faith in God, can cast out the devil. If you just have faith and courage — you must also have courage. The devil may grasp a person, but if that person has courage, she casts it out.

Reviving the Spirit in Inner City Baltimore

In *Reviving the Spirit,* Beverly Hall Lawrence describes how "a generation of African Americans goes home to Church." She illustrates this unexpected development by telling the story of Bethel African Methodist Episcopal Church, which once served a largely middle-class constituency in Baltimore. In the seventies, its membership dropped to 310, but it now has a dynamic congregation of 10,000. As she describes the change that has come about in the last twenty years under the influence of pastors she identifies as "Neo-pentecostal," it is abundantly clear that the secret of the change lies in what we have been describing in this and the preceding chapter:

The pastor who initiated this new era in the life of the church, the Reverend John Bryant, speaks of this experience as that of "being full of the Holy Ghost," "embracing God as a Living Spirit." He speaks of our society as one that sees human beings only as mind and body, and he notes, "I preach that man is a Trinity of mind, body, and spirit." "I maintain that the spirit transcends the other two." The Reverend Frank Madison Reid III, the present pastor, declares that "Holy Spirit power provides an individual with encouragement and a sense of spiritual strength that enables him or her to face the problems and possibilities of life."[1]

This spiritual reality finds expression in worship, which offers a rich and compelling emotional experience. In it, African Americans can reconnect with their cultural and historical heritage, in which music and dance, religion and life, are blended together in a holistic experience. And as Lawrence observes, pastors with this spiritual orientation who were influenced in the 1960s by "black liberation theology" have developed what she calls the "Bethel model," "a synthesis of the Holy Spirit, African-American culture, and progressive social programs for the goals of salvation, empowerment, liberation and peace."[2]

Consequently, a new relationship with God and a powerful experience of the Spirit make it possible to "revive the spirit" of the people, as they learn to affirm themselves, help each other, and work together

---

1. Beverly Hall Lawrence, *Reviving the Spirit* (New York: Grove Press, 1996), p. 138.

2. Lawrence, *Reviving the Spirit,* p. 97.

on issues of health, education, work, and economic survival. Members coming from the suburbs get involved in the struggles of those in the inner city, while evangelism reaches those in most desperate need and deals with the total life of individuals and community. The church has become what Lawrence calls "the Grand Central Station of a modern-day Underground Railroad," where underground networks work to hear and respond to those in trouble, those facing crises in relationships, or those without work. Reverend Reid has dedicated himself especially to a ministry to black men. Each Monday night he leads a group of 400 to 500 men in Bible study related to issues of today. And in a special effort to appeal to young men in the inner city, he has created a disciplined group, the Mighty Men of God, whose members have a chance to overcome the drug culture, violence, and unemployment. This effort, combined with a wide variety of social outreach ministries and active involvement of church members in politics, gives expression to the conviction that "it is economic empowerment that African Americans feel we must stress."[3]

In her conclusion about the significance of this ministry, the author declares: "Now we are looking not only for personal salvation but social salvation. So-called authentic churches like Bethel are working to stabilize communities by working with substance abusers, mentoring youth, reuniting families, bridging the gap between black males and females, proclaiming a gospel of holy esteem that spills over into a healthy self-esteem, and enabling people to think of economic development while at the same time avoiding greed by putting community interests first."[4]

Transformed by the Witness of Snake Handlers

As we have become more aware of the experience of poor Pentecostals in life in the realm of the Spirit, we have also talked with or read about a number of women and men who are completely outside of these circles, both by religious affiliation and social class, but who have embarked on a new spiritual journey because of contact with them.

3. Lawrence, *Reviving the Spirit,* p. 161.
4. Lawrence, *Reviving the Spirit,* p. 163.

One of them is Dennis Covington, a college teacher and journalist in Alabama, who wrote a fascinating story of his experiences with snake handlers in southern Appalachia, *Salvation on Sand Mountain,* and has spoken more recently, in an interview in *Sojourners,* about how all this has affected his own personal journey.

As he mingled with snake handlers, he found himself among the most marginal and impoverished people in that region who, when they came out of the mountains, discovered that they were surrounded by a hostile and spiritually dead culture. But it was this peculiar people who, when their own resources failed, called down the Holy Spirit, drank poison, took up serpents, and encountered the dominant culture. In Covington's words: "Running smack up against a culture that seems to have lost its sense of the sacred causes spiritual people to reach deep down inside themselves and their faith to find something that is actually of lasting and permanent value."[5]

What is important for me here is not merely this discovery Covington made, but what happened to him as he moved among these people. This man who, as he himself admits, was cynical, given to drink, and without any sense of meaning in his life, was strangely attracted by the spirit of this movement and eventually became a snake handler for a short time. As a result, this extremely marginal Pentecostal movement became the instrument by which he was transformed and felt called to commit himself to the struggle of the poor of the world for life. Through snake handlers he was able to discover that Christianity is a matter of passion, danger, and mystery. With them he not only saw the movement of the Spirit healing wounded people and transforming broken lives, he also came to know this reality for himself. "I felt I was somehow being led by the Spirit. . . . If you accept the idea of a universe set into motion by an intelligent hand, then it seems to me you have to consider the possibility that the hand may still be at work in its movement."[6]

Consequently, surprising, life-giving things happen. More than this, among people who experienced spiritual ecstasy, Covington realized that, through this experience of ecstasy, men and women found them-

5. Dennis Covington, "From the Mountain," *Sojourners* (July-August 1996): 29.
6. Dennis Covington, *Salvation on Sand Mountain* (New York: Penguin Books, 1995), p. 202.

selves in tune with one another. They experienced being of one mind, one accord, part of one body. Love for the Lord expressed itself in love for brothers and sisters. And from this, as he reports, "I had to take up serpents before I saw other ways to reach spiritual ecstasy." Thus his discovery that the entry into ecstasy is abnegation, letting go, putting everything on the line, and that denial of self through service to others is a way to do that.

It is thus hardly surprising that, as a result of this experience, Covington, while continuing as a writer and teacher, is primarily concerned about giving expression to "the fruits of the Spirit," which for him has meant taking up well-drilling in places of the world where there is no clean water. As he and his wife have discovered, when they have taken this step of abnegation and commitment and have prayed, surprising things have begun to happen. As the result of unexpected contacts with persons in university circles who were into well-drilling, they were led to someone who gave them well-drilling equipment that he had in his back yard.

Being Led through Modernity to a New Future

While I was still reflecting on the parallels between Covington's experience among the snake handlers and my own response to involvement with Pentecostals in Brazil, I came upon a book in which the author appears to be moving in a similar direction but from a very different starting point: *Synchronicity,* by Joseph Jaworski.

As I began to read it, my first reaction was: How could this man's journey have any relationship whatsoever with what we are here exploring? Jaworski is not someone from a poor marginal community but was the founder and CEO of the American Leadership Forum and head of Global Scenario Planning for Royal/Dutch Shell. Jaworski was living and acting in the center of our dominant Western culture and was a student of the latest developments in physics, not someone immersed in a traditional culture by-passed by modernity. Furthermore, he makes no mention of any contact with Pentecostals or with the poor and exploited people who make up so much of their membership.

Yet as I read his story, I became aware of a number of surprising things. He never knew the pain of hunger, poverty, or exploitation, but as a very young boy, he learned from his father, Leon Jaworski, about the unimaginable horrors of what happened in the Nazi concentration camps. Years later, his father, who served as a Watergate Special Prosecutor, told him about the extent and depth of evil in the highest places of government, about unscrupulous laders who abuse power, and about lazy, self-indulgent citizens who allow it. All of this convinced him of the inhumanity of which human beings are capable and also left him with a sense of his own powerlessness to make lasting change.

Reflecting on the state of our society in the light of all this, while at the same time pursuing a brilliant career as a successful partner in a law firm in Houston, Jaworski became captivated by a dream of doing something to prepare men and women for an urgently needed new type of leadership. Obsessed with this dream, but with no idea as to how to achieve it, he nevertheless decided to leave his position and risk trying to find some way to work toward his goal. To his great surprise, after having taken this step, unexpected things began to happen. People appeared who shared and supported his dream, and things came together time and again in ways he could not have imagined. He soon came to the conclusion that, as he freed himself to follow his dream, he was being carried forward by what he describes as "a powerful force beyond ourselves and our conscious will."[7] In this context, the important thing was to surrender himself and, in an attitude of expectancy, allow himself to be carried forward.

Caught up in a new world of experience that simply did not fit into the Western scientific-materialistic worldview he had taken for granted all his life, he knew he had to move beyond it. At this point he began to explore recent developments in human understanding taking place in the new physics and other disciplines. This led him to the realization that the world cannot be conceived of primarily as *substantial,* predetermined, and fixed, but rather as an open world, primarily consisting of relationships. A world that is *unfolding* and thus offering possibilities that go far beyond what our logical minds have defined as possible.

Jaworski also turned to the writings of the Christian mystics as well as outstanding spiritual leaders in other religious traditions. He came to realize that the rigid boundaries our Western secular world has estab-

---

7. Joseph Jaworski, *Synchronicity* (San Francisco: Berrett-Koehler, 1996), p. 119.

lished between our day-to-day reality and the realm of the Spirit are eroding. He goes so far as to speak of his own experience of a loss of boundaries between God and self and an emerging sense of identity that is
expanding to include God. Moving in this realm, he perceives that "there
exists beyond ourselves and our conscious will a powerful force that helps
us along the way and nurtures our growth and transformation. Our journey is guided by invisible hands with infinitely greater accuracy than is
possible through our unaided conscious will."[8] He concludes this book
describing his personal life journey with the words over the entrance to
Carl Jung's home in Switzerland, "Invoked or not invoked, God is present."

Jaworski finds himself living and working in an *open world*. Rather
than being bound by what is defined as possible, he is able to perceive
new possibilities and undertake the impossible. Assuming the existence of
a powerful and purposeful force beyond our conscious will, he is free to
surrender to it. He is able, as he puts it, to "allow creative forces to move
through me without my control" and thus to expect "predictable miracles." In this context, as he seeks to contribute his part to the transformation of the world in which he is living, he expects to be surprised all along
the way by the appearance of others with similar concerns and by opportunities he had not anticipated.

Jaworski's language may be very different from that of Pentecostals,
but who is better prepared than they to connect with his worldview and
experience? Women and men who experience being connected with the
realm of the Spirit, which penetrates and transforms all aspects of their
day-to-day struggle. Women and men whose experience of the Holy
Spirit as presence and power in their midst leads them to expect miracles,
to surrender to the flow of the Spirit, and to find the courage and energy
to do the impossible. Women and men who, often in spite of inherited
rigid dogmas and moral rules, discover that living by the Spirit sets them
free from imprisonment in rational structures in order to follow the leading of the Spirit in their personal lives and in their response to their
neighbors in need, and to perceive that they are living in and can participate in an open world unfolding before them.

All this suggests the potential for a new dialogue from which many

---

8. Jaworski, *Synchronicity,* p. 119.

of us might profit. For Pentecostals, it might provide encouragement for them to value more highly the new form of Christian faith and life emerging in their midst, and see with greater clarity how different it is from that of the older mainline churches. At the same time, ongoing dialogue with those who are exploring the new ways of thinking mentioned by Jaworski might contribute significantly to the efforts being made by Pentecostals and others of us who are living in dialogue with them to develop further the new theological paradigm we see emerging, and thus have greater resources for thought and action as we struggle for a more human future.

6 The Spirit: The Presence in History of the Resurrected Jesus

In our efforts to identify those elements in Pentecostalism that we sensed were pointing toward a new paradigm of Christian faith and life, we have focused our attention on two thus far: (1) the shift in the understanding and experience of redemption and (2) a perspective on life and the world in which the realm of the Spirit is the supreme reality to which human beings are connected and which, through the Holy Spirit, becomes the source of life.

But it was also evident that, in conversations about what was happening in the lives of Pentecostals, as well as in their preaching, there was something else of crucial importance. They were always talking about Jesus. This, in itself, did not surprise us, given our experience with conservative Evangelicals over the years. But what did surprise us was the way they spoke about Jesus: as Someone who was not only very real and close to them but who could be counted on to do amazing things in their day-to-day struggle for life.

My first conclusion was that this was simply a logical consequence of their religious worldview. Starting out from their grounding in the realm of the Spirit and their experience of life flowing from it, it seemed quite natural for them to feel a special closeness to Jesus, who experienced this same reality and believed in and lived out this presence and power of God in his life. Moreover, his ministry was directed toward people like them, and who better than they could understand the price he paid for this expression of solidarity?

This Jesus declares that the divine presence and power in which he lives and moves is of a God who is grace and compassion. Thus he can say that, because the "Spirit of the Lord is upon [him]," he is the bearer of "good news" to the poor, proclaims release to the captives, and the recovery of sight to the blind. He is empowered to set at liberty those who are oppressed and to proclaim the year of Jubilee, in which God's reign of life and justice especially for the poor and excluded is coming to fulfillment (Luke 4:18-19). As he proceeded to draw on this power to heal the sick, feed the hungry, announce the radical new age that was dawning, and challenge the powers that opposed it, those who listened to him and responded experienced this same divine presence and power giving them life, creating a new quality of relationships with others, and empowering them to move into the world as instruments of this redemptive power. At the same time, this experience and power of God leading to identification with the poor and outcasts not only challenged the forces of evil but also aroused their bitter opposition, so that this Jesus, who identified himself with the victims, ended up sharing their rejection, condemnation, and death.

Most Evangelical preaching I know is quite far removed from this dimension of the life of Jesus. To the extent that Pentecostals are closely connected to it, their experience as well as their way of speaking about Jesus would naturally be different.

Yet this explanation did not seem to be sufficient, and eventually I discovered why. *In Pentecostalism, poor and broken people discover that what they read in the Gospels is happening NOW in their midst.* This same Jesus is present with them, doing what he did in Galilee two thousand years ago. For them, the incredible witness of the Gospels to the resurrection is confirmed in their day-to-day experience. The impossible, the supreme miracle, has indeed happened. The crucified Jesus not only overcame death. He is present in the world, doing in their lives and communities what he did then — through the Holy Spirit.

In other words, whatever theological explanations they may or may not have, Pentecostals somehow know what Paul affirms, in 2 Corinthians 3:17: "The Lord is the Spirit." In their experience, the risen Christ lives now in the form of the Spirit. It is through the Holy Spirit that Jesus enters history. Consequently, the presence and power manifest in Jesus is no longer limited to one particular place at one particular moment in history but is accessible here and now, to the ends of the world and to the end of time.

It is thus hardly surprising that many of those who live by this faith are able to live every day with body and soul filled with God, know this as a life-giving and life-transforming reality, and find a new future opening before them. And all this becomes something contagious, as they cannot avoid making known to others what they have found. Moreover, to the extent that the experience of the Holy Spirit is identified with Jesus of Nazareth, his presence and action in their world and their lives now is seen as manifesting a sign and foretaste of God's reign, just as happened during Jesus' earthly ministry two thousand years ago.

The richer their life in the Spirit, the more aware they are that this life is a constant movement toward the kingdom. Miracles happen in and around them, or, as Paul describes it, the Spirit is daily making possible the formation of a "new creature." Their experience is similar to that of the earliest Christian community in the book of Acts. New doors are being opened and distressing problems are being faced and solved in unexpected ways. Thus, the Christian life is a dynamic one, always open to surprise, to creative new possibilities as well as unexpected calls for them to explore new realms of thought and action.

As we listened to the witness of those being drawn to Pentecostal churches, this is what we heard time and time again. At the same time, we were aware of the contrast between the vitality and expectancy of these women and men and the lack of this same spirit among so many of us who have not only everything we apparently need for a full life but also the capacity and resources necessary to work dynamically to change our world.

Once again, the major issue before us was not our judgment of what Pentecostals were or were not doing, but rather the challenge they present to us to reexamine our own faith and practice. Or, to speak more specifically in relation to what we are discussing here, What are we who are not Pentecostals being challenged to be and to do in the face of this extraordinary dynamism? Earlier in our study of these movements, my answer would have been that we are discovering how we might grow in our experience of the presence and power of the Holy Spirit. I continue to be convinced of the importance of this, but I now believe that it can happen only as we take into account the intimate relationship of Jesus with the Spirit. This, I believe, calls for further biblical study in relation to a number of issues.

The Historical Jesus and the Spirit

One of the most important contributions liberation theology has made in Latin America has been what it has done to restore the historical Jesus to a central place in our Christian faith and to open our eyes to dimensions of his life and teaching that had been given little importance or ignored completely. Now that this has happened, we must go one step further in our rediscovery of the historical Jesus: to recognize the absolute importance he gave to life in the Spirit, the cultivation of a vital relationship of communion with God.

As we indicated earlier, from his baptism onward Jesus not only lived every moment in intimate relationship with God; he also claimed that all that he did manifested this divine presence and power. As the British New Testament scholar James Dunn has put it, "Jesus' awareness of being uniquely possessed and used by the divine spirit was the mainspring of his mission and the key to its effectiveness."[1] He experienced God as a supernatural power compelling him to speak and to act. In line with the experience of the prophets and others in the history of Israel, Jesus knew the reality of God's Spirit that, in the words of Leonardo Boff, "invades a person and gives that person a power that otherwise would not be possible."[2]

This intimate relationship with God leads Jesus to identify himself with the poorest and the outcasts. More than this, he declares that all that he

1. James Dunn, *Jesus and the Spirit* (Philadelphia: Westminster Press, 1975), p. 54.
2. Leonardo Boff, *Church, Charism and Power* (New York: Crossroad, 1985), p. 148.

does through this divine power is intimately related to and pointing toward the coming of God's reign — thus the excitement and expectancy he aroused wherever he went. The working of God's Spirit through him in healing the sick, feeding the hungry, including the excluded, and giving life to the dead — all these are manifestations of the kingdom and thus signs of the end time. "If it is by the Spirit of God that I cast out demons, then the kingdom of God has come upon you" (Luke 11:20). His power to cast out demons is visible evidence that the power of God is flowing through him and is available to his disciples, to overcome the forces of evil, even superhuman powers, and thus restore and make life whole.

In the Gospel of Matthew, this statement is followed by the admonition that every sin and blasphemy will be forgiven except that against the Spirit (12:31-42). Reflecting on what Jesus means by these words, Dunn says: "to slander and reject the manifest power of God in overcoming illness and evil was to commit the unpardonable sin," because it is to ignore the plain evidence that the power of the age to come is present. "To refuse to recognize that presence, to live in the power of it and in the expectation of its continued manifestation, is to reject God."[3]

The Resurrected Jesus and the Spirit

In the epistles of Paul, as in the writings of Luke and the Gospel of John, we find repeated assertions regarding the close relationship of Jesus with the Spirit. In his commentary on the Gospel of John, Raymond Brown goes so far as to affirm that the Holy Spirit is nothing less than the presence of Jesus when Jesus is absent.[4] In the Spirit, the risen Christ is now active in the world. The presence and power of God, incarnate in one time and place in Jesus of Nazareth, is now exploding into all of the world and moving toward the end of time. On the basis of her study of the Gospel of Luke and of Acts, Odette Mainville concludes that with the resurrection and the manifestation of the Spirit in Pentecost, "henceforth the actions of the Spirit will be the continuation of the earthly mission of Je-

3. Dunn, *Jesus and the Spirit,* p. 53.

4. Raymond Brown, *John,* Anchor Bible (Garden City, N.Y.: Doubleday, 1982), p. 1141.

sus; they perpetuate his actions, his options, his ideas, his perception of God and of the human being."[5]

The Holy Spirit is "the force and means by which the Lord remains present in history and so continues his work of inaugurating a new world."[6] Thus, through the experience of the Spirit we are not only caught up in the life-giving and transformative work of Jesus but also empowered to carry it forward beyond all established boundaries, whether they be of race, class, culture, or nationality.

To know the risen Christ is to know and participate in the ever-renewed miraculous work of Jesus and to live by a power from beyond ourselves that can only be experienced as an exciting journey toward an ever fuller life and a transformed world. It is grounded in and flows from an inward experience that fills us with confidence and finds expression in joy and celebration. The richer our experience and the greater our growth, the more compelling is the call to witness — as individuals and as a community of faith: witness to the life we have received (evangelism) and struggle to make real the promise of God's new order of life and justice especially for the poor and excluded (social and political action).

The Experience of the Resurrected Jesus and the Spirit at Pentecost

Pentecostals compel us to take much more seriously the nature of the experience that gave birth to the church, what happened on the day of Pentecost and immediately thereafter, as recorded in the first chapters of the book of Acts.

In their encounter with Jesus immediately after the resurrection, the disciples make clear what they expected: that now the risen Christ would establish the promised new order through the restoration of the nation of Israel. This is not unlike the expectation many of us have had as we have taken part in the struggle for political liberation in recent decades. But they must have been shocked when Jesus informed them that his resurrection called for a radically different perspective and agenda. This hum-

5. Odette Mainville, *L'Esprit dans l'oeuvre de Luc* (Montreal: Fides, 1991), p. 333.
6. Boff, *Church, Charism and Power,* p. 150.

ble band of disciples are called to dedicate themselves to the cultivation of their communion with God through prayer until they receive the power of the Holy Spirit. Then they, and those who join them, will be empowered to continue doing what Jesus has been doing, as witnesses to the kingdom and its extension to Jerusalem, all Judea, Samaria, and "the very ends of the earth."

On the day of Pentecost, all this became possible. Those who experienced the presence and power of the Spirit in their lives discovered that they were not only able to undertake the impossible but were being swept forward by the Spirit into a world of ever-expanding possibilities.

Everything is being turned upside down. Young people will see visions and those who are old will dream dreams. Servants and slaves, men and women alike, will announce the events relating to God's kingdom.

Those who have been locked into their past, and have acquiesced in submission to the "present evil age," can now, through forgiveness, step into a new world and discover that they are free from this perverse age.

Those who are caught up in living only for themselves now share in a new quality of life in community, which becomes a reality as they learn to share their material possessions with each other, a life in communion with God and others that is filled with joy.

Living this reality, this small community of faith is led by the Spirit, with rapid succession, to venture into new areas and undertake new tasks, tasks they had never imagined and they never dreamed they were capable of doing:

- Within a few days, they are confronted by a lame man and are led to heal him, thus discovering their calling and power to continue one of the things that had been most central in Jesus' ministry. As Peter tries to make sense out of what is happening, he declares not only that Jesus has given them strength to heal, but that through this new people of God now being constituted, the promise that "all the families on earth shall find blessing" is being fulfilled.
- As this community grows, a new problem arises: The Grecian Jews protest against the Palestinian Jews because their widows are being neglected in the distribution of food. In the face of this crisis, the Spirit leads them to the creation of a new "order" of deacons, commissioned to respond to this need.

Very soon thereafter, the Spirit led Peter to undertake a mission that seemed to be contrary to what Jesus himself had done and had asked of his disciples: Peter is led by the Spirit to the home of Cornelius, where he is confounded by the fact that the Holy Spirit has been poured out on the Gentiles. He has no choice but to respond by baptizing Cornelius and thus opening this formerly closed community to those outside.

It is hardly surprising that Karl Barth, when he speaks of the baptism of the Holy Spirit in his *Dogmatics* (IV.4), declares that "the work of the Holy Spirit is always and particularly always a new work. Consequently, each time it is produced, it constitutes a change that calls for new radical transformation."

The Holy Spirit and "Life in Christ" according to Paul

Paul the Apostle expresses this same dynamic understanding of the Christian life as life in the Spirit by speaking repeatedly in his epistles about life in Christ as a constant process of transformation, the remaking or reforming of human beings to the image and likeness of God. This represents such a radical novelty that Gerhard Ladner, in his classical study of *The Idea of Reform: Its Impact on Christian Thought and Action in the Age of the Fathers,* declares that "the idea of reform may be considered as essentially Christian in its origin and early development and finds its most profound and categorical expression in the writings of Paul."[7]

In Romans, those in whom God's Spirit dwells, who "possess the spirit of Christ" (8:9-11), are called to undergo a complete transformation of life, not to be conformed to the pattern of the present world, but to be "transformed by the renewal of your minds" (12:2). In Ephesians, this means to put off "the old man" and put on a new nature. This new nature takes shape as the two completely hostile nations, Jews and Gentiles, are united to create one new humanity. In Colossians 3:10, the believers are exhorted to discard the "old human nature" and to "put on the new nature that is constantly being renewed in the image of its Creator" (REB). In 2 Corinthians 5:17, "anyone who is in Christ is a new

---

7. Gerhard Ladner, *The Idea of Reform: Its Impact on Christian Thought and Action in the Age of the Fathers* (Cambridge: Harvard University Press, 1959), p. 9.

creation: the old order has gone; a new order has already begun"
(REB).

If our perception of the nature of the Pentecostal experience is correct, then its unique nature and power lies not just in the fact that Pentecostals discover that all aspects of their daily struggle for life are situated
in the context of the realm of the Spirit, from which they receive life and
by which they are empowered. To this must be added what we have described above: their discovery that through the Holy Spirit, Jesus of Nazareth, risen from the dead, is now present in the world and in their lives,
manifesting the same divine power, and doing what he did in Galilee.
This presence and action is now as then a sign and foretaste of God's
reign, which even now is breaking into our lives and our world.

7 *The Gifts of the Spirit and the Life of Faith*

The Reformation was a powerful experience of God's gracious gift of forgiveness and justification that transformed lives, energized believers, and gave them a compelling sense of vocation in the world. Until recent times, this experience continued to provide the foundation and motivation for Christian life and service for many in our mainline Protestant churches. Today, however, this same message has lost much of its transforming and energizing power; rarely does it lead men and women to leave all to follow Jesus in his ministry to a suffering world. It often seems that, if communities with such vitality exist in our churches, they are to be found mainly among fundamentalist and more conservative Evangelical groups whose orientation owes little to this Reformation heritage or who, while trying to preserve it, have distorted it.

To a great extent this crisis is due to the ease with which middle-class Christianity has accommodated itself within our American culture, dominated as it is by the values sustaining our capitalistic economic system. But even if we take this fully into account, the question still remains to haunt us: Why has mainline Protestantism not even attempted to challenge this accommodation or demonstrated the power to re-create itself, taking into account especially the nature of the Reformed heritage?

At the same time, many Christians across the world are finding new life, as well as tremendous energy for putting their faith into practice, comparable to the experience of people at the time of the Reformation. They are demonstrating a faith that is as compelling in its power to change and motivate lives as was the faith of the Reformers. But this power for the re-creation and transformation of life is the product of a perspective on the gospel and an experience of faith quite different from that which we have taken for granted for centuries.

Pentecostals address themselves primarily to those who are poor and marginal where they are — overwhelmed by the struggle for survival, in the face of the disintegration of personal and social life. They invite them to open themselves to the realm of the Spirit, entrust their lives to God, and receive power that enables them to respond with new life and energy to all that threatens to destroy them. At the heart of this experience is the reality of the risen Christ, present through the Spirit, active in their lives in the same way that he was during his earthly ministry in Galilee.

What is distinctive here in the shaping of the Christian life is the centrality Pentecostals give to what Paul the Apostle calls the *charismata,* the gifts of grace bestowed by the Spirit, which empower and determine the life of the believer. As Jesus Christ is the supreme charisma, the concrete expression of new life, it is these gifts that make it possible for women and men today, especially those in a situation similar to that of those to whom Jesus ministered, to receive the healing and resources for living offered by Jesus. It is through these gifts of the Spirit that they are called and equipped to express, in their lives, the quality of life and the reality of love that was present in the person of Jesus of Nazareth. As Bishop Macedo has put it, Christians "must take on the character of the Lord Jesus Himself. Think like Jesus thought, speak like Jesus spoke, act like Jesus acted, feel like Jesus felt."[1] Pentecostals today have learned from Paul that anyone who receives and lives by these *charismata* participates in the movement of the world toward the reign of God, which aims at filling all of life and the whole creation with this reality.

1. Edir Macedo, *O perfil do homen de Deus* (Rio de Janeiro: Editora Gráfica Universal, 1994), p. 9.

I believe that Pentecostals, with this understanding and experience of Christian faith, open a number of new avenues for the cultivation of the Christian life, avenues that we would do well to explore, even though our exploration of them may lead us to conclusions quite different from those which many Pentecostals have reached.

The Source and Power of New Life: Baptism by the Holy Spirit

At the time of the Reformation, people were transformed and energized as they heard and responded to the word of God's gracious forgiveness and justification as proclaimed in the Sunday church service by sermon and song and repeated daily in the family gathered around the Bible.

Today in Pentecostal services, frequently held every day of the week, in churches, small shacks, or on street corners, people — especially the poor, the disoriented, the broken — have a similar experience. This experience becomes a reality as they open themselves to the presence of the Spirit in their midst, and experience a conversion in which the Spirit takes possession of their lives and redirects them. Thus, all that happens in regular worship in the church or in evangelistic campaigns is oriented toward bringing people to this point of conversion and to experiences that confirm the Spirit's presence and action: preaching and singing, often accompanied with speaking in tongues and dancing, praying for and healing of the sick, and, on some occasions, the casting out of demons.

In this context, the preaching is such that those attending often feel that the preacher recognizes their particular burden and is speaking directly to their situation. They also know that their often miserable and confused lives are being touched by God, and that they are being grasped by a power that can put their lives together and support them in their daily struggle against demonic forces. If hearing and responding to the proclamation of God's forgiveness provided the dynamic for Reformation faith, among Pentecostals today it is this experience of the presence and power of God in the baptism of the Holy Spirit that changes everything and gives life a new direction and a call to mission in the world.

It took me quite a while to perceive this fundamental shift and the importance of it. I well recall one of our first interviews with a small group of pastors of the Assembly of God in Rio. This was, I suspect, their first encounter with members of a research team who spoke openly of their own faith as they were doing a sociological study of their church. When one of the members of our team attempted, in the course of the conversation, to establish a closer rapport with them, she described her own faith and what it meant for her. When she finished, the pastors had only one comment: "Have you been baptized by the Holy Spirit?"

An interview with Dona Juliana, whose story we told earlier, revealed why this is, for them, the most important issue. She spoke about her early life and struggles, her contact with various religious groups, and then her first visits to a Pentecostal church. As she described it, very soon after she started going to this church, she had one overwhelming desire, a "yearning for the baptism of the Spirit," which soon happened for her. It was an experience she found no adequate words to describe: "something so beautiful," "a light noise like the wind," the compulsion "to speak something I didn't understand," which left her "feeling the Holy Spirit." From this moment she was a new person, filled with enthusiasm to evangelize and also to care for her own children as well as those of others, to provide food and clothing for those in need, to visit prisons, and to become a lay worker.

As I listened to similar testimonies on other occasions, I had a new sense of what must have been the vitality and power of the Reformation faith that made it possible for the Reformation to spread across Europe so rapidly, fill people with life, and lead to dynamic action in the world. I had to ask myself what has happened if most of us no longer have that type of experience or even feel the compulsion to seek what we are missing. I came to the conclusion that, if we have lost this fire and regret this loss, we might be surprised by new experiences of the leading of the Spirit as we relate to and live with those who today experience the fire of Pentecost. When we find that many of the Pentecostals we know have turned this experience inward or have become more concerned about some of the superficial outward signs of it than about what was for Paul the greatest gift, love, this should not be a sufficient reason for us to ignore what the Spirit may be doing in their midst. The alternative open to us is to discover how to be more receptive of the Spirit in our lives, and struggle, as Paul did in the communities he established, to discern and live by the Spirit as manifest in Jesus of Nazareth.

Freedom

To the surprise and shock of many moralistic Protestants in Brazil, especially those in older Pentecostal movements, the IURD has categorically affirmed the freedom of the Christian life. They have done so in a way that has made a much more widespread and profound impact, in a few years, than anything those of us in more progressive Protestant circles have been able to do over many decades. By doing this on the basis of their confidence in the presence and power of the Holy Spirit, they present a new challenge to all of us.

Those whose lives are anchored in the experience of the Holy Spirit have an experience of God that frees them from undue concern about a world or a moral order collapsing around them. They also experience the Spirit as always on the move, opening new opportunities and directions in their lives and in the lives of others. To the extent that life in the Spirit is life in communion with Christ, it has a center that transcends the self and strives to approach all dimensions of life from the perspective of Christ. At the same time, the believer expects to receive *gifts,* the specific nature of which cannot be predicted, but which give direction to a new quality of life as well as the power to live it. Any attempt to limit life in the Spirit by imposing on it rigid moralistic rules is undermined, and it may be only a matter of time until such moralism is recognized as alien to the essential nature of Pentecostalism and should give way to a more biblically based ethic.

One of the most interesting aspects of this that we have found in the witness of some Pentecostals is their sense that this experience not only frees them from subservience to rigid rules but also provides them with an unusual capacity for discernment: discernment of what is going on in their own lives, in the concrete situations in which they find themselves, and especially in the lives and struggles of other people. Those who discover that they have this capacity for discernment realize that it also contributes to their discovery of what to do in concrete situations. This makes it impossible for them to make absolute any biblical text or tradition in order to be free to respond more faithfully to God's will.

Those who are thus being led by the Spirit and are open to receive the *charismata* offered to them are called, as Paul makes very clear, to a life of love, which by its very nature cannot be a principle or an obligation. It is rather, as James Dunn points out, a matter of the inner compulsion of the Spirit coming to concrete expression in loving word and act.[2] When I was much younger, I made an attempt to take all the ethical exhortations in the Pauline Epistles and come up with a coherent set of norms for the Christian life. It didn't take long for me to realize, however, that this was not only an impossible task but also seemed to be imposing something on Paul that just did not fit. That apparently was not what he was doing in his exhortations to the communities to which he ministered. For him, what is important is to follow the leading of the Spirit, which by its very nature can only find expression in concrete manifestations of love in everyday life. Or, as the New Testament scholar Ernst Käsemann has said, Paul's instructions are "navigation lights."

One can question how far the pastors and theologians of the IURD have gone in their exegetical studies of Christian freedom in the Pauline writings or in their theological reflection on what we have just mentioned. There can be no doubt, however, that they have broken with the rigid moralism of traditional Pentecostalism and of many of the more established Protestant communities in Latin America. Their rapid growth has raised this issue in an inescapable way, especially in Pentecostal circles.

As IURD members frequently said to us: the women and men we are evangelizing — those addicted to alcohol or drugs, prostitutes, those whose lives have been broken by the stresses of poverty, those who are caught up in conflict and violence in their own families and communities — these people will not be touched or transformed by a type of preaching that constantly tells them that they are condemned sinners. They know that what they are doing is wrong and that they are victims of evil. Their problem is that they find themselves caught in a situation from which they cannot escape. They have neither the will nor the power necessary to break with it.

In the IURD the emphasis in preaching and evangelism is on this experience of the Spirit that breaks the control of evil over their lives and offers them power to overcome whatever is destroying them. Through frequent attendance at religious services, which reinforce all this, and as they are supported in their struggle by pastors or small communities of

2. James Dunn, *Jesus and the Spirit* (Philadelphia: Westminster Press, 1975), p. 224.

church members, converts gradually find themselves led by the Spirit to find their way and change their lives. Bishop Macedo has expressed categorically what this means for him: "Those who have been transformed by the Spirit practice the word of God naturally. An orange tree does not have to go through contortions to produce oranges."[3]

We all know that making ethical decisions calls for much more than this, but in the responses to questions we raised about ethics in our interviews, two things stood out: (1) Those who have gone through a profound experience of conversion in which the traditional moralism is absent have not found in this a justification for lack of concern about the ethical life. Liberation from moralism means rather that they are not dominated by the "Law" and are thus free to follow the leading of the Spirit, which means a process of moral transformation. Many of them seem to find, within the community, the support they need to follow this path.

(2) While we found many instances in which certain ethical norms deeply rooted in the traditional culture — especially in the areas of sexuality and family life — were still preserved without questioning, we were more impressed by the way in which their religious experience had led them to be more open and flexible than others around them on many issues. While often living in the most precarious conditions in a society in which their future was very uncertain, they did not seem to be unduly anxious about it. Nor did they try to shore up what was crumbling around them by sacralizing the established order and its values.

While I believe that Neopentecostalism has made a significant contribution in this area in a very short period of time, I'm also convinced that, if it hopes to develop a new ethic of freedom, solidly grounded in the Scriptures, it will have to give much more attention than it has thus far to some major problems in the Pentecostal community for which there are no easy answers. Fundamentalistic moralism, with the biblical literalism that accompanies it, is so deeply rooted in many communities that it cannot be overcome without much theological struggle. As a number of charismatic movements have shown, it is very easy to use a certain type of individualistic spiritual experience not only to make people feel quite at

3. Edir Macedo, *Aliança com Deus* (Rio de Janeiro: Editora Gráfica Universal, 1993), p. 95.

home in their self-centered materialistic culture but also to become enthusiastic defenders of it. Men and women who find, in Pentecostalism, the resources they need to overcome one or another form of addiction may be so involved in that struggle that they have little time or energy to explore wider areas of Christian freedom, leading to participation in the struggle for social transformation.

How prepared are those of us who are not Pentecostals to deal with these issues, especially since our faith communities have done so little to face these same issues or to respond to them? Perhaps only as we undergo a major shift in our ethical stance, give priority to the cultivation of life in the Spirit, and rediscover what was so important for Paul the Apostle in the "gifts of grace" will we be prepared to develop and live an ethic of freedom that will challenge the fundamentalism and moralism in our midst, and to help those who feel most threatened by the crisis of our modern world and the changing values that accompany it to overcome the fears and insecurities that are driving them to seek political and religious movements that will sustain their belief in the survival of a world they desperately want to hang on to. Only out of such a renewal of our faith and life in the Spirit will we be in a position to engage with Pentecostals in ecumenical reflection on this issue from which all of us might profit.

Daring to Affirm Oneself before God

In traditional Protestant churches, the emphasis upon God's gracious initiative in forgiveness and justification and the response of the believer in acceptance of this gift and gratitude for it is so central that it is difficult for us even to conceive of anyone questioning it. It is thus hardly surprising that many Protestants in Brazil find what is happening in the IURD scandalous. Neopentecostal preaching affirms categorically that God can be counted on to act to heal sick and broken lives and grant blessings to those who believe only as they dare to demand that God respond to their need. In this context of faith, our relationship with God is that of *believing and demanding*. Faith is the conviction that God will bless you if you ask with passion.

Leila, a young woman in her early twenties, who had left the Assembly of God for the IURD, remarked, "If you really have faith that something is going to happen, it happens. When one is feeling tired or sick, or low in spirit, and believes in God and prays, certain that one is going to be healed, it will happen."

Bishop Macedo declares repeatedly that those who pray to God thinking that they can do nothing to change their situation will indeed not be able to do anything. All God's blessings, he says, "can be obtained only through an arduous and constant struggle on the part of those who desire them passionately."[4] He uses this approach most powerfully when pleading for money — "an offering to God." As we observed previously, when anyone makes a special offering, an offering of what he or she often doesn't have, this act creates a new situation of interaction with God in which God is obligated to respond.

We may with good reason be scandalized by the way in which IURD pastors use this approach to get money from their people. We may also have good reason to raise serious theological questions about it. But we should not ignore the fact that this emphasis on the power of a gracious God to change the situation of believers, and God's willingness to offer them blessings if only they dare stand up to him and demand them, is a powerful factor in the transformation of the lives and destiny of those believers, especially those who have no place in society, have a low self image, are convinced that they can do nothing to change their situation, and, because of all of this, have given up. We heard frequently, from people thus transformed, this declaration: "I put a challenge to God." In the case of Leila, it was this type of faith that transformed her from a passive, retiring person lacking in self-confidence into a dynamic young woman now taking all sorts of initiatives in her life and in service to others. "My attitude changed completely. I am another person, now I am a jewel in the eyes of God."

Once Again: Life as a Journey

For the people of the Reformation — for Calvin, the Puritans, the early Wesleyans — the Christian life was conceived of as a dynamic, exciting,

---

4. Macedo, *Aliança com Deus,* p. 31.

and very serious journey. It was a constant ongoing process of overcoming sin, drawing closer to God, and being ever more faithful in discipleship. Today we rarely find this vision or the passion to pursue it in our comfortable middle-class churches.

In Brazil and elsewhere, among Pentecostals, this is being recovered and expressed in ways that respond especially to the situation of poor and broken people.

People who have been victims of addiction know the intensity of the struggle in which they are involved, the need for constant community support, and the importance of their marking and celebrating little victories along the way. For them, nothing is more essential than the daily experience of the power of God in their midst, and the movement of the Spirit in the community that daily supports them.

For many, the experience of conversion brings with it a radical change in perception of what is happening around them. It makes them much more aware of the destructiveness of the society of which they are a part, the demonic powers at work in it, and thus of the need of participating in a long and arduous struggle against these forces in their own lives and in the world around them. For them also, life in the Spirit is a journey that follows its own rhythm and that they can trust. In talking with mothers of adolescent children and other believers, we noted how often they spoke of those who had at some point turned to Christ, had been active in the church, and had later strayed from the path. However, what most caught our attention was the confidence so many of them had that the Spirit continued to be present and active in the lives of those who had strayed. This meant that their journey was continuing. Their relatives and friends could patiently continue praying for them and expect them to find their way in God's good time.

Because of the nature of their life in the Spirit, those who are Spirit-filled can expect to be led, time and again, into new and unexpected paths. The Spirit that gives and transforms life is always doing new things. That Spirit gives people vision and calls them to specific forms of discipleship. Those who receive the call know that they must accept it and count on the Spirit to sustain them in it. For some of us this may bring to mind examples such as that of the two Swedish immigrants in Chicago who felt called to go to Belem, in the Amazon, to establish a Pentecostal mission and who had to find an atlas in order to discover where they were called to go. But for many with whom we spoke, what was important was their belief that, time and again, God presented them with a new and unexpected opportunity of service. Thus, they were open to new challenges and ready to respond to them. To the extent that they had lived this way in the past and their lives had been blessed, they looked toward the future expectantly.

While teaching in Costa Rica recently, I met a Brazilian Pentecostal pastor and his wife who, over the last decade, had started a new church in Fortaleza. The church had grown and had become the center from which seventeen new congregations and centers of evangelism had been established. They, with three small children, were about to return to Brazil to continue this work. What most caught my attention was the fact that this couple had a divine uneasiness that was leading them to envision what they might be called to do in the future. The wife spoke to me of her experience with the suffering and struggle of abandoned adolescent girls in her city, and of her plan to begin to develop a small center from which to work with them. She had no money, no promise of any governmental or private support, and no expectation of receiving a salary for this work. She was determined, however, to start this project with the assurance that God will make it possible for her to sustain it.

Her husband was exploring how they might become involved in mission work in Africa. They had no missionary board or church to support them and understood very well what they might have to do to make this possible, but that did not stop them from exploring the possibility and expecting to be led as they did so. When I expressed my admiration for this spirit as well as my uneasiness about the risks involved in living this way, their response was that this was nothing unusual in Pentecostal circles. It was rather for them an essential element in the life of a faithful Christian.

The Gifts of the Spirit

I can't remember ever hearing a sermon or taking part in a theological discussion in Reformed circles on this theme. Yet, when I read the epistles of Paul, I can't understand how we have ignored, for so long, what for him is at the heart of the ethical life of the Christian: the *charismata,* "gifts of grace," or "gifts of the Spirit." It has been primarily through the witness of Pentecostals that our eyes have been opened to this dimension of life. I can't here attempt a thorough study of this, but one thing seems very clear in the thought of Paul: Living in the Spirit means that the life of the believer flows out of an experience of receiving a charisma, a gift of grace.

For Paul, a charisma is always a gift of grace, mediated by the Holy Spirit, and Jesus Christ is the primal charisma. Consequently, the most important charisma we can receive and live is that of love, for only thus can we lead a life that is an authentic expression of following Jesus. In his letters to the communities with which he is related, Paul is compelled to dedicate a great deal of attention to the rich variety of *charismata* manifest in services of worship, while declaring categorically that love is the one to be most sought after and cherished.

Pentecostals today not only remind us of the centrality and richness of this outpouring of the Spirit, through which each of us receives a special charisma. They also demonstrate that, as in the churches Paul nurtured, this invasion of life by the divine expresses itself in a spirit of ecstasy and joyfulness, of liberation and freedom. If we pursue further the instructions Paul offers, we realize that these gifts are at work in each "for some useful purpose" (1 Cor. 12:7, REB). As we receive a gift of grace we also become a gift of grace to others. The specific *charismata* all contribute to openness to the other and to Christ in the other, and thus contribute to the building up of the community. In the words of Jean-Jacques Suurmond, "the gifts of grace put people in a position to receive in wonderment the totally other in the neighbor, and thus in Christ."[5]

This comes to expression most powerfully in Romans 1:11-12, where Paul speaks of his yearning to impart these gifts of the Spirit so that the community will be strengthened as people, by their faith, and encourage each other. Life in the Spirit is a matter of constantly giving and receiving in a way that contributes to the growth of each and all. As the Spirit present in the life of Jesus led him into ever closer identification with the poorest and most excluded people, to the point of his being excluded and condemned on the cross, so those who receive these gifts of the Spirit, the greatest of which is love, are being led to follow the same

---

5. Jean-Jacques Suurmond, *Word and Spirit at Play: Towards a Charismatic Theology* (Grand Rapids: Eerdmans, 1994), p. 183.

path. We cannot ignore the fact that, in Paul, the centrality of his focus on the future manifestation of Christ implies that each gift of the Spirit has an eschatological dimension to it.

If we make room for these experiences of the reception of God's gifts of grace, we, whether we be Pentecostals or mainline Christians, will probably have to struggle as much as Paul did to find our way, as individuals and communities of faith, so that these gifts "serve some useful purpose" in the community and are not limited to personal experiences of spiritual satisfaction. At the same time, we might find ourselves exploring new depths of relationship with others and also re-creating in our time what was so central for Calvin, the sense of God's purpose for each life and God's calling to service, evangelism, and the struggle for social transformation.

Conclusion

For me, all the elements mentioned above add up to one thing: Pentecostalism has demonstrated and continues to demonstrate that Christian faith, when it is true to its nature and origins, has the power to transform life, give direction and energy to it, and pass on that experience from one generation to another. This, in my judgment, is the most important gift Pentecostalism continues to offer those of us who belong to other religious traditions and communities.

A concern about this, which has haunted me for a long time, came to focus in a conversation I had in the mid-seventies with Bishop K. H. Ting. Before the communist victory in China, Ting had been the Secretary of the World Student Christian Federation for North America and later worked out of its international office in Geneva. Then he returned to China and was a member of the Chinese delegation to the General Assembly of the Federation in 1955. I met him there and came to admire him a great deal but lost all contact with him during the Cultural Revolution. When he was able, for the first time after that, to leave China, to attend a conference of World Religions and Peace, in Princeton, we met again.

In the midst of our conversation about many things, I asked him: "Returning to North America after this long absence and your experience in China, what is your first reaction?" He replied immediately: "Moral decadence." When I seemed surprised by his answer, he added: "Decadence is the inability of one generation to pass on to the next generation the vision and convictions by which it has lived."

After that conversation, I began to take a new look at what was happening around me and what I had been doing. My own life, since childhood, had been grounded in a compelling faith in Jesus Christ, which had produced a passion to explore, live, and share that faith and to strive to revitalize or create communities of faith dedicated to express this faith and life in transformative action in the world. I had no doubts that what I and many others were doing in the church would orient and sustain a new generation capable of responding in new ways to an ever-changing situation.

In my work with young people in the churches, and especially with students, I often got a positive, even enthusiastic response. As time went on, however, many of those who responded this way failed to find a context for further growth in the church. Some settled down to limited participation in congregational life. Others left the church. But those who stayed in the church rarely seemed to do very much to revitalize or re-create it or to pass on to others, in or out of the church, a contagious faith.

Among those who left the church, I found very few who felt compelled to keep on searching until they found a vital community, or who attempted to find a few others like themselves with whom to create a new faith community. Many were led by their early faith experience to become involved in social action for fundamental social change, and some chose their professions with this in mind. But I couldn't escape the conclusion that, as they reached a dead end in one after another of the movements for social change in which they were involved, they tended to concentrate more and more of their efforts on advancement in their professional life, rather than risking taking initiatives in experiments and actions that might open new possibilities. But whatever option they or I chose, we rarely succeeded in communicating a contagious faith committed to social transformation to a significant number of a new generation.

I spent most of four decades teaching seminary students. I did this because I was convinced that those who had a vital faith experience and a sense of calling to service had gone to seminary determined to discover how to spend their lives supporting, renewing, or re-creating communities of faith as the source of life and instruments of God's transforming presence and coming reign. If they could not find the right opportunity to live out that calling in the pastorate, then they would at least seek ways to find new expressions of faith and community, in relation to the needs and suffering of an ever more desperate human situation. What I have seen, however, is that those who have not found a place in the church to cultivate and live out that vision turn sooner or later to another "profession" that largely determines the direction of their lives. In it they may be doing many good things, but somehow the compulsion to strive to create a contagious community of faith rarely seems to be a priority.

Others do find their place within the institutional church or one of its institutions, and they do what they can to follow their ideals within it. Yet the question of whether the institution they are serving is really a faithful church of Jesus Christ or is contributing to the coming realization of the reign of God seldom seems to be a burning concern that might lead them to give up the position, prestige, and income they have secured in order to reproduce, in new forms of church life, the vision and conviction out of which their faith was born and nurtured. Without taking that step, we may be able to do very little to reproduce, in a new generation, the quality of church life that nurtured and sustained us.

My immersion in Pentecostalism has been so important for me because it has thrown me into the midst of people who have a faith so meaningful and so compelling that it determines their life and destiny, a faith that is contagious and that comes to them as a calling to which they assume they must respond, a calling that is not a burden but a gift of grace. At any one time and place it may be visibly present in only a few women and men. Among lay persons, it manifests itself as a commitment to evangelism, to be followed wherever it may lead. Or as a vision of service to others that leads people to change the direction of their business or dare to undertake new ventures more related to the need around them. Furthermore, while many Pentecostal pastors sooner or later feel the attraction of the status and economic rewards that accompany successful pastoral work, I continue to meet women and men for whom a commitment to evangelism sets the terms for their lives, or who are willing to risk starting new churches without any financial support from a new church development program, or to embark on other ventures of faith, however insecure. For them, confidence in the presence and power of the Spirit somehow tends to break the hold over them of our commonly taken-for-granted middle-class professional values.

In the face of their witness, the issue, as I see it, is to be involved with those, wherever they are, who are keeping this vision alive and are thus making available, to a new generation, a form of Christian faith and life that has the power to plant the seeds of new life and community in a world becoming ever more destructive of individual and community life.

8 The Pentecostal Experience: Source of Power for Social Transformation?

I f there was ever a time when the world desperately needed women and men on fire with the power of God, motivated for and committed to the struggle for its restoration, it is now. For what is at stake at the present time is not only the survival of hundreds of millions of broken and impoverished people, but the re-creation of conditions for a human existence in society and the salvation of this planet from threatening ecological disaster.

In this situation many Christians around the world are discovering or rediscovering the centrality, in our biblical heritage, of God's concern for the poor and exploited and Jesus' passion for the "reign of God," God's new order of life. In response to this word, and the calling which accompanies it, faith in Christ is leading many to enter into solidarity with the poor and the struggle for justice through the transformation of economic, social, and political structures.

Yet when we turn to our churches, we see little evidence that this experience of God or the passion it creates has come to occupy a central place in their life and work. In the older, more established churches, if that passion was once present, it has been largely lost, except as it manifests itself from time to time in a few individuals or small groups responding to urgent and specific human needs. While these persons and groups have shown a great deal of vitality for a time, they seem strangely incapable of reproducing themselves in response to new situations. The one exception to this has been more conservative Evangelical groups, which have shown greater vitality and staying power but have often been limited by a rationalistic fundamentalist theology and a static and rigid ethical stance.

In Latin America, the Christian base communities became the incarnation of this faith that created a new life in community among those dedicated to the struggle for liberation and that grew rapidly across the continent. Today the vitality and impact of these communities in society are much less evident, and they seem to have largely lost their former capacity to reproduce themselves.

Moreover, it is now evident, as we have shown earlier, that any hope for the reconstruction of human life in society today depends first of all upon initiatives and energies coming from significant numbers of the poorest and most marginal people, through the transformation of their *religious* life. Consequently, for those of us who hope to be faithful to our rediscovered heritage and participate in any significant way in this struggle for life as it is now taking shape, the burning question is that of how to discover and be bearers of God's passion for life and for justice, how to communicate it to others, and how to relate, from this position, to the religious world of the poor and marginal and live in solidarity with them in their struggle. For those who are the victims of the established order, the issue becomes that of cultivating and communicating a compelling and transformative experience of faith powerful enough to make them subjects and drive them to dynamic action in response to God's call to struggle for social transformation. In the face of this challenge, most of us in our middle-class churches have to recognize that we have little or no connection with the victims of our present order, are at a loss to know how to change that situation, and by and large are lacking the richness and depth of experience of the presence and power of God necessary for dynamic participation in this struggle for life.

The Growing Involvement of Pentecostals in the Struggle for Life

At the same time, our engagement with Pentecostals has convinced us that they not only have this richness and depth of experience but that many individuals and communities are becoming increasingly involved in a variety of forms of social action as a direct result of this faith experience. Bernardo Campos, a leading Latin American Pentecostal theologian, has put it this way: "Today's Pentecostals have achieved a new level of maturity. Increasingly they desire to become subjects of their own history and are casting their lot with the new forces emerging in our societies," close to and identified with the "people as an organic unity."[1]

Moreover, they have demonstrated their ability to reach and convert vast numbers of the most impoverished and broken people who, because of their social position, have the strongest desire to change the existing order of things in the direction of greater equality and justice. It is now evident that the passion to do this was an integral part of the Pentecostal experience from the very beginning. Walter Hollenweger declares that for William Seymour, "Pentecost meant more than speaking in tongues. It meant to love in the face of hate, to overcome the hatred of a whole nation by demonstrating that Pentecost is something very different from the success-oriented American way of life." It is thus not surprising that the first Pentecostal community cut across class and racial lines, something which, in that time and place, was most revolutionary.[2] As the growth of Pentecostalism continues especially in Africa and Latin America, among people whose lives are rooted in cultures that do not separate the body and the spirit, as we do in the West, or the individual and social well-being, many of these movements are becoming increasingly involved in diverse struggles for societal transformation.

Our study of these churches in Brazil found little evidence of the development of a theology of social responsibility. The sermons we lis-

---

1. Bernardo L. Campos M., "In the Power of the Spirit: Pentecostalism, Theology, and Social Ethics," in *In the Power of the Spirit. Pentecostals in Latin America: A Challenge to the Historic Churches,* ed. Benjamín F. Gutiérrez and Dennis A. Smith (Mexico: AIPRAL, 1996), p. 45.

2. Quoted by Cheryl Bridges Johns, *Pentecostal Formation: A Pedagogy among the Oppressed* (Sheffield: Sheffield Academic Press, 1993), p. 67.

tened to rarely revealed careful study of the social dimensions of the biblical witness or of the structures of injustice in society. While the pastors are showing a rapidly growing interest in the presence of the church as a political force, thus far this interest has been directed primarily toward the support of political parties identified with the status quo, from whom the pastors might gain favors of one kind or another for the church.

At the same time, we found massive evidence of the power of these movements to touch the lives of the poorest and most excluded, to help them reorganize their lives, and to give them a new sense of identity and hope for the future. In a society in which all forms of life in community are in crisis, they are creating new human relations in community at the most basic level of society. All of this indicates that they may become a more significant force for changes throughout society than we can imagine at this time.

The Need for a Radical Change of Attitude of Mainline Churches

As awareness of these developments grows in mainline churches, we can see a significant shift in attitude. Rather than speaking of Pentecostal churches as an expression of "alienation," or a refuge from the world for those most harmed by it, we hear more about the need to recognize their positive contributions and make efforts to relate to them, even to see them as our partners. Alexandre Brasil Fonseca, writing "Pentecostals and Society: A History of Desires," in a publication of Koinonia, a leading Brazilian ecumenical organization, speaks about this changed attitude: "It is fundamental that other sectors of society, concerned about a more just society, recognize Pentecostal churches as possible partners. This calls for a dose of 'patience' that might permit dialogue with Pentecostals and their peculiar language."

This certainly represents an important change in attitude, but it doesn't go far enough. With all that it represents in a new openness to Pentecostals, it still assumes that we can approach them without expecting to be called into question. We assume that our understanding of faith and of social reality is superior to theirs. Thus, in any dialogue or collaboration with them, we must be "patient" and find ways to relate to their "peculiar language."

If, however, the conclusions we have reached in this study are valid, then the nature of the dialogue must be quite different. We also are well aware of what seems to us a "peculiar language," as well as the limitations of their articulation of their theology, especially when judged from the perspective of our theological systems. We're convinced, however, that something much more important is taking place here. As we have affirmed repeatedly, they are presenting us with a new interpretation and experience of the Christian faith, which could contribute to the development of a new paradigm from which to re-create our theology and orient and motivate a more dynamic response to the growing crisis of our society.

If this is the case, then we enter into dialogue with them not from the security of our position, but rather with the recognition that, as we relate to them, *we might be radically changed.* For this to happen, it will be imperative for us to allow them to open our eyes to the reality of their world and their struggle, as well as to the nature and power of their faith as understood, experienced, and lived by them. As we do this, we will probably not be converted to their position, but we may find ourselves struggling to articulate a new paradigm that is authentic for us, our history, and our situation. As we do this, we will not only discover new resources to help us find our own way. We will also learn what it means to be real partners, in a relationship of mutual respect and give-and-take, in which each of us grows as we enable the other to be more faithful.

For us, what this means specifically is that we must be willing to start with their witness to the centrality of the presence and power of the Holy Spirit in our experience of the faith and our reflection on it: the Spirit that spoke through the prophets; the Spirit that filled the life of Jesus leading him to identify himself with the poor and excluded and empowering his mighty works as signs of the coming reign of God; and the Spirit manifested on the day of Pentecost as the continuing presence and work of Jesus reaching out through his witnesses to the ends of the world for the fulfillment of the biblical promise of a new heaven and new earth, where justice and compassion reign. Our engagement with Pentecostals around this vision of a transformed world can, we believe, lead us into further exploration of a number of areas of Christian social responsibility.

Hearing and Living the Fullness of the "Good News"

For centuries in much of Protestantism the "good news" of the gospel has been limited to a message of *spiritual salvation for the individual.* Consequently, most members of our churches pay little attention to social sins and have little spiritual motivation to struggle for social transformation.

This is quite contrary to the theology of the Reformation, especially in Calvinism, but it is rarely taken into account in our churches, except among small groups. In recent decades, however, the theology of liberation, in its diverse expressions, has demonstrated, through thorough biblical and theological studies, that God's salvific work has to do with the fullness of human life, spiritual and material, individual and social. Many theologians and biblical scholars in Europe and North America have been influenced by this and have done their own work to develop it further in their context.

Liberation theology has gradually transformed the faith and action of significant numbers of women and men in both Catholic and Protestant circles but has left those captivated by this vision more acutely aware of how few have heard about or embraced this understanding. Thus far, it is evident that few of our churches have been willing to give this a central place in their preaching, teaching, and action.

When we look for resources for changing this situation, we rarely if ever turn to the Pentecostals with the expectation that we might learn something from them. This, I believe, is a very serious mistake. While they have not made many efforts to develop a theology of social responsibility clearly integrating the personal and the social, a number of things are happening in their communities in which this integration is a reality. As it takes place, it does so in such a way that challenges our generally accepted theological perspective, and it could set new terms for dialogue.

(1) We usually start out with people who are relatively at home within the structures in which they live, without any earth-shaking experience of the divine that creates a state of tension with their world. If at some point in their lives they are moved by a vital religious experience, it is usually a limited "spiritual" experience leading, at most, to the transformation of personal life. For those socially concerned, the issue becomes how to open their faith to dimensions of discipleship that are not an essential part of their overall religious perspective.

Pentecostals, however, start out as victims of a society that has excluded them, dominated by forces of evil that are destroying their lives and the world. Moreover, for many of them, in the religious realm, the separation of body and spirit, the personal and the social, is alien to their perception, and thus the integration of the two is not of primary concern. What is important is their profound experience of the Spirit as an all-encompassing reality that has given them new life. This Spirit of God is doing powerful, even incredible things now not only in their lives but also in their world.

In this context, the question to be posed by Pentecostals for themselves is not how to bring together the individual and the social. It is rather how to be aware of and faithful to the biblical witness to the nature of the Spirit and its action in the world rather than to be subject to imported theologies that are alien to their background and faith. The question posed by this witness for us is how we can be grasped by an experience of the Spirit that opens our eyes to the dehumanizing and demonic forces in our culture and society and provides us with the motivation and the drive to struggle for the manifestation of God's reign in our midst.

(2) We attempt to overcome the dichotomy between the individual and the social by working out an overall theological position based on the Bible and then developing the implications of it for diverse areas of society. Or, if we have been influenced by liberation theology, we seek to achieve this same end by an integration of theory and praxis, which still relies very much on a rational ordering of our understanding of the gospel and of the functioning of the structures of society. In Pentecostalism, a new social consciousness and commitment is emerging in a quite different way.

This is developing, as I see it, as a consequence of what we might call the leading of the Spirit in the lives of people trying to find their way in the midst of their struggle for survival in a world in transition. This has been expressed best by two Pentecostal theologians we have cited earlier.

Juan Sepulveda speaks of what has happened in Chile as people experiencing the overwhelming reality of hunger, poverty, crisis in the family, and despair have processed all this in the context of the spiritual reality they are living in prayer and worship. This, according to Sepulveda, has become, for many congregations, an "imperative call to action" and has resulted in the enrichment of worship, which, in turn, has sustained "daring action in the face of adversity."[3] According to Bernardo Campos, "the transforming power of Pentecostalism resides not in the coherence of its doctrine, but in its flexibility and its capacity to give expression to new social practices in the defining moments of a society in transition."[4]

(3) What I perceive here is not that Pentecostals consider unimportant or unnecessary any attempt to arrive at a rational understanding of their world or their faith, but that they come to the Bible and social reality with a different type of perception. With it, they find ways to put their world together, to order their life by their faith and to respond to issues confronting them in society. We may not understand how all this works, and we may raise serious questions about the conclusions to which they are at times led. However, we cannot ignore the fact that they often find resources for thought and action that others around them do not have. More than that, if we make the effort to understand what is going on with them, we may find that they are perceiving dimensions of reality and ways of relating experience and reason that we thus far have not explored.

One example of this is reported in a long article in the *Philadelphia Inquirer* about the desperate situation of miners in communities in Appalachia where the mines in which they worked all their lives have been closed. The report speaks primarily about their loss of jobs and income, their loss of their self-worth and of hope, and about how many of them, in their desperation, have committed suicide. Yet the article also tells the story of one Kenneth Cox, who became a Pentecostal pastor, which made it possible for him to re-create his life and his family, become actively involved in the life of the community, and experience a rebirth of hope. In his words: "I guess a lot of men around here thought about hanging it up when the mines went down, but the chickens, the Little League I coach and the church, I guess that's what kept me from suicide. I haven't lost my dreams. I may have lost my paycheck but not those dreams."

I have gotten new insight into what this is all about by reading a book written by Deborah Levenson-Estrada regarding the long struggle by Guatemalan workers in the Coca Cola factory in Guatemala.[5] In it she

3. *Signos de Vida* 2 (1992).

4. Campos, "In the Power of the Spirit," p. 49.

5. Deborah Levenson-Estrada, *Trade Unionists against Terror: Guatemala City, 1954-1958* (Chapel Hill: University of North Carolina Press, 1994).

tells the story of the persistence of members of the union over a period of thirty years in their struggle in the face of terror and all that goes with it. Her primary concern is to discover how they were able to resist and finally win out in the face of increasing impoverishment, constant threats on their lives, and the assassination of several of their leaders and members. She discovered that some workers were motivated and sustained by socialist ideology, others by their Mayan identity and culture. She realized, however, that the workers drew their inspiration largely from Christianity. Some were oriented and sustained by the resources they found in progressive Catholic Action groups and in liberation theology. Yet of greater significance was a deep-rooted popular Christianity in which "no line existed between suffering and joy, camaraderie and mockery, life and death, celebration and mourning."

We may never really get inside the logic of faith as expressed by these individuals and groups, and we certainly cannot expect them to pay much attention to the theology of social responsibility or of liberation as we have articulated it thus far. However, what we are going to see, I believe, is a growing commitment, in Pentecostal circles, to the poor and their struggle, which will need a solid biblical and theological foundation to sustain it.

To cite only one example, found where one might least expect it, in the leading editorial of the 24 September 1995 issue of *Folha Universal,* the paper published weekly by the IURD: the author affirms that while the gospel is for all, at the same time Jesus gave special attention to the poor. "To them he directed his most tender and comforting words, promised the most precious blessings, and guaranteed the greatest rewards. . . . Even if the dominant and powerful call them 'alienated' or 'weak in the head,' the Lord grants them permanent company, relief, rest, and calls them to learn with Him."

As this type of awareness grows, it might be greatly enriched by the work of many biblical scholars and theologians in Latin America that has been done and continues to be performed when the right conditions for dialogue can be found. This will not be easy. For whether we who are not Pentecostals have been oriented by the theology of liberation or the social consciousness emerging from more Evangelical circles, we tend to be satisfied with our own theological stance and hope that Pentecostals will accept it, or at least be more open to it. Perhaps we are now being called to rely less on our well-defined systems and risk centering our reflection on the presence and power of the Spirit as the source of surprising new insights and directions. With this, we are challenged to explore new ways of thinking theologically and biblically as we take much more seriously the type of rationality and the structure of the thought of poor and marginal people.

What this means we will only come to know as we venture along this road. I think it significant, however, that Bernardo Campos is convinced that this should lead Pentecostals to develop their insights more in contact with indigenous religions and popular Christianity, for they will find there something more accessible and useful theologically than the rational categories and systems of the ancient Christian tradition — Hebrew, Greek, and Latin. This might be worthy of consideration by those of us who are not Pentecostals as well.

9 *Spiritual Formation:*
Growth toward the Reign of God

I f the Christian community is to be a force for social transformation, it must be a community of people who undergo an experience of conversion to the crucified and risen Christ, now present in the world through the Holy Spirit, who is calling and empowering them to participate with him in the transformation of human life and the world in the direction of God's reign. A conversion of this sort opens up for us a radically different perception of life and the world and gives a new center and direction to our lives. Thus, to become a disciple of Christ means to follow a disciplined process of growth in awareness of this world and what Christ is doing in it. *It also calls for a process of growth in response to Christ's call to discipleship.* As this experience is a gift of new life and hope, response to it leads inevitably to dynamic witness to an ever-widening circle of people. As the reign of God coming to reality in Christ is "good news" especially for the poor and marginal people of the world, discipleship leads us inevitably toward solidarity with them in their struggle for life.

For those of us at home in our more established churches, all this may sound rather scandalous. At the very least, it is quite outside the pale of what happens in our churches and their programs. But for those of us in positions of privilege, more or less at home in our world, following Christ calls for nothing less than a radical change of values and lifestyle, which can only happen as we make a clear decision to change the direction of our lives and then make a *constant* effort, over time, to work out the implications of this in our personal lives, our work, and our relation to our society and its problems.

For those who are denied an opportunity to a full life in the existing order, this also involves an experience of conversion and a process of change and growth. For them it is an experience of the presence and power of God that can open their eyes to what is really happening around them, break its hold over them, give them a new sense of worth and self identity, and empower them to act to change their lives, community, and society. In both instances, life becomes a serious and exciting journey in the direction of God's reign, an ongoing process of growth and change.

In our various faith traditions, Catholic and Protestant, this has often been a matter of crucial importance: in Catholic circles, a rich heritage of spiritual formation; in Calvinism, the centrality of spiritual and ethical disciplines in each local congregation; in Methodism and the Holiness movements, the central importance of sanctification. Yet in most of our churches in recent times, this emphasis on a disciplined process of spiritual formation for the life of faith has largely been lost.

Today, with the renewed interest in spirituality, we have an opportunity not only to re-create but to go beyond what we have inherited and participate in the development of models of spiritual formation responsive to the leading of the Spirit in a new historical situation. However, the efforts being made thus far have, in my judgment, serious limitations. Some of them are leading many to a growing concern for human need and suffering, but I have not found much evidence that their fundamental theological orientation — their understanding of God and God's relation to the world, and thus of the Christian life — integrates the individual "spiritual" relationship with God with the wider dimensions of God's salvific action. In mainline churches at least, even our most vital models of spiritual formation mean very little for the masses of poor and broken people at home or abroad.

At the same time, something is happening among Third World Christians, which could mark the beginning of a new era in spiritual formation. In Latin America, it manifested itself first in the Christian base communities, in which poor women and men with a vital religious faith became increasingly aware of their situation of oppression and the causes of it at the same time that they were, through Bible study in small groups, discovering that the God they worshipped was on the side of the poor, active on their behalf, and very close to them in the midst of their struggles for life.

As priests and pastoral agents worked with the poor, they realized that the poor were, by and large, submerged in a closed world that they did not understand, and they were unable to break its hold over them. If they were to appropriate and give expression to their faith, they had the urgent need of a process by which they could become aware of the nature of the reality of the poor, overcome its power over them, develop a new sense of self, and discover how they could be engaged in the struggle to transform their world and continue to grow in their faith and commitment to the process. In other words, a new understanding and experience of the fullness of the gospel message called for a new type of spiritual formation that would incorporate this dimension of faith.

As these pastoral agents worked at this with a group of educators, attempting to develop resources for such a process, one of the educators, Paulo Freire, developed a radically new philosophy of education and a pedagogical methodology that, while focused on the wider problem of liberating education rather than on spiritual formation, responded to this need. It provided the base communities with a philosophical undergirding and a methodology for such a process of growth in faith and discipleship, which became a major factor in the development of a new process of spiritual formation, which could mark the beginning of a new era in this realm.

Freire, facing daily the depth of suffering of the poor and marginalized in a world where the whole system contributed to their exploitation and oppression, nevertheless perceived the world as open, in a process of becoming, and human life as unfinished, striving for completeness. In this context, every human being has an "ontological vocation" to become a subject acting to transform the world and thus move toward ever new possibilities of a fuller and richer life individually and collectively.

Yet human beings, especially those oppressed, are submerged in the world that oppresses them. They are thus unable to objectify their world or know it in a critical manner, and as long as they are in this situation, they cannot emerge as subjects capable of acting to change it. Moreover, a new identity as subjects is not something that can be "given" to them; it is something they must acquire "by conquest." Perceiving the human situation in this way, Freire dedicated all his thought and educational efforts to the development of a process of "conscientization." By finding the central themes dominating their lives, making visual images of them, and creating conditions for dialogue about them, the educator made it possible for people submerged in this reality to "problematize" it. Engaging in dialogue about it, they were enabled to identify the conditions that imprisoned them and see them as "limit situations" which they could confront and overcome. This process gave them an experience of freedom and empowerment for action. This action, in turn, led to new insights into their situation and their own lives as well. From this would come a new process of "problematization," creating conditions for a new stage of dialogue leading to action.

In the Christian base communities, this became a powerful instrument for a new type of spirituality. Poor Christians with a vital faith, studying the Bible in their situation of oppression and drawing on Freire's process of conscientization, developed a process of interaction between their study of the Bible and their situation, which led to a profound transformation in their perception of the world around them and of their own potential and empowered them to act dynamically in movements for social change and liberation. Along this path, many of them experienced a deepening of Christian faith and of commitment to this struggle, which led them to risk their lives, even to the point of martyrdom. In other words, this integration of a new understanding and experience of the gospel with the pedagogical perspective and methodology provided by Freire produced a radical new process of spiritual formation of particular appeal and relevance for Christians in situations of dehumanization and injustice.

Since that time, Freire's thought, best expressed in his *Pedagogy of the Oppressed,* first published in English in 1970, has become known around the world. It has made a major impact in educational circles, and its implications for Christian education have been developed by a number of scholars in North and South America. Unfortunately, thus far our mainline churches have paid little attention to the work of Freire or to the revolutionary significance of the Christian base communities.

Now, even with all the interest being shown in spirituality and in growth in the experience and practice of the Christian faith, I'm aware of only one effort on the part of communities of women and men committed to spiritual formation to enter into dialogue with and draw on the resources of Freire to develop a process of conversion and spiritual formation through which women and men who come to vital experience of God in Christ are caught up in a process of formation that leads them more and more into dynamic involvement in community reconstruction and social transformation. This unique effort is being made by a team of scholars at the Church of God School of Theology in Cleveland, Tennessee. The key person on the team is Cheryl Bridges Johns, author of *Pentecostal Formation: A Pedagogy among the Oppressed* as well as a number of articles on the same topic.

I'm not in a position to assess the significance of her work within the Pentecostal context. But since what she is doing is, in my judgment, breaking new ground in the area of spiritual formation and can be an important resource for those of us who are not Pentecostals as well, I want to present briefly what I believe she is contributing to the type of reflection and action called for above. It is important for us to keep in mind something that she mentions at the beginning of her work: Both Freire's theory of conscientization and Pentecostalism have arisen out of the experience of Third World peoples and aim at helping them to become aware of their socio-cultural reality as that of injustice and oppression, and to discover how to struggle dynamically to change that reality.

Bridges Johns declares that Pentecostals as well as those who follow Freire's pedagogy are essentially committed to and engaged in a process of conscientization, which aims at a radical change in the perception of reality, social as well as personal, and which in turn leads to commitment to an ongoing struggle for personal and social transformation. While they function out of different frames of reference, each has a contribution to make to the other.

Pentecostalism had its origin in William Seymour's vision of a radical transformation of American life. Central in the Holiness movement was a utopian vision of reality. From time to time in its relatively short history, those experiencing the power of the Spirit in their lives and in the world have been led to dedicate themselves to "ushering in the kingdom of God." This, according to Bridges Johns, is the foundation for a process of conscientization initiated and maintained by a transforming encounter with God, "which prefigures the corresponding historical action."[1] Consequently, Pentecostalism is in a position to connect with and be transformed by the pedagogical work of Freire, which might make it possible for it to "both retain and recapture its revolutionary nature as a movement which can change the course of human history."[2] At the same time, Pentecostalism is able to offer an alternative process of conscientization to that of Freire. By taking seriously the religious experience of the marginalized, Pentecostalism is in a position to transform the process into a more effective instrument in their struggle for liberation.

Freire, as we have seen, perceives the world and human life as unfinished and in the process of becoming. In the world as it is now structured, oppressed people are caught, but through the dynamics of conscientization they can learn to examine social, political, and economic injustices in order to take action to correct them. Furthermore, Freire has developed a pedagogy that provides the instruments needed for achieving this goal.

For Pentecostals, the world and human life are also unfinished, in the process of becoming. They perceive all of this as set in the context of and permeated by a divine reality that, through the presence and power of the Holy Spirit, is actualizing the reign of God, the signs of which are already present. Thus, the everyday reality of the world and life as we know it concretely is constantly being acted upon by God in a way that contradicts the world as it is and opens up before us a compelling new reality. Those who experience the impact of the world as it is and at the same time live in the Spirit and bring their experience of the world into dialogue with the biblical narrative are living a process in which they make ever new discoveries of the falseness of the closed world in which they are immersed, and also of an alternative reality in which they can participate "to make God's history upon the earth."[3]

In a serious engagement with Freire, Pentecostals, according to Bridges Johns, are challenged to recover elements of their own heritage,

1. Cheryl Bridges Johns, *Pentecostal Formation: A Pedagogy among the Oppressed* (Sheffield: Sheffield Academic Press, 1993), p. 65.

2. Bridges Johns, *Pentecostal Formation,* p. 9.

3. Bridges Johns, *Pentecostal Formation,* p. 71.

which could undergird, orient, and motivate their life in the world. They are also challenged to relate the movement of the Spirit toward the reign of God to their concrete historical situation and to draw on Freire's pedagogical and methodological resources for the articulation of a process of spiritual formation more faithful to their own heritage.

At the same time, in what I consider to be her most original and creative contribution, Bridges Johns claims that Pentecostalism has the potential to transform the process of conscientization and the methodology developed by Freire, thus making it a more faithful pedagogy of the oppressed. If taken seriously, this could have revolutionary consequences far beyond Pentecostal circles.

- It creates a process of conscientization that is not primarily a cognitive process, elevating reasoning skills above all other forms of knowledge, but one enriched by a blending of the rational with the affective, thus bringing it much closer to the thought and experience of the poor.
- In Pentecostalism the effort to know reality is not limited to abstract rational analysis of the world in an objective way. Rather, reality is explored and known in and through the experience of women and men who are struggling to understand what is happening to them and why this is happening in the context of their faith.
- By giving priority to *oral* means of communication among people in oral cultures, it is able to start with the thinking — and way of thinking — of the people. This helps those with special skills and training to overcome the temptation to approach the poor with a predetermined agenda, rather than entering into and honoring their own ways of perceiving and reflecting upon their reality.
- Such a process of conscientization has the possibility of taking seriously the full experience of people in their social reality, including the religious experience of the poorest, which rational analysis is incapable of doing.
- By situating this whole process in the context of the experience of the Holy Spirit oriented toward the establishment of the reign of God, the signs of which are appearing all along the way, it can provide a much more powerful motivation for struggle than any political ideology or social analysis can produce.

In Brazil, we have met or have known of members as well as pastors of Pentecostal communities who have lived or are now living a process of conscientization, even though they have never heard of Paulo Freire or of the process of spiritual formation developed by Bridges Johns and others. This was evident in the decade of the sixties, when the Peasant Leagues were very strong in northeast Brazil. At that time, many members of the more conservative Assemblies of God, without pastoral support and with only the Bible, especially the prophets, to nourish them, not only joined these Leagues but often provided leadership for them. In more recent times, Pentecostal peasants without land or whose land has been taken from them have reacted energetically and at times become leaders of groups acting to occupy land not being cultivated or to reclaim land taken from them. One such leader declared: "this business of being a brother only in church doesn't hold up any longer. What matters is being a brother in everything, including in the struggle."

Whether Pentecostals in Brazil will discover the resources provided by Freire's process of conscientization for the development of a process of spiritual formation more in tune with their own heritage and faith remains to be seen. However, those of us who are not Pentecostal could take on the challenge presented here to develop a process for our own spiritual formation that would be more biblical, both in its theological orientation and in its revolutionary social witness.

10 *Laying the Foundation for a New Order*

A s is evident in the last two chapters, our study has convinced us that Pentecostals are not only making a tremendous contribution to the reorganization of the lives of individual women and men but also engaging in creating new elementary forms of community and social life. While not yet possessing a clearly worked-out theology of social responsibility and often limited by an "individualistic" and "spiritualistic" approach, they are in many instances emerging as an important force for social transformation, especially among poor and marginal people. In fact, their witness, with all its limitations, has led us to the realization that the foundational experience of the Holy Spirit, which is not limited to Pentecostalism, may come to have a transformative impact on society far beyond anything we have imagined until now. The limited and often inconsistent witness of Pentecostals points to this reality as well as this potential in a number of ways.

(1) Entrance into the realm of the Spirit along with the experience of conversion often results in a new way of perceiving the world as well as what is happening in daily life, which makes it possible for Pentecostals to envision a different world and gives them power to struggle for it. In the words of Donald Dayton, the experience of Pentecostal worship and ec-

clesiastical life "seems to create an alternative reality that not only sustains one in the course of a mundane and monotonous existence, but generates the energy with which one can imagine a new and more just world, not just beyond this world, but transforming life in the here and now."[1]

(2) Especially among women, who constitute the majority in most Pentecostal churches, this spiritual experience produces an extraordinary new quality of life, which has a decisive impact on the family and also on the church and society. Senia Pilco Tarira, a Pentecostal educator in Ecuador, speaks of the amazing results of this experience:

> The desire on the part of Pentecostal women to serve God is so great that they dedicate and give themselves completely to the work of the church even in the midst of unfavorable circumstances. When they join a congregation, they come with a profound sense of their own lack of worth, abandonment, and oppression, sharpened by the strong competition existing in society, even among women, who struggle to get a few of the "crumbs" that society offers.

When they are welcomed in Pentecostal churches, they find "communities of healing" where sisterly love helps them to recover from the fierce individualism characteristic of the society in which they live. In this atmosphere of support and solidarity women experience great changes in their lives and feel the compelling need to witness to others about what God and the brothers and sisters of the churches, their "extended family," have done to bring about the complete transformation of their lives.[2]

(3) One sociologist in Brazil, Paul Freston, declares that he and other sociologists now see Pentecostalism as a source of effective changes because it creates communities of discontinuity and transformation, confronts machismo more effectively than feminism, deals convincingly with matters of money, sickness, moral crises, and family problems, and is able to offer the principal alternative to the drug culture by giving people a new identity and values.[3] We might add to this one other fact: By calling

1. *Bulletin of CELEP* 107, p. 92.
2. Senia Pilco Tarira, "Testimonial de la Mujer Pentecostal en Ecuador," in *En la fuerza del Espiritu. Los Pentecostales en America Latina: un desafío a las iglesias historicas,* ed. Benjamín F. Gutiérrez and Dennis A. Smith (Mexico: AIPRAL, 1996), pp. 240-41.
3. See *Veja,* Rio de Janeiro, 10 October 1994.

upon the poor to give rather than receive, Pentecostals contribute significantly to breaking the attitude of dependency so deeply rooted among
marginal peoples. As Cecília Mariz puts it: By not giving to the poor, Pentecostals "make it possible for the poor to no longer be subjectively poor."[4]

Seeking the Path to Social Reconstruction Today

While affirming all this, there still remains, for me, an important and dis-
turbing question. Even if what is here claimed is happening and growing,
how important is it as a means of social change? What contribution can it
make to the construction of a new, more just, and more egalitarian society? Good actions of service, however necessary they may be for some in
the daily struggle for survival, will not bring about the structural changes
so urgently needed at the present time.

At the same time, those of us who have focused our efforts on clearly
defined political strategies in the hopes of bringing about such change
must take into account the implications of the new social reality that un-
derlies much of our reflection here. In a relatively stable society, in which
the most basic social, economic, and political structures are more or less
intact and play a major role in maintaining human life in society, effective
action to transform these structures must have a clearly defined political
character. Any action to relieve human suffering or overcome oppression
or injustice must, of necessity, focus on this task. However, that's not the
reality vast numbers of poor and excluded people are living today. They
experience daily what I think we must now identify as a crisis of civilization, in which all major structures and institutions — centralized governments, political parties, bureaucracies of all sorts, economic structures,
and many organizations that are most basic to life in society — are not
only in a state of crisis but are in many instances in a process of disintegration. How do we contribute to the reconstruction of society when this
is happening?

In this situation, many of us, accustomed to working for change in

4. "Pentecostalism and Confrontation with Poverty in Brazil," in *In the Power of the Spirit. Pentecostals in Latin America: A Challenge to the Historic Churches,* ed. Benjamín F. Gutiérrez and Dennis A. Smith (Mexico City: AIPRAL, 1996), p. 47.

an earlier era, may be at a loss to know what to do. I would claim that it is precisely in moments of such acute crisis that we have a historic opportunity to participate in social reconstruction that could turn out to be more radical than what we have been doing until now because it means nothing less than the re-creation of life in community from its very foundation. If this is the case, then the poorest and most excluded can be the primary agents of such reconstruction, whether or not they perceive their struggle in this way.

As I expressed this three years ago in a lecture at the Seminario Bíblico Latinoamericano in Costa Rica, "It is possible that the most elementary efforts to reorganize and reconstruct life in community among the poorest may be much more important in the creation of a more human and more just society than we have tended to think until now: the formation of new types of extended families, initiatives in the informal economy on the part of individuals and groups that could point the way to alternatives to the present economic system, initiatives of young gang leaders toward reconciliation and toward the creation of work for their members, the formation of groups of Evangelicals in the worst slums and in prisons in which their members help each other to survive in the midst of violence and work to diminish it, and initiatives of drug addicts who undergo a conversion experience, overcome their addiction, and work together to solve their problems of housing and work."

Bishop Samuel Ruiz, of San Cristobal, Chiapas, has gone much further than I have in expressing what this might offer. As he perceives it, in situations where no total alternative exists, political or economic, people in civil society are simply going ahead and creating a transitional society. The people are becoming the government, deciding what needs to be done and doing it, and then demanding that the established government and others with power not only give them support but act responsibly.

The majority of those most involved in this are not functioning in terms of rational political ideologies but are more often people empowered by the Spirit who are coming to perceive their reality in a new way and respond to it. As they do this, they are calling for and helping to create new forms of social organization. As they work together to improve their economic situation and be more self-sufficient — starting with such basic needs as food, health care, and medicines — they may be creating alternatives to the "savage capitalism" now rampant. Working together to solve their problems, they have a sense of ownership of their creations and are thus less inclined to fall victims of corruption. In the midst of this common struggle — especially in the context of their religious faith — a new utopian vision may emerge.

In this situation, with this potential for social reconstruction, all of us, Pentecostals or mainline Christians, face the same challenge: to work together in order to draw fully on the resources of the Spirit at work in community to empower such efforts and to develop new forms of theological reflection on society, new processes of conscientization, and new strategies for action, which can contribute to the eventual emergence of a new and more just order.

Bibliography

Alves, Rubem. *Protestantism and Repression*. Maryknoll, N.Y.: Orbis Books, 1985.

Antoniazzi, Alberto, et al., eds. *Nem anjos nem demônios: Interpretações sociológicas do Pentecostalismo*. Petrópolis: Editora Vozes, 1994.

Bastide, Roger. *As religiões no Brasil: Uma contribuição a uma sociologia das interpenetrações de civilizações*. São Paulo: Pioneira, 1989.

Berger, Peter. *A Rumor of Angels*. New York: Anchor Books, 1990.

Beyer, Peter. *Religion and Globalization*. London: Sage, 1994.

Birman, Patrícia, Regina Novaes, and Samira Crespo, eds. *O mal à brasileira*. Rio de Janeiro: Editora UERJ, 1997.

Boff, Leonardo. *Church, Charism and Power*. New York: Crossroad, 1985.

Bridges Johns, Cheryl. *Pentecostal Formation: A Pedagogy among the Oppressed*. Sheffield: Sheffield Academic Press, 1993.

Burdick, Donald W. *Tongues — To Speak or Not to Speak: A Contemporary Analysis of Glossolalia*. Chicago: Moody Press, 1981.

Burdick, J. *Looking for God in Brazil*. Berkeley: University of California Press, 1993.

Campos, Luís de Castro, Jr. *Pentecostalismo*. São Paulo: Editora Ática, 1995.

Certeau, Michel de. "Cultura popular e religiosidade popular." *Cadernos do CEAS* 40 (Salvador) (November-December 1975).

Cleary, Edward L., and Hannah Stewart-Gambino, eds. *Power, Politics, and Pentecostals in Latin America.* Boulder, Colo.: Westview Press, 1997.

Comblin, José. *The Holy Spirit and Liberation.* Maryknoll, N.Y.: Orbis Books, 1989.

Conde, Emílio. *História das Assembléias de Deus no Brasil.* Rio de Janeiro, 1960.

Consejo Latinoamericano de Iglesias (CLAI). "Pentecostalismo: La fé que moviliza multitudes." *Signos de Vida* 3 (Quito, Equador) (1993).

Corten, André. *Pentecostalism in Brazil: Emotion of the Poor and Theological Romanticism.* New York: St. Martin's Press, 1999.

Covington, Dennis. *Salvation on Sand Mountain.* New York: Penguin Books, 1994.

Cox, Harvey. *Fire from Heaven.* New York: Addison-Wesley, 1995.

daMatta, Roberto. *A casa e a rua: espaço, cidadania, mulher e morte no Brasil.* São Paulo: Editora Brasiliense, 1985.

D'Épinay, Christian Lalive. *Haven of the Masses: A Study of the Pentecostal Movement.* London: Lutterworth Press, 1969.

———. "Religião, espiritualidade e sociedade." *Cadernos do ISER* 6 (Rio de Janeiro) (March 1977): .

Desroche, Henri. *Sociologia da esperança.* São Paulo: Edições Paulinas, 1985.

———. *O homem e suas religiões.* São Paulo: Edições Paulinas, 1985.

Dunn, James. *Jesus and the Spirit.* Philadelphia: Westminster Press, 1975.

Eliade, Mircea. *The Sacred and the Profane.* New York: Harper & Row, 1961.

Fernandes, Rubem César. "O debate entre sociólogos a propósito dos pentecostais." *Cadernos do ISER* 6 (Rio de Janeiro) (1977).

———. *Os cavaleiros do Bom Jesus: Uma introdução às religiões populares.* São Paulo: Editora Brasiliense, 1982.

———, ed. "Censo Institucional Evangélico — CIN." Rio de Janeiro: Núcleo de Pesquisa, ISER, 1992.

Freston, Paul. *Evangélicos na política brasileira: história ambígua e desafio ético.* Curitiba: Encontrão Editora, 1994.

Gomes, Wilson. "Cinco teses equivocadas sobre as novas seitas populares." *Cadernos do CEAS* 139 (Salvador) (1992): 40-53.

———. "Demônios do fim do século: curas, ofertas e exorcismos na Igreja Universal do Reino de Deus." *Cadernos do CEAS* 146 (Salvador) (July-August 1993): 47-63.

Gondim, Ricardo. *"O evangelho da nova era, uma análise e refutação bíblica da chamada Teologia da Prosperidade."* São Paulo: Abba Press, 1993.

Gromacki, Robert G. *The Modern Tongues Movement.* Grand Rapids: Baker Book House, 1972.

Gutiérrez, Benjamín F., and Dennis A. Smith, eds. *In the Power of the Spirit. Pentecostals in Latin America: A Challenge to the Historic Churches.* Mexico City: AIPRAL, 1996.

Gutiérrez, Gustavo. *A força histórica dos pobres.* Petrópolis: Editora Vozes, 1981.

Hollenweger, Walter J. *Pentecostalism: Origin and Developments Worldwide.* Peabody, Mass.: Hendrickson, 1997.

―――. "The Pentecostal Elites and the Pentecostal Poor: A Missed Dialogue?" In *Charismatic Christianity as a Global Culture,* edited by Karla Poewe. Columbia, S.C.: University of South Carolina Press, 1994.

―――. *The Pentecostals.* Peabody, Mass.: Hendrickson, 1988.

Justino, Mário. *Nos Bastidores do Reino: A vida secreta na Igreja Universal do Reino de Deus.* São Paulo: Geração Editorial, 1995.

Lawrence, Beverly Hall. *Reviving the Spirit.* New York: Grove Press, 1996.

Léonard, Emile-Guillaume. *O Protestantismo brasileiro: Estudo de eclesiologia e história social.* Rio de Janeiro/São Paulo: JUERP/ASTE, 1981.

Macedo, Edir. *Orixás, Caboclos e Guias.* Rio de Janeiro: Universal Produções, 1990.

―――. *A liberação da teologia.* Rio de Janeiro: Editora Gráfica Universal, 1992.

―――. *Aliança com Deus.* Rio de Janeiro: Editora Gráfica Universal, 1993.

―――. *O perfil do homen de Deus.* Rio de Janeiro: Editora Gráfica Universal, 1994.

―――. *O perfil da mulher de Deus.* Rio de Janeiro: Editora Gráfica Universal, 1995.

Machado, Maria das Dores Campos. *Carismáticos e pentecostais — Adesão religiosa na esfera familiar.* Campinas: Editora Autores Associados/ANPOCS, 1996.

Mainville, Odette. *L'Esprit dans l'oeuvre de Luc.* Montreal: Fides, 1991.

Maraschin, Jaci C., et al. *Religiosidade popular e misticismo no Brasil.* São Paulo: Edições Paulinas, 1984.

Mariano, Ricardo. "Os Neopentecostais e a teologia da prosperidade." *Novos Estudos* (CEBRAP) 44 (São Paulo) (March 1996).

Mariz, Cecília. *Coping with Poverty: Pentecostals and Christian Base Communities in Brazil.* Philadelphia: Temple University Press, 1994.

Mariz, Cecília, and Maria das Dores Machado. "Sincretismo e trânsito religioso: comparando Carismáticos e Pentecostais." *Comunicações do ISER* (Rio de Janeiro) (1994).

Martin, D. *Tongues of Fire: The Explosion of Protestantism in Latin America.* Oxford: Basil Blackwell, 1993.

McAlister, Roberto. *A esperiência Pentecostal — A base bíblica e teológica do Pentecostalismo.* Rio de Janeiro: Igreja da Nova Vida, 1977.

―――. *Dinheiro: um assunto altamente espiritual.* Rio de Janeiro: Carisma Editora, 1981.

Meeks, Wayne A. *The First Urban Christians.* New Haven: Yale University Press, 1983.

Mendonça, Antônio Gouvea. *O celeste porvir: A inserção do Protestantismo no Brasil.* São Paulo: Edições Paulinas, 1984.

Mendonça, Antônio Gouvea, and Prócoro Velasques Filho. *Introdução ao Protes-tantismo no Brasil.* São Paulo: Edições Loyola, 1990.

Novaes, Regina R. *Os escolhidos de Deus. Pentecostais, trabalhadores e cidadania.* Rio de Janeiro: ISER/Marco Zero, 1985.

Oliveira, Pedro A. Ribeiro de. "Movimentos carismáticos na América Latina; uma visão sociológica." *Cadernos do ISER* 5 (Rio de Janeiro) (November 1975).

Oro, Ari Pedro. "Religions pentecôtistes et moyens de communication de masse au Brésil." *Social Compass* 39.3 (Louvain) (September 1992).

Paleari, Giorgio. *O Deus fragmentado.* São Paulo: PUC, 1992.

Pierucci, A. F. O. "Liberdade de cultos na sociedade de serviço: em defesa do consumidor religioso." *Novos Estudos* (CEBRAP) 44 (São Paulo) (March 1996).

Pierucci, A. F. O., and Reginald Prandi. *A realidade social das religiões no Brasil.* São Paulo: Editora Hucitec, 1996.

Reily, Ducan A. *História documental do Protestantismo no Brasil.* São Paulo: ASTE, 1984.

Richard, Pablo. *A força espiritual da igreja dos pobres.* Petrópolis: Editora Vozes, 1989.

Rolim, Francisco Cartaxo. *Pentecostais no Brasil: Uma interpretação sócio-religiosa.* Petrópolis: Editora Vozes, 1985.

———. "Pentecôtisme et vision du monde." *Social Compass* 39.3 (Louvain) (September 1992): 401-22.

Schäfer, Heinrich. "El fundamentalismo y los carismas: La reconquista del espacio vital en América Latina." San José, Costa Rica, mimeo., 1992/1995.

———. *Protestantismo y crisis social en América Central.* San José, Costa Rica: ULS/DEI, 1992.

Schultze, Quentin J. "Orality and Power in Latin American Pentecostalism." In *Coming of Age: Protestantism in Latin America,* ed. Donald Miller. Lanham, Md.: University Press of America, 1994.

Seminario Bíblico Latinoamericano. *Vida y pensamiento — Las iglesias y nuevas perspectivas* 15.2. San José, Costa Rica, 1995.

Shaull, Richard. "From Academic Research to Spiritual Transformation: Reflec-tions on a Study of Pentecostalism in Brazil." *Pneuma* 20, no. 1 (1998): 71-84.

———. "Renewed by the Spirit." *The Other Side* (November/December 1998): 20-24.

Sherrill, Edmund. "Carismá tico e ecumênico" (interview). *Comunicações do ISER* 18 (Rio de Janeiro) (1986).

Soares, Luiz Eduardo. "A guerra dos pentecostais contra o afro-brasileiro: dimensões democráticas do conflito religioso no Brasil." *Cadernos do ISER* 44 (Rio de Janeiro) (1992).

Souza, Luiz Alberto Gómez de. *Classes populares e igreja nos caminhos da história.*
    Petrópolis: Editora Vozes, 1982.
Stoll, D. *Is Latin America Turning Protestant?* Berkeley: University of California
    Press, 1990.
Suurmond, Jean-Jacques. *Word and Spirit at Play: Towards a Charismatic Theology.*
    Grand Rapids: Eerdmans, 1994.
Synan, Vilson, ed. *Aspects of Pentecostal Charismatic Origins.* Plainfield, N.J.: Logos
    International, 1975.
Weber, Max. *Ensaios de sociologia.* Rio de Janeiro: Zahar, 1963.
Willems, W. *Followers of the New Faith: Culture Change and the Rise of Protestant-
    ism in Brazil and Chile.* Nashville, Tenn.: Vanderbilt University Press, 1967.